Routledge Revivals

Lessons from the Past

In times of financial stringency and conservatism in the public sector, social work, with its diversity and differentiation, is often criticized for its lack of efficiency and cost effectiveness. First published in 1990, *Lessons from the Past* demonstrates the need for a more refined theory and practice to benefit social workers, their clients, and their agencies, as well as influencing government legislation and policies.

Richard Roberts criticizes and evaluates a significant body of social work writings from the 1970s in its search for a 'grand', all-encompassing theory. Variously described as 'generic', 'integrated' or 'unitary', these theories attempted to construct propositions that would accommodate social work's broad domain, regardless of setting, method of intervention, or socio-political context.

Crisp and innovative, *Lessons from the Past* will prove invaluable to professionals and students of social work, social policy, and the social sciences.

Lessons from the Past

Issues for Social Work Theory

Richard Roberts

Routledge
Taylor & Francis Group

First published in 1990
by Routledge

This edition first published in 2025 by Routledge
4 Park Square, Milton Park, Abingdon, Oxon, OX14 4RN

and by Routledge
605 Third Avenue, New York, NY 10158

Routledge is an imprint of the Taylor & Francis Group, an informa business

Publisher's Note
The publisher has gone to great lengths to ensure the quality of this reprint but points out that some imperfections in the original copies may be apparent.

Disclaimer
The publisher has made every effort to trace copyright holders and welcomes correspondence from those they have been unable to contact.

A Library of Congress record exists under LCCN: 89010326

ISBN: 978-1-041-14644-5 (hbk)
ISBN: 978-1-003-67544-0 (ebk)
ISBN: 978-1-041-14647-6 (pbk)

Book DOI 10.4324/9781003675440

LESSONS
FROM THE PAST
Issues for Social Work Theory

RICHARD ROBERTS

R

TAVISTOCK/ROUTLEDGE
London and New York

First published in 1990
by Routledge
11 New Fetter Lane, London EC4P 4EE

Simultaneously published in the USA and Canada
by Routledge
a division of Routledge, Chapman and Hall, Inc.
29 West 35th Street, New York NY 10001

Printed in Great Britain
by Richard Clay Ltd, Bungay, Suffolk

British Library Cataloguing in Publication Data

Roberts, Richard
Lessons from the past: issues for social
work theory. – (Tavistock library of social
work practice).
1. Welfare work. Theories
I. Title
361.3'01

Library of Congress Cataloging in Publication Data

Roberts, Richard, 1945–
Lessons from the past.
(Tavistock library of social work practice)
Bibliography: p.
Includes index.
1. Social service. I. Title. II. Series.
HV40.R576 1989 361.3 89–10326

ISBN 0–415–00819–0

By definition, generic qualities are wider and more encompassing than specific characteristics. But merely to say that all lions and tigers are just cats, and henceforth only cats are to be recognized, not only makes for a bad taxonomy but also might confuse those who wish to know how to catch mice or go big-game hunting.

David Howe (1980: 318)

CONTENTS

CONTENTS

CONTENTS

GENERAL EDITOR'S FOREWORD

I

In recent years, the question of social work – how to define it and its objectives, how to determine its worth and its effectiveness – has become the centre of controversy and debate. The intellectual foundations of social work are being re-examined once more, and a great deal of attention is being paid to the ways in which its knowledge base is communicated to students and how it influences practice. Further, the rapid and relatively substantial increase in the number of social workers, and the expansion in their statutory responsibilities, has posed new, and as yet unresolved, relationship problems with clients and employers.

An anti-social work critique has emerged to foster some improbable alliances between groups of social administrators, sociologists, doctors, and the *Daily Mail* and *Daily Telegraph*. The criticisms vary in content and emphasis, and are often contradictory in their conclusions. Some are of the view that at a professional level social workers are still far too dominated by therapeutic concerns and the significance of the relationship, and inflict on their clients a watered-down psychoanalysis, under the guise of casework, in place of a proper concern for their social rights.

An opposing view criticizes social work for assuming a political role, expounding radical ideas which raise clients' dissatisfaction with their disadvantaged position, and, in the process, failing to consider psychological explanations for motivation and actions. Others suggest that social workers are no more than agents of control, maintaining the status quo, enforcing the views of the ruling establishment, constituting a threat to individual freedom and rights. Contrary opinion argues that social workers sanction, and provide pious excuses for, social transgression and lawlessness, and encourage a cult of social and personal irresponsibility.

An American observer claimed that social work has 'champagne pretensions and a root beer performance',[1] adding credence to the suppositions that, first, there is nothing particularly difficult about social work and that anyone with a kind heart can do it; and second, by professionalizing the activity a great number of people are prevented from contributing to their own satisfaction and the well-being of others. These last ideas suggest that social work can be no more than a statement of values and describe efforts to do good to others, and that all the talk of scientific understanding and analysis is trite and absurd – so much hocus-pocus and mystification.

Perhaps the most important and significant discontent relates to the discrepancy between society's expectations – what the public assumes – and what is actually possible. The needed proliferation of statutory responsibilities and growth in the duty of social work 'to provide services to the people', to cope with the ever-increasing demand for services, have not yet been provided. This has led to public disapproval which has shown itself in a hostile media, critical of what it sees as the failure of social work to socialize the delinquent, restrain parents who abuse their children, prevent old people from dying alone, and to provide a satisfactory level of community care for the mentally disordered and the chronically sick and disabled.

Whilst criticism is not unknown in social work, the severity of the recent barrage, together with public censure, has taken the profession by surprise. The effect on the individual social worker is serious. It compounds the stress felt by many workers constantly faced with large-scale human need and misery, without institutional support, public approval, adequate knowledge and skills, sufficient resources, and the mechanisms developed by the established professions for protecting their members. The results are that the morale of social workers is low, and individuals are despondent and bedevilled with a deep sense of frustration and hopelessness. This loss of confidence makes many unwilling to experiment and to announce their achievements and blame is indiscriminately attributed to colleagues and to the hierarchy. Overall there is a feeling of powerlessness when attempting to respond to the hurt and privations of their clients – many have taken flight.

II

Whilst it is true that many of these criticisms owe more to impression and vested opinion than objective analysis, it is also true that in large part this situation is due to the propounding of social work theories dogged by inexactitude and of little proven value in practice, and to the profession being unable to evidentially defend itself in public. The solution to these dilemmas was accurately summed up by Howe some 120 years ago, during the laying of the cornerstone of the New York Institution for the Blind in 1866[2] – 'Good intentions and kind impulses do not necessarily lead to wise and truly humane measures . . . meaning well is only half our duty; thinking right is the other and equally important half.'

This book, the first major text of its kind, contributes to that effort by critically examining the major social work writings and theories which emerged during the 1970s, in terms of the manner in which the theories were developed, the evidence which supports them, their relationships to other constructs, and their value in social work practice. The 'lessons' to be learned from the accumulative and inherent weaknesses of social work theory are pursued, and the criteria for sound theory-building in the future are highlighted. It should prove invaluable to scholars and practitioners alike.

III

The Tavistock Library of Social Work Practice series was prompted by the growth and increasing importance of the social services in our society. Until recently there has been a general approbation of social work, reflected in benedictory increases in manpower and resources, which have led to an unprecedented expansion of the personal social services, a proliferation of the statutory duties placed upon them, and major reorganization. The result has been the emergence of a profession faced with the immense responsibility of promoting individual and social betterment, and bearing a primary responsibility to advocate on the behalf of individuals and groups who do not always fulfil or respect normal social expectations of behaviour. In spite of the growth in services, these tasks are often carried out with inadequate resources, an uncertain knowledge base, and as yet unresolved difficulties associated with the reorganization of the personal social services in 1970. In recent years these difficulties have been compounded by a level of criticism unprecedented since that attracted by the Poor Law.

These developments highlight three major issues that deserve particular attention: first, the need to construct a methodology for analysing social and personal situations, and prescribing action; second, the necessity to apply techniques that measure the performance of the individual worker, and the profession as a whole, in meeting stated objectives; third, and still outstanding, the requirement to develop a knowledge base against which the needs of clients are understood and decisions about their care are taken. Overall, the volumes in this series make explicit and clarify these issues. They contribute to the search for the distinctive knowledge base of social work; increase our understanding of the aetiology and care of personal, familial, and social problems; describe and explore new techniques and practice skills; aim to raise our commitment towards low status groups which suffer public, political, and professional neglect; and promote the enactment of comprehensive and socially just policies. Above all, these volumes aim to promote an understanding which interprets the needs of individuals, groups, and communities, in terms of the synthesis between inner needs and the social realities that impinge upon them, and which aspires to develop informed and skilled practice.

M. Rolf Olsen, 1989

ACKNOWLEDGEMENTS

The ideas in this book are developed from my Ph.D. thesis. The research was carried out between 1980 and 1986. This period witnessed a change in my attitude to 'integrated' theory from initial acceptance, indeed enthusiasm, to one of scepticism that this approach did not contribute to social work being more effective or more efficient.

Given the volume of material written about this genre of social work theory, I believe the lessons from its critical evaluation are salutory in our continuing efforts to better understand the nature of social work.

I appreciate the encouragement given to me by Professor Emeritus Rolf Olsen to develop my thesis into a book. He was one of the examiners of my Ph.D. thesis, and, along with Professors Emeritus Edna Chamberlain and Herb Bisno, provided useful criticism to assist my thinking.

I wish to acknowledge the assistance of Mrs Margaret Lewis and Professor John Lawrence. In addition, the following colleagues, either directly or indirectly, stimulated my ideas: Mrs Lynne Muir, Mr Roger Evans, Mr Peter Baird, Dr Brian English, Ms Jennifer Wilson, Dr Damian Grace, Professor Tony Vinson, Dr Martin Mowbray, Dr Sandra Regan, and Dr Diane Zulfacar.

Needless to say, the writings of the protagonists provided the impetus for this study. I have had the privilege of personal discussions with many of these authors.

Ms Heather Gibson and Ms Louise Clairmonte of Routledge were extremely helpful in the transformation of the manuscript into the finished product. Mrs Frances Landreth proved an excellent typist.

ACKNOWLEDGEMENTS

The personal assistance of Bruce Jarrett and my daughter Rebecca Roberts is gratefully acknowledged.

Richard Roberts,
University of New South Wales,
Sydney, Australia,
June 1989

Chapter One

INTRODUCTION

THE SEARCH FOR INTEGRATIVE CONCEPTS IN SOCIAL WORK THEORY

From time to time, social workers have searched for concepts and ideas which bring together and consolidate the variety of tasks which they undertake, and the diversity of theory which they use. They have sought to develop social work theory to cover the whole of social work, rather than limiting it to one or more aspects of the many and diverse assignments which social workers undertake. This search for 'commonness' in social work dates back to the beginning of this century (Richmond 1917, 1930; Addams 1910; Lee 1937). In the United States of America, this search has been reinforced periodically by conferences and meetings, commencing with the Milford Conference in 1929. The conferences of the 1950s, the Madison Conference of 1977, and the Chicago Meeting of 1981, all had as their goal the identification and reinforcement of what was common about social work, and what made it different from other professions and disciplines.

In the United Kingdom, this search was less well articulated until the Seebohm Report in 1968, because until then social work in the UK had been more closely identified with particular agencies and fields of practice than in the USA. However, after the Seebohm and Kilbrandon reorganizations, and the formation of the British Association of Social Workers in 1970, the search for unity and commonness increased.

While there are historical concomitants influencing the development of this search for integrative concepts, the actual motivation on the part of social workers, as evidenced in their writings, remains ambiguous. Two major influences would seem to be important.

First, social work is a relatively new profession. In order to establish its legitimate place alongside other professions, the development of a unique knowledge and theory base is seen to be of fundamental importance (Flexner 1915; Greenwood 1957; Gilbert 1977; Bartlett 1970; Rosenfeld 1983; Loewenberg 1984). The explanation of its actions in terms of theory has been a high priority, not only to justify its existence to other professions, but also to develop better practices in order to assist its clients.

Second, because social workers have developed both professional and industrial organizations, it is important for them to reaffirm, from time to time, what these organizations have in common, and what their goal should be. The search for integrating concepts and 'centre-moving ideas' (Billups 1984) is related to a need to consolidate the membership of these organizations. Thus the search for integration can be seen as both an academic pursuit in the development of knowledge and theory, as well as an aid to establishing the legitimacy of identifiable professional and industrial organizations.

Whatever the underlying reasons, a significant genre of social work theory emerged during the 1970s, heralded by Bartlett's *The Common Base of Social Work Practice* in 1970. Since this time the number of books and articles about 'integrated', 'generic', 'unitary', 'ecological', and 'systems' approaches to social work practice has burgeoned. In terms of volume alone, the significance of this material cannot be underrated and hence it is necessary to review its contribution to social work and the strengths and weaknesses this broad and all-embracing approach has.

In the eleven conceptual frameworks studied and evaluated in this book it will be seen that each of the authors, in one way or another, is attempting to develop theory for the *whole* of social work. Their work is not limited to attempting to account for and explain a limited set of social work activities relating to practice within particular settings, to particular social problems, or even practice within particular social or geographic contexts. Nor is their work limited to attempts to explain particular practice behaviours related to particular outcomes. Their theory has been developed to apply to all social work with an unacknowledged historic or socio-political location. It is intended to relate to both the grand purposes of social work, as well as to the ways these can be operationalized. There are many parallels to the search for a 'grand theory' in sociology. Thus the scope of this theory, at least in its rhetoric, is massive.

This enthusiasm for attempting to deal with the whole of social work is understandable, given that social workers have become involved in a wide range of activities and practices, from individual therapy through to being active participants in social and political movements. Furthermore, social work has had to carve its own niche alongside the other helping professions, and in so doing has claimed a special interest in the 'person-in-environment' interface as its domain. This wide interest has led social workers across the boundaries of many other disciplines and professions in their attempts to be holistic, and as such has led to the need to understand the theory from a wide range of socio-behavioural sciences.

The need to invoke the knowledge and theory developed within other disciplines and professions has often led to social workers being seduced by these often more-powerful providers of theory, and hence the temptation to neglect social work's own mission (Bartlett 1970 : 71). However, while social work has always been tempted to define its own domain in very ambitious terms (Howe 1980; Rosenfeld 1983), the implications of this for social work theory-building have been demanding. Social work theorists have had to both contend with problems relating to the rather immodest delineation of social work's domain, and at the same time deal with the discipline's propensity to rely heavily upon 'borrowed' theory from other sources.

While attempting to 'integrate' theories from other sources with the needs of social work practitioners and with social work theory itself, there has remained an uncertainty about the specific purposes of social work within a widely-defined domain. This uncertainty about the nature of social work's goals has made the assignment doubly difficult, because without a clear direction or purpose, it is not possible to justify the means used in terms of operational techniques and skills.

The ambition, or dream, to integrate this mass of material is commendable, provided social work has an established and rigorous approach to its subject matter. However, the search for integration and for 'grand theory' commenced in the profession's relative infancy, well before the profession had a chance to consolidate what it was *doing*, rather than merely what it was saying. Furthermore, the attitudes prevailing in social work have often resulted in its theory being developed by an academic sub-culture and thus not only reflecting an incomplete picture of reality, but remaining somewhat apart from much mainstream practice. In these circumstances, the persistence in the search for 'integrated' theory portrays a fundamental naïvety on the part of social workers toward their theory construction.

I am not suggesting that social workers should stop dreaming and talking about their ideals. These provide an important impetus and keep our visions high. I am not suggesting that social work should remain characterized only by piecemeal and limited accounts of its undertakings. This would be inaccurate, and limiting to the vision of the pioneers of social work. Social work does need an overall professional framework on which to plot its activities. It does need a mission. However, this mission must be realistic, it must reflect, to some degree, the resources over which social workers have control, their power and authority, as well as the skills and techniques at their disposal. Furthermore, social work will only be able to justify the use of its techniques and skills, that is its 'means', when a clearly delineated purpose, or set of purposes, that is its 'ends', has been established.

Given that social work activities are carried out by members of a profession within particular contexts, agencies, communities, and countries, it is doubtful if a mission for social work can be divorced from a historical and socio-political context. In this sense, social work is not an 'applied social science', because its application of social and behavioural theory takes place against a backdrop of contextual sanctions, both prescriptive and proscriptive. Any theory which will be of use to its practitioners must take this into account. Any theory which ignores the normative issues related to both personal well-being, as well as to the broader socio-political contexts of practice, will be deficient.

While social workers will continue to dream about ideals for the future, they cannot afford to ignore the current realities faced by a relatively young profession operating with increasingly limited resources, and being called to demonstrate to clients, agencies, and governments their efficiency and effectiveness. This is why any significant group of writings about a particular genre of social work theory must be critically evaluated.

AN INTRODUCTION TO 'INTEGRATED' THEORY

During the 1970s the writings of Bartlett, Pincus and Minahan, Goldstein, Baker, Compton and Galaway, and Loewenberg had a certain appeal in that they attempted to answer some fairly basic questions about the nature and purpose of social work. These writings attempted to construct a broad social work frame of reference to which a diverse range of social work activities could be related, and which would help in the choice of theory from other sources. This frame of reference helped to establish and maintain a social work focus which was not eclipsed by the goals of another discipline or profession, and which helped to provide some purpose over and above that defined by a particular agency or a particular government.

I saw in these 'integrated' approaches to social work some attempt to address such questions as the following:

1. Who were my clients? How could I differentiate my clients from the wide variety of people I saw every day? Was everyone my client?

2. What was *real* social work? When in my office (or occasionally making a home visit) with someone I thought was a client, and when talking to them (interviewing, assessing, doing 'therapy'/ counselling/'casework') I labelled this 'social work'. But I was quite unsure how to label all the other kinds of work I did on behalf of clients, for example mediating, advocating, acquiring resources, making referrals, writing submissions, doing research, consulting. Were these activities *really* social work? They took up a lot of time, and hence reduced the number of 'real' clients I saw each day. The attitude of some other social workers often relegated the activities not directly involving a 'client' to ancilliary chores, and many tried to circumvent them as much as possible.

3. How should I relate to the range of people with whom I had contact? With clients, this was easy, because my social work education had taught me how to be 'accepting', 'non-judgemental', 'facilitating', 'non-directive', and most of all how to develop a 'helping relationship'. In this 'helping relationship' the client was supposed to feel free to unburden him or herself, and eventually to begin the process of 'self-actualization'. Some of the time this worked with clients. It rarely worked with 'non-clients'. I found myself wondering how to relate to 'directive', 'demanding', and 'manoeuvring' teachers, administrators, doctors, clerks, magistrates, and so on. What I learned from painful experience was that a non-directive, warm, facilitative, and helping relationship was not appropriate for everyone.

4. Where was I going? Was I representing the 'cause' of some person or some interest? Whose side was I supposed to be on where there was conflict? (Husband against wife, parent against child, principal against pupil, departmental clerk against recipient of a benefit.) Usually each side of a conflict could be argued. There was nothing within social work which told me where my allegiance should be *as a social worker*. Perhaps it was part of my personal ideology which led me, most often, to take the side of the person who appeared to have the greatest disadvantage. This, however, became increasingly difficult where the grounds on each side were fairly well balanced. Was I supposed to remain 'neutral'? There was no clearly articulated mission of social work to which I could refer. The focus seemed to be an individual's social functioning; and that applied to everyone.

5. What rights did I have, as a social worker, to challenge the way certain social structures and certain social institutions were affecting my clients? What sanctions allowed me to practise? What authorities and rights did I have? Further, what skills did I possess in order to influence the structures I wished to change? The skills I had acquired in one way or another focused solely on the 'helping relationship' with clients. Once the client's potential had been unleashed through this experience, it would be the client, through the use of self-determination, who would bring about the necessary changes in his or her environment, not me! This idealistic and unrealistic view left me impotent when faced with recalcitrant individuals, systems, and institutions.

6. How could I effectively explain to others what I did? Most often I would resort to my psychological background and talk about 'therapy', 'counselling', and helping individuals 'sort themselves out'. Occasionally I resorted to social work terminology: 'working with person and environment', helping with 'social functioning'. Mostly, I hoped people wouldn't ask.

7. Was there a coherent frame of reference I could use to give some meaning, some order to the very wide range of activities I was involved in? Without this my perception of 'real' social work was very much limited to 'personal adjustment', 'coping', and 'helping individuals to relate better to others'.

What my initial understanding of 'integrated' theory did was to put back the 'social' in its rightful place alongside the 'psychological', by considering social work activities around a social work purpose (no matter how vaguely defined this was) or a constellation of elements (like Bartlett's 'common base' (1970)). Without the benefit of closer scrutiny and focusing on the strengths of this theory, I initially saw its usefulness and major contribution in the following ways.

1. It attempted to take into account the wide range of activities which I had undertaken as a social worker, and to put them together in a cohesive and coherent way. Although there appeared to be superficial differences in the way this was done in the different frameworks, each one attempted to outline a range of tasks and roles which seemed to acknowledge the variety of social work activities, and in particular to address activities and roles when dealing with both clients and others (non-clients). Thus this approach legitimized social work's contribution in working with individuals, groups, organizations, and communities.

2. There was an attempt to define 'client', and thus recognize the possibility that social workers worked with a range of people, and not everyone was a 'client'.

3. This approach recognized the need for different types of relationships with different people and groups. Thus the 'helping relationship' of the therapist was only one type which was required for social work intervention. The recognition of 'conflict' and 'bargaining' as other types of relationship, by Pincus and Minahan (1973, 1975, 1977) at least legitimized the fact that social workers were not professionally confined to 'helping' consensual relationships.

4. In attempting to establish a purpose for social work, usually invoking the 'person-in-environment' concept, the theory appeared, at first sight, to provide a more balanced approach to these two components than the more psychologically-based 'casework'. In this regard it recognized the contribution of knowledge and theory from other sources, and emphasized the necessity of relating this to social work's own purposes. In this way it could be used by the social worker, to further social work purposes. This was appealing, because it had seemed to me that many social workers were directed in their practice by only one or two theories (usually of a psychological type), or were heavily influenced by the needs and wishes of other occupational groups (particularly in secondary settings like hospitals).

5. This approach attempted to establish what was *common* about

7

social work, and thus establish the characteristics which made it different from other occupations and other disciplines. Some frameworks attempted to construct a 'process' model which helped the practitioner to identify common phases of intervention: from the identification of a problem, through assessment, planning, intervention, and evaluation.

6. This theory rejected the orthodox delineation of practice into 'casework', 'group work', 'community work', and 'administration'. Such 'artificial' boundaries were seen to adversely limit the assessment of and subsequent intervention in a problem. Likewise, the orthodox division of social work into particular social problems, fields of practice, and agency setting were rejected. According to these writers a problem should be observed and assessed in its own right, without the orthodox 'blinkers' of one kind or another.

7. In recognizing the links between 'direct' and 'indirect' service, frameworks drew attention to the connections between 'private troubles' and 'public issues' (Schwartz 1969). The rhetoric of the 'public issues – private troubles' debate linked neatly to the 'person–environment' interface. It was here at the 'interface' that social work's very own piece of 'turf' was seen to be located.

8. Development of 'practice theory'. It was claimed by some authors that this was the development of 'middle-range' practice theory: broad enough to take into account the purposes of social work, yet not so specific that it would prescribe the finer details of practice interventions. Although ambiguous as to whether the frameworks represented accurate descriptions of practice, or were being put forward as justified prescriptions, it was claimed they were at an early stage in their development. Furthermore, this 'practice theory' was differentiated from 'theories for practice' or 'foundation knowledge' which was borrowed from other disciplines.

These apparent positive characteristics led me to contemplate the use of this type of social work theory both for practice and for social work education. Upon closer scrutiny, it became increasingly apparent that my initial expectations of this genre of social work theory could not be realized. In 1982 I concluded that in relation to its use for curriculum design:

> the utilization of unitary approaches increases curriculum choice, but I believe they do not provide a strong rationale for one set of options over another. The positive [sic] which I believe an

introductory course has, based upon unitary frameworks, is it provides a framework for establishing the broadest parameters of practice. On to this map, various specializations in terms of fields, social problems or technologies of practice can be fitted.

(Roberts 1982 : 254)

As difficulties in operationalizing this type of theory became increasingly apparent, this led to a much closer scrutiny of this writing. This scrutiny progressed by examining more closely the expectations of the individual writers, as well as considering some key issues related to theory construction in general and its application within a social work frame of reference. It is the analysis and evaluation of eleven conceptual frameworks of practice, as representative of the genre of 'integrated', 'unitary', 'generic' theory, which is the subject of this book.

ORGANIZATION OF THE BOOK

This book is set out in four parts. Part One, Chapters 2 to 4, is an essay-review of selected key issues related to the construction of theory in social work. Out of this, a list of important criteria to be observed in each of the frameworks is developed. Part Two, Chapter 5, provides a summary and critique of four conceptual frameworks. Part Three, Chapters 6 to 10, examines the general findings, taking into consideration the issues developed in Part One as well as the expectations set by the various writers. Part Four, Chapter 11, outlines the contribution I believe this genre of theory makes to social work.

SOME PARAMETERS

Before proceeding, the reader's attention should be drawn to the parameters of this study. First, it was undertaken by a social worker for the primary benefit of other social workers. This is important, because this same exercise may have been undertaken quite differently had the author been a philosopher, a sociologist, an historian, or a political scientist. Professions construct their 'communities' in particular ways: not only in relation to the particular activities they engage in, and the particular goals they hope to achieve, but also in the questions they ask, and the methods they use to find answers

(Kuhn 1970). The language and concepts of discourse are different (Duncan 1962, 1968, 1969), and this is illustrated when trying to comprehend the language and concepts of a discipline other than one's own.

The norms and mores of professional 'communities' often create insularity, so there is no desire for interdisciplinary discourse. However, even when interdisciplinary discourse is desired, the barriers created by differential language and concepts help reinforce insularity within each community. Even between the disciplines of sociology and social work, such a gap persists (Evans and Webb 1977; Bowker and Cox 1982). Thus the professional community in which I have been educated and socialized has provided a particular set of language and concepts, a particular perspective for viewing issues and their resolution. I assume this is the case for the social workers who are my readers. My aim therefore is to use a language and set of concepts familiar to our occupation. In so doing I have limited the study by excluding issues which the philosopher, the sociologist, the psychologist, the historian, or the political scientist may have considered to be of greater importance.

Second, my study and conclusions are based upon study and contemplation of others' writings, as well as my own experiences as a practitioner and educator. This is not a study which observes practice *in vivo*. I will strongly argue that for theory to be relevant, it must be explicitly linked to action, and furthermore, both the 'academic' and 'practice' sub-cultures must maintain effective working communications with a greater overlap of roles. However, I recognize that my contribution is only one side of the story, albeit within a context where I have searched the literature relating practice applications of the theory under review.

Third, I am very much aware that my own practice context is Australian, and that most of the writers I review are North American or British. While I am weary of using my background to evaluate the work of others from different backgrounds, this position has provided me with the opportunity of seeing the relevance of this theory when used within another social welfare system and socio-political context. This is particularly valuable for examination of a theory which places little importance on context, and thus implies a universal application.

Fourth, in making some of the criticisms about this kind of theory, I am well aware of some of the shortcomings of other social work writing taking, for example, a 'methods' or 'fields' orientation.

A consideration of this material is outside the brief of this study, however.

It is my conviction that the past teaches us many lessons. To ignore these often means going through the painful experience of repeating the same mistakes. Social work in the current economic and political climate does not have the time to keep repeating the mistakes of the past. Nowhere has an analysis of 'integrated' theory been recorded with its strengths and weaknesses. This book, if it serves no other purpose, will put on record my attempt at this task. Hopefully this record of an important group of social work writings in the 1970s will serve as a salutary reminder to future writers. It is imperative for social work's survival that they avoid some of the errors of the past.

Part 1

THEORY

Chapter Two

ORIENTATION TO 'THEORY' AND THEORY CONSTRUCTION

The term 'theory' is often daunting to students and practitioners, either because it is seen to have an uncontested definition of which the user is not sure, or its user fails to relate, in a proper way, theory to action. In the latter case one often hears both students and practitioners saying they are not interested in 'theory' but rather they are 'practical' in their social work. The real problem for these people is that they are operating from an implicit theory, and this is dangerous because they are not able to account for or justify their behaviour. If they did, this would form the theory on which they based their actions.

It is not the case, either in social work or in other disciplines, that 'theory' has an uncontested meaning. It is this ambiguity which is rarely recognized, and hence causes some of the confusion which students and practitioners face. In order to help deal with these issues this chapter will (i) demonstrate the ambiguity which exists in the terms 'theory', 'knowledge', 'model', 'framework', and their relationships; (ii) observe different types of 'theory', its construction, and different expectations which people have of 'theory'; and (iii) consider the effects of developing theory and knowledge within different paradigms which are underpinned by different sets of assumptions.

As noted by Lecomte (1975 : 25–6) the term 'theory', both in social work and social science, is full of ambiguity. The differential usage of nomenclature causes problems for discourse both within the discipline of social work and between social work and other disciplines. A review of key terms and their relationships demonstrates this.

'THEORY' AND 'KNOWLEDGE'

Substantive differences can be noted in formal definitions. According to Dubin (1971 : 58), 'A theory is the attempt to model some aspect of the empirical world.' The underlying motive for this modelling is that either (i) the real world is so complex that it needs to be conceptually simplified in order to understand it, or (ii) that observation by itself does not reveal ordered relationships among empirically-detected entities. A theory tries to make sense out of the observable world by ordering the relationships among 'things' that constitute the theorist's focus of attention in the world 'out there'.

The process involves choosing the 'things' (units) whose relationships are of interest. This can be an arbitrary list selected by the theorist as being of particular interest. It involves suggesting how these selected units are related to each other, thus establishing 'laws of interaction'. 'The process of putting things or units together in lawful relation to each other establishes the fundamental building blocks out of which a theory is constructed' (Dubin 1971 : 59).

Theories have a domain over which they are expected to mirror the empirical world: beyond that domain it is problematic whether the theory holds. A boundary is required, and so every theoretical model, if it is complete, must specify the boundary within which the units interact lawfully. In addition it is necessary to specify the states in which the model or theoretical system operates (Dubin 1971 : 58–60).

Such a definition leaves ample scope for the development of specific criteria upon which the theory can be developed – in particular, ample scope in the *choice* of 'things' whose relationships are considered to be of interest; how these relationships are determined; and the extent of the domain over which these suggested relationships will operate. Thus, while helping to accurately describe and understand the world, the construction of theory in the first place is value-based, depending on the importance placed upon *which* particular 'things' are considered of interest, and therefore whose particular relationship becomes worthy of study.

The importance of the role of the theorist in constructing a theory (see, for example, Feyerabend 1975; Fay 1975 : Chs 4 and 5; Middleman and Goldberg 1974; Berger and Luckmann 1966; Bakan 1966) is not always taken into account, thus reflecting epistemological differences in how theory can be constructed. Some definitions are presented as if the theorist was of no importance at all. A definition offered by Compton and Galaway is an example of one which ignores the idiosyncratic value position of the theorist:

> A *theory* is a coherent group of general propositions or concepts used as principles of explanation for a class of phenomena – a more or less verified or established explanation accounting for known facts or phenomena and their interrelationship. If one thinks of knowledge as discrete bits of truth or discrete facts and observations like a pile of bricks, theory can be likened to a wall of bricks. In a theory the observations of the real world are ordered and put together in a certain way and held together by certain assumptions or hypotheses as bricks in a wall are held together by a material that cements them in place. Thus theory is a coherent group of general propositions, containing both confirmed and assumptive knowledge, held together by connective notions that seek to explain in a rational way the observed facts of phenomena and the relationship of these phenomena to each other.
>
> (Compton and Galaway 1979 : 41)

While some aspects of this analogy may be helpful in understanding the relationship between concepts, assumptions, and hypotheses, the visual analogy to a wall of bricks offers something rather too permanent and impervious to change to accurately reflect the state of most theories, particularly in social work. The ontological leap from 'ideas' to 'bricks and mortar' provides an analogy which is far too permanent and static to cope with the rapidly-changing realities with which social workers have to deal. In contrast to Dubin's definition, that of Compton and Galaway presents theory as much more objective, observable, and static.

Similar *types* of definition (without the physical analogy) are provided by Johnson (1981) and Siporin (1975). Each focuses upon the processes involved in constituting a theory:

> A theory is a set of logically interrelated and systematically stated propositions that describes (at a high level of generality) and explains some set of empirical phenomena.
>
> (Johnson 1981 : 41)

> A good theory can aid our understanding of the facts, helping us to explain them and to make valid predictions from them; this is

essential to planning for the future, both in our personal lives and in public policy.

(Johnson 1981 : 3)

Theory is a system of related, consistent *concepts* and *propositions* [my italics] about reality . . . a theory may be stated in the form of hypotheses, generalizations, principles, laws, facts.

(Siporin 1975 : 361)

This latter definition relies on the defining of *concept* and *proposition*, which Siporin does as follows:

Concept is a mental abstraction, or symbol, that represents a class or unit of events, actions, or objects having common properties. It is a general idea, of which varied phenomena are seen to be a case, and also a rule for evaluating and organizing the materials of experience. *Ego, psychosis, social type, social functioning* are concepts.

(Siporin 1975 : 355–6)

Proposition is a formal statement, in which at least two concepts are logically related to each other, so that the statement can be judged as true or false. Propositions can be 'empirical', based upon direct, sensory observation; or 'theoretical', based on rational, logical inferences, or generalizations; or 'concrete', based on personally experienced, intuitive, and intersubjective observations, as by participant observers.

(Siporin 1975 : 358)

All the above definitions of 'theory' focus on the *relationships* or *connections* between 'concepts' and 'propositions' of one kind or another. Thus 'facts' or 'knowledge' are seen to be component parts of a theory. However, not all writers see the relationship between 'theory' and 'knowledge' in this way. Kahn (1954), for example, suggests that 'knowledge' in a given field is the sum total of available theory that is considered to be highly confirmed.

This is a similar position to that of Rychlak, who believes that 'knowledge' encompasses both theory and the method used in determining whether a theory is true or false. Knowledge is theory which has passed the test of methods (Rychlak 1968 : 43). For him,

A theory may be thought of as a series of two or more constructions (abstractions), which have been hypothesized, assumed, or even factually demonstrated to bear a certain relationship one with the other. A theoretical proposition, which defines the relationship between constructions (now termed 'variables') becomes a fact when that proposition is no longer contested by those individuals best informed on the nature of the theory, and dedicated to study in the area of knowledge for which the theory has relevance.

(Rychlak 1968 : 42)

Thus it can be seen that a *particular* relationship between 'knowledge' and 'theory' is not accepted universally and so needs to be clarified each time the terms are used.

In addition, the commonly undifferentiated range of discrete meanings attributed to 'theory' in social work is noted by Blyth and Hugman:

Use of the words 'theory', 'practice' and 'integration' seem to imply that each refers to some discrete, unambiguous concept, but closer examination reveals each to be complex and ill-designed, and their interrelationship to be highly problematic.

(Blyth and Hugman 1982 : 61)

Pilalis (1986 : 81–6) has brought together the work of Blyth and Hugman (1982), Leonard (1975), Durkheim (1971), and Habermas (1974) to illustrate the different meanings of 'theory'. This is presented in Figure 2.1. She concludes that 'theory' means many different things in social work. Hence, it is not surprising that students and practitioners are often unsure exactly what 'theory' is, and users of the word find difficulties in effectively communicating *their* meaning.

TYPES OF 'THEORY' AND ITS PURPOSES

Further difficulties arise when using the word 'theory' in a general sense, because of the different expectations different people have of this descriptive term and its level of application. In any discipline it is expected that the theory underpinning its practice will be made explicit rather than remaining implicit (Johnson 1981 : 7–11). However, the making explicit of certain assumptions over others is not always done. It is suggested that this is associated with the argument of Berger and Luckmann (1966) that social systems and their associated world views are socially contrived and maintained. Thus, in highly stable societies with one dominant cultural world view, people

19

Figure 2.1 Meanings attached to 'theory'

Meanings of 'theory' (Blyth and Hugman 1982, p. 62)	Paradigm type (Leonard 1975)	Theory type (Durkheim 1971)	Goal of theory type (Habermas 1974)
1. General rule or law, as yet unchallenged, which is testable against observable evidence	Physical Sciences A (Empirical objectivity)	Non-normative	Quantification
2. Speculative explanation, or hypothesis, awaiting confirmation	Physical Sciences B (Empirical probability)	Non-normative	Quantification
3. Description of an 'ideal state' or statement of principles in the light of which everyday events are understood or controlled (provides understanding)	Human Sciences C (Subjective understanding)	Normative	Understanding
4. Theories of political, sociological or psychological nature, which are understandings or statements of intent based on moral, philosophical or religious values (i.e. have ideological base)	Human Sciences D (Ideological base to science)	Normative	Emancipation
5. Information or knowledge as opposed to practice (e.g. designing as opposed to building bridges)	—	Non-normative or Normative	
6. Idealized statement, often seen to be unrealistic (e.g. 'that's all very well in theory')		Normative	

Source: Pilalis (1986 : 84)

experience this as based upon an ultimate and unchanging reality that seems independent of their culture. In a more fluid or pluralistic social structure and culture, there develops a multiplicity of competing world views and cultural patterns, each based on alternative social definitions or beliefs, among which individuals have to make choices. In such a context the need to make assumptions explicit in order to justify choices becomes mandatory.

It must be accepted, then, that any scientific social theory, in order to be validated, has to be explicit in the way it is constructed. Furthermore, because social reality is socially constructed through symbolic communication, 'it is imperative . . . that social scientists develop their ever distinctive strategies to deal with the symbolic and socially constructed nature of much of social reality instead of simply attempting to imitate the strategies of the other natural sciences' (Johnson 1981 : 32).

In constructing theory, Schrag (1967 : 220–53) proposes three distinct modes: *inductive* (from observed evidence to concepts to generalizations); *deductive* (from assumptions and concepts to observed evidence); and *retroductive* (from observed evidence to assumptions to concepts).

These modes are linked to formal and informal theory construction by Lecomte (1975 : 149) who argues that the formal mode of theory construction tends to adopt the assumptions held by the proponents of the inductive and deductive approaches, while the informal mode will be inclined toward the assumptions held by the retroductive model. Lecomte (1975 : 152–3) argues that in the formal mode of theory construction, induction and deduction are two sides of the same coin, because both have a concern for the search for 'law-like' and/or 'truthful' statements in a systematic way. Their aims are to 'cleanse the formulation of theory of metaphysics and ideology' (Lecomte 1975 : 153). To exclude these considerations they impose strict criteria of verifiability, of testing, and of evaluation, such as theories outlined by Schrag (1967 : 250–1): criteria of logical consistency, parsimony, testability, congruence between theoretical claims and empirical evidence, and pragmatic adequacy: the utility of the theory in controlling the phenomena of interest.

Further, Lecomte (1975 : 157–60) notes that any dispute which arises about an 'objective' theory can be settled by demonstrative reasoning of the empirical methods, i.e. by actual observation or measurement. This is because demonstrative reasoning is based on terms which stand for observable objects capable of identification and measurement. Thus a formal mode of theory construction will tend to build theories that are expressed in a hierarchical, axiomatic, set-in-laws, and causal processes form. 'Integration' is stressed; that is, bringing together theoretical constructs and propositions into a more or less consistent and unified whole. When a theory is pulled together into an interdependent unity, this is termed 'formal' theory.

This is a similar position as the one proposed by Smith *et al.* (1981 : 13), where theory is described as having the following characteristics:

> it is an inter-related set of concepts, definitions, and propositions arranged in a logical deductive/inductive system. This set must present a systematic view of a phenomenon by specifying relationships and variables with the purpose of explaining and predicting the phenomenon. The form that this process of explanation and prediction takes is through a series of testable hypotheses.

This conceptualization of 'theory' leads Smith *et al.* (1981 : 3) to conclude, 'At present we are doubtful whether there is anything in social work which takes this stringent form, although the task of building and developing theories must continue.' However, such a position neglects an alternative mode of theory construction: the 'informal'.

The informal mode of theory construction takes quite a different form. Whereas the formal mode believes in the superiority of method, the informal mode assumes that theory comes first, and that it *selects* and *moulds* method. Informal theory construction does not limit the definition to highly structured systems of thought, nor does it limit its theory building to a range which includes only theories compatible with the experimental method. This mode involves conjectures, speculations, hunches and guesses, and the method of theory construction must vary with the 'image of reality' of the subject matter. Theory develops over time, and produces not laws but better ways of knowing and viewing (Lecomte 1975 : 164). It also emphasizes the importance of historical context and the use of qualitative methodology. Lecomte notes (1975 : 166) that sometimes those who take a qualitative approach do not refer to their work as theory generation, because they have been too concerned with formulating their ideas within the rhetoric of verification. Thus, in social work, qualitative phenomena, feelings, 'relationships', and other behaviours difficult to quantify and verify, are either neglected, or reports of them are not given the status of 'theory'. When this occurs it is often the result of significant variables being ignored as a result of the predominance of *one* particular *method* of theory construction.

Informal modes of theory construction work simultaneously with both the data of observation (the observed evidence) and the logical abstractions inherent in theoretical concepts and assumptions. By a technique of successive approximations, the concepts and assumptions of theories are brought into closer alignment with relevant evidence while at the same time maintaining the logical consistency of deductive systems. This method has been called *retroduction* (Hanson 1958).

It must be noted, as well, that informal modes of theory construction are more open to the influence of ideology. While noting the differences between 'theory' and 'ideology', Loewenberg (1984 : 320) admits that while 'there are real differences between ideology and theory, in social work practice these two elements inter-penetrate'. Because social work is a normative activity, its ideologies have a profound influence on its theories (e.g. see Smid and Van Krieken 1984; Epstein 1986; Gammack 1982; Rojek 1986). Furthermore, because there are competing and complementary ideologies (Rojek 1986), any social work theory must be able to recognize these differences.

Thus it can be seen that the method of theory construction is itself open to debate with different writers having different expectations of what will count as 'theory', depending on its mode of construction. While it has been argued that 'formal' theory has not yet been developed in social work (Smith *et al.* 1981), it remains open to debate whether this is the proper line for social work theory construction in any case, taking account of the arguments related to informal theory construction, and the need to recognize ideology.

The debate about formal and informal theory in social work is an important one, because social work is increasingly required to be more publicly accountable for the efficiency and effectiveness of its interventions. In justifying their actions, social workers are required to invoke theory of one kind or another. If, for example, they choose to justify their actions only by theory which has been formally constructed, then it may be the case that only *one* particular type of criteria will be used, that which emphasizes observable phenomena, verification and so on. Hence it is possible that the recognition only of variables within this particular *methodology* of theory construction will exclude a consideration of some other variables which might better account for and explain the *modus operandi* of social work, like ideologies of practice, as well as a range of qualities like the 'helping relationship', feelings, and values. It is often the case, however, that adherents to one type of theory construction do not recognize the legitimacy of an alternative type. This narrow view limits the possibilities of the varying effects of the perceived data on theory construction, and in turn this theory for explicating perceived data.

'MODELS'

A review of definitions of 'models' reveals differential and inconsistent usage of the term. A common theme in the definition relates to a model's pictorial capacity and its providing directives for practice. These qualities are demonstrated in the following definitions. A model is:

> a symbolic, pictorial structure of concepts, in terms of metaphors and propositions concerning a specific problem, or a piece of reality, and of how it works.
>
> (Siporin 1975 : 361)

> a symbolic representation of a perceptual phenomenon . . . a pattern of symbols, rules, and processes regarded as matching, in part or totality, an existing perceptual complex.
>
> (Hearn 1958 : 10)

> a coherent set of directives which state how a given kind of treatment is to be carried out. A model is basically definitional and descriptive. It usually states what the practitioner is expected to do or what practitioners customarily do under given conditions.
>
> (Reid and Epstein 1972 : 7–8)

This symbolic or pictorial structure, in order to be of use, must reflect reality to some degree or other. As Meadows notes:

> The formulation of a model consists in conceptually marking off a perceptual complex. It involves, moreover, replacing part or parts of a perceptual complex by some representation, or symbol. Every model is a pattern of symbols, rules and processes regarded as matching, in part or in totality, an existing perceptual complex. Each model stipulates thus, some correspondence with reality,

some relevance of items in the model to the reality, and some verifiability between the model and reality.

(Meadows 1957 : 4)

Likewise, Goldstein sees that:

A model is useful only in its 'goodness of fit' to the reality it is intended to represent. While one model may adequately portray the functions of practice, it may be less depictive of the stages through which change takes place. Therefore each model can be regarded in terms of its utility for gaining greater organization and comprehension of the elements or processes it intends to describe rather than as an all-encompassing prefiguration of practice.

(Goldstein 1973 : 187)

Models are usually given a more tentative status than 'theory'. As Breshers (1957 : 34) notes, models are usually not themselves tested, but rather, are used to develop hypotheses which can be tested. Thus Breshers proposes two criteria for the development of models: they should be convenient and facilitate the processes of research design, hypothesis formation, and data analysis; and they should be plausible and congruent with the data they are supposed to represent.

But, this *tentative* status is not always accorded to models. As Meyer (1973 : 89) observes, 'The models with which we work, our present roadmaps that provide us with guides to action, seem to lie in the solution category rather than the problem category'. Later Meyer remarks:

Recalling that models are by design *metaphors* or *constructs* of reality, and are to be short-term at that, all would be well if the schools and the field at large would use the models in a tentative way. But we don't; we tend to marry our models, we don't just court them.

(Meyer 1973 : 89)

RELATIONSHIP BETWEEN 'THEORY' AND 'MODEL'

The relationship between 'theory' and 'model' is viewed quite differently by different authors. Kettner (1975 : 630ff.) reviews these different relationships. At one end of a continuum is Klein who views a model as:

a way of stating theory in relation to specific observations . . .

models are built from theories around a problem . . . one can build
a theory without building a model . . . but it is doubtful if one can
build a model without a theory.

(Klein 1970 : 9)

A similar position is argued by Evans (1976 : 192 and 180). He sees
model-building as 'sophisticated description'. Models are conceptually complex ways of *describing* reality; they do not necessarily *explain*
the relationship between the elements, this can only be done by
theory.

However, Pincus and Minahan (1973 : *xii*) take a contrasting
view on the relationship between 'theory' and 'model'. For them, 'the
social work model for practice . . . should clearly be differentiated
from any substantive theoretical orientations being utilized.' In other
words, a social work model should be able to interact with a range of
theoretical perspectives, and should not be fashioned by any *one*
theory.

For Kettner a middle-of-the-road course of action between the
extremes expressed in the views of Klein and Pincus and Minahan
should be taken, for:

On the one hand intertwining model and theory into one
undifferentiated position or posture can . . . lead to theory
dictating the purpose of practice. On the other hand, a model
without theoretical underpinnings reduces practice to mere
technical competence.

(Kettner 1975 : 630)

For Meyer (1973 : 88–9) it is the building of 'models' which
results in theory development. As such she notes the inappropriate
reductionism and premature closure which results when models are
'married rather than courted' (Meyer 1973 : 89). She asserts that
there is a 'tendency to jump on bandwagons before they are even out
of the garage.' Her argument relies on Willer, who takes the position
that a model is a

conceptualization of a *group of phenomena*, constructed by means of
a *rationale*, where the ultimate *purpose* is to furnish the terms and
relations, the propositions of a formal system, which, if *validated*,
becomes theory.

(Willer 1967 : 15)

This position however places model-building within the context of theory construction, and leaves open the question of what the dependency is of a model on a particular theory or theories.

'FRAMEWORK'

Siporin defines a 'theoretical framework' or 'conceptual framework' as:

> a structure of concepts, propositions, theories, facts and models used as an orienting and ordering perspective with regard to some problem or set of problems. Technically, it is a structure of variables and theories, given explicit statement and definition, as part of a research project, or to explain and justify a specific practice program.
>
> (Siporin 1975 : 362)

This definition is particularly useful when considering the genre of writings which is the subject of this book. These can be regarded as 'theory' in the broad sense of the word, given that theory can be both 'formal' and 'informal' in the manner in which it is constructed, and given that 'theory' can be differentiated from 'action', in that it is about contemplation and conceptualization. However, because 'theory' is often differentiated from other notions such as 'concepts', 'propositions', 'knowledge', 'facts', and 'models', it is much less confusing to refer to each author's conceptualization as a 'framework', which on Siporin's definition at least, can then be seen as containing a mixture of concepts, propositions, theories, facts, and models.

'PARADIGM'

A paradigm is 'the system of ideas, beliefs and attitudes which provide both the background and framework for theory development and associated research endeavours' (Chamberlain 1977 : 1). This definition is closely related to that developed by Kuhn (1970) which refers to the underlying intellectual assumptions scientists make about their subject matter. Johnson (1981 : 49) notes that Kuhn is not consistent in the use of this term but argues that the definition in Kuhn's original work implied that 'a paradigm consists of the fundamental world view (*Weltanschauung*) shared by scientists in a particular discipline.'

27

As Leonard notes:

> Kuhn uses the term paradigm to denote the assumptions, theories, methods and results of a particular scientific discipline within which it normally develops. Within a particular paradigm the work of what he calls 'normal science' is carried out, it provides an overall framework for communication in the discipline and through which new scientists are socialized, by their education, to the dominant culture of the discipline.
>
> (Leonard 1975 : 325–33)

Friedrichs (1970) likewise argues that a paradigm influences the fundamental image a discipline has of its subject matter. However, as noted by Johnson (1981: 50), his usage focuses on self-images and political orientations rather than basic world views described as *Weltanschauungen*.

The importance of giving recognition to the influence of scientific paradigms results in the fact that 'theory construction is normatively constrained', and that it is socially constructed within scientific communities which have their own sets of values. Thus, as Evans (1976 : 179) points out, the task for social work theory is 'to develop consciousness of its own social location.'

Evans further argues:

> Where paradigms indicate the social location of science, theories constitute its content and consist of sets of concepts related in such a way as to explain particular natural or social phenomena. The important point about this relationship is that the assumptions underlying particular theories may be crucially affected by the nature of the paradigm within which the theory is developed.
>
> (Evans 1976 : 179)

The differential effects of four major paradigms on theory development, the creation of knowledge, its relationship to values, and the acceptance of particular criteria and methodologies for determining knowledge, are demonstrated by Leonard (1975). However, it can be observed that only rarely are the assumptions of the different paradigms made explicit. In particular, the effects of the unpostulated and unlabelled assumptions or 'background assumptions' (Gouldner 1970 : 29) often remain unacknowledged. It is these assumptions which operate alongside an explicitly formulated set of assumptions. At every stage, these 'background assumptions' influence a theory's formulation and the practices to which it leads (Lecomte 1975 : 31).

'Background assumptions' also play a key role in the 'social career' of theory, influencing the responses of those to whom it is communicated. 'For, in some part, theories are accepted or rejected because of the background assumptions embedded in them. A theory is more likely to be accepted by those who share the theory's background assumptions and find them agreeable' (Lecomte 1975 : 31). Such a view challenges a rational approach whereby a theory's acceptance or rejection is determined in empirical terms, that is, a deliberate inspection, rational evaluation of the theory's formal logic and supporting evidence (Lecomte 1975 : 32).

Background assumptions are important in social science, and particularly in social work, because as Lecomte remarks:

we think it probable and prudent to assume that social workers do, at this historical juncture, . . . tend to commit themselves to certain assumptions about man and society, the nature of social problems, with significant consequences for their choice of theory and modes of theory development.

(Lecomte 1975 : 33)

It is Kuhn's (1970) thesis that most of the time scientists work within the framework of a dominant paradigm without challenging it. As anomalies (or negative cases) gradually accumulate, it becomes more difficult to account for them within the prevailing paradigm, and so there is a need to develop a new competing paradigm.

However, conflict between representatives of opposing paradigms is not carried out on a purely rational, scientific basis. There is a political dimension to the conflict which reflects scientists' indoctrination during their training and their scholarly commitments and sources of prestige within the discipline. This means that a non-rational element characterizes scientists' acceptance or rejection of fundamental world views.

An example of this is developed by Bakan (1966) who studied the implications of a particular socio-economic context on the development of behaviourism, and more particularly the behaviourism of J. B. Watson. The implication is that the socio-economic context in which knowledge is developed plays a significant part in what kinds of questions are asked and how they are answered. These normative influences and their effects upon the development of theory and knowledge challenge the positivist school of thought that knowledge can be value-free (Fay 1975). This recognition does not necessarily mean 'that the great body of empirical data which has emerged out of the behaviouristic orientation [for example] . . . is to be discounted.' Rather one must 'take a new look at this contemporary situation and attempt to decide the direction that [one] wishes to go, to decide whether [one] is handicapped or enriched by this or that element in [one's] background' (Bakan 1966 : 26).

WORKING WITHIN MULTIPLE PARADIGMS

It is important to recognize that one can describe and differentiate paradigms on the basis of both explicit and background assumptions. Thus the delineation of a paradigm will provide vital information on the meta-theoretical assumptions being made in terms of both the nature of the theory being developed as well as the particular means used to construct the theory.

Ritzer (1975) has distinguished three fundamental paradigms: the 'social facts' paradigm, the 'social definition' paradigm, and the 'social behaviour' paradigm. These three paradigms can be differentiated on the basis of the fundamental assumptions they make regarding the nature of social reality.

The social facts paradigm (represented, for example, by Durkheim and presently in functionalism and conflict theory) emphasizes the idea that social facts are real, or should be treated as real, just as fully as facts about the individual. In addition, social facts have a reality of their own and are not reducible to individual facts.

The social definition paradigm emphasizes the subjective nature of social reality, rather than its existence independent of the individual (represented, for example, by Weber and later by Parsons's social action theory, and presently by symbolic interactionism). These theories are characterized by the view that social reality is based upon individuals' subjective definitions and evaluations.

The social behaviour paradigm emphasizes the objective, empirical approach to social reality. Theorists within this paradigm believe that the social facts paradigm is excessively abstract, while the social definition paradigm is excessively subjective. This paradigm emphasizes the importance of developing sociology as a science firmly grounded in measurable empirical data. The empirical data of social reality are simply the overt behaviours of individuals, and explanations of individuals' overt behaviour are possible in terms of measurement of specific and empirical environmental stimuli.

The differences between these paradigms are most patently observed when a representative of one particular paradigm attempts to define his or her position as opposed to that of others who have differing emphases. It is Ritzer's position that all three paradigms are necessary for us to understand social reality. 'In fact, no aspect of social reality can be adequately explained without drawing on insights from all of the paradigms' (Ritzer 1975 : 211).

'META-THEORY'

Meta-theory, according to Bromberger (1963), is concerned with the 'theory of theory or the theory of theories'. The way theory is viewed, as well as the way in which it is constructed, is determined by and dependent upon a more fundamental set of assumptions having to do with philosophical concerns about the nature of the subject matter under consideration, the choice of concepts used to describe and analyse this subject matter, the selection of specific problems for investigation, and the strategies used in the process of analysis.

In addition, the views of the theorist in relation to his or her purposes form a part of the meta-theoretical assumptions of a theory. An example of this is Friedrichs's (1970) differentiation between opposing value orientations of 'prophetic' sociology versus 'priestly' sociology. The prophetic mode takes a critical stance towards the status quo, 'arguing that an appropriate role for sociology is to identify deficiencies and inconsistencies in the social structure and to provide enlightenment regarding more humane possibilities. The priestly mode operates comfortably within the framework of the established structure' (Johnson 1981 : 47–8). By failing to provide a critique of the status quo, the priestly or establishment sociologists are providing tacit support for the status quo by default. The critics, or prophetic sociologists, claim that neutrality and impartiality are impossible and that unless a sociologist is devoted explicitly to promoting a more humane social structure, he or she is basically accepting the legitimacy of the status quo.

It is the case, especially in social work, that the assumptions which form the meta-theory remain, in most instances, unacknowledged. In these situations, 'theory' takes on a status of greater importance and authority than that which might be accorded if due recognition were given to its own assumptions. This might in part result in the 'marriage' rather than the 'courtship' with theory, suggested by Meyer (1973 : 89). Further it might in part cause the hoarding and accumulation of theories (Sheldon 1978a : 1–3), resulting from an inability to assess their usefulness over and above their eclectic potential (Loewenberg 1984).

It is accepted that the complex maze of underlying, mostly unstated, assumptions related to the nature of theory and its construction play a significant role in the development of social work. However, because the meta-theory has to be *implied*, it is often ignored or interpreted incorrectly. Johnson (1981 : 54) points out that 'Understanding and interpreting a theory involves learning the ideas that are explicitly stated and also being sensitive to the broader intellectual and ideological implications, including the basic world view underlying them.' But in order to get at these unstated 'world views' it is often necessary to 'read between the lines' to determine what they are. In much social work theory there is far too much 'blank space between the lines', leaving considerable latitude for the reader's imagination to construct these underlying assumptions. Furthermore, there is often a failure to acknowledge the influence of various ideologies on theory construction. The importance of understanding the effects of paradigms and meta-theory in social work is developed further in Chapter 4.

CONCLUSIONS

This chapter has been primarily concerned with explicating the key terms 'theory', 'knowledge', 'model', 'framework', 'paradigm', 'meta-theory' and outlining some connections between these concepts. It is noted that there is no agreed and consistent usage of these terms, and this creates difficulties when attempting to use and apply them. The differential use of nomenclature causes problems in any enterprise. It would be impractical to ask for a uniformity of definition at this point in time. However, to avoid some of the ambiguities identified in this chapter, writers should be asked to make explicit their particular usage. Likewise, students should be encouraged to question the meaning of these key terms, rather than assuming there exists universal agreement on their meaning.

In addition to the differential and inconsistent usage of these terms, it has been noted that theories are constructed in different ways, that the importance of the role of the theorist in theory construction is viewed differently by different writers, and that both a theory's construction and its 'career' depend upon both the explicit and background assumptions forming the paradigm in which it is developed. A recognition of the influence of differently constructed paradigms on a theory is fundamental. The critical student and practitioner needs to keep these realities in mind in order to judge the worth of a theory for use within his or her own practice. Furthermore, future writers need to be diligent in making explicit as many assumptions as possible in order to minimize the 'reading between the lines' where both assumptions and definitions of key terms remain implicit.

The recognition of different types of theory and their forms of construction ('informal' and 'formal') is important in order for the student and practitioner not to become unnecessarily dominated by one particular type and its methodology. In a bid to emulate the 'respected sciences' and to help document its efficiency and efficacy, there has been a tendency to search for formal modes of theory construction. However, this neglects the significant role of ideology and values and, together with a positivist epistemology, has the effects of ignoring certain types of qualitative and emotional experiences and phenomena, which are recognized by many as an essential part of social work.

Chapter Three

'THEORY' AND 'ACTION', 'PRACTICE THEORY', AND 'THEORY FOR PRACTICE'

THE RELATIONSHIP BETWEEN 'THEORY' AND 'ACTION'

It is argued here that because of the linkage between 'theory' and 'action' in social work, there is no substantive difference between 'social work practice theory' and 'social work theory'. As the words themselves imply, 'social work' is about 'action', 'intervention', and 'interference' in social events and in people's lives. This 'action' component historically has been characteristic of social work (Kamerman *et al.* 1973; Polansky 1975; Pilalis 1986; Pemberton 1982; Rosenfeld 1983; De Maria 1982; Hernandez *et al.* 1985).

Thus social work can be differentiated from those disciplines which have as their major concern the study of events, actions, and social conditions, without a responsibility to try to change these. A distinction is sometimes made in terms of 'applied' and 'pure' science; or in terms of clinical or practice studies in contrast to foundation disciplines. Examples can be found in medicine and education. In the former case clinical medicine is supported by the sciences of physics, chemistry, biology, and so on; in education, practice is supported by educational psychology, education philosophy, sociology, and so on.

The attitudes of members of different disciplines vary in the degree to which they believe theoretical considerations should be influenced by or influence the practical concerns and actions of practitioners in their day-to-day activities and interventions. At the one extreme, a totally *intrinsic* view of theory development is reflected in the adage 'Here's to pure science, may it never be of use!' (Leonard and Skipper 1971 : 273). In this case the generation of theory and the discovery of knowledge is seen as laudable, irrespective of its utility for application.

34

For social work, however, a study of foundation knowledge subjects such as psychology, sociology, economics, political science and so on, aims not only at clarifying and gaining a deeper understanding of events in themselves, but at understanding *in order to change or modify* behaviour and events. Thus, understanding of events for the social worker has a *utilitarian*, not just an *intrinsic* purpose.

'Theory' and 'action'[1] can be conceptualized in ways which link the two with varying degrees of relationship. At one extreme 'theory' and 'action' can be seen as relatively separate, with 'theory' referring to the development of connected thoughts, ideas and contemplations in relation to a particular subject matter, and 'action' referring to behaviours and acts of individuals (e.g. the demonstration of particular skills), with no explicit links between these two activities.

Such a position, however, has been argued against (Johnson 1981 : 7–11) on the assumption that 'action' is the behavioural outcome of a particular theory, whether the latter is explicit or implicit. In the case of a person who believes his behaviour is not connected to any theory, it can be assumed, argues Johnson (1981), that the action *is* connected to a theory of some kind, but this theory remains unacknowledged by the person because he or she may be unaware of the assumptions being made.

In supporting such a proposition Lecomte comments:

> We contend that the real issue is not whether practitioners operate from theory, but rather 'what' theory they use and how they should evaluate its usefulness for practice. For it seems evident that those who feel that they can operate entirely without theory are usually basing their behaviour on vaguely defined 'implicit' theory.
>
> (Lecomte 1975 : 208–9)

These practitioners may not be working from a scientific theory, but a moral one instead (Plant 1970; Simey 1968). Lecomte (1975 : 209) further argues that 'It is the theory used by a practitioner without knowing he is using it that is dangerous to practitioners and their clients.' Such a proposition is demonstrated by Wallace (1980) in relation to community workers, for example.

For Leonard, 'theory' (or 'thinking') and 'action' are intimately related, and he argues that 'theory' can 'just as well be determined

35

by past action as it can be a guide to future action' (Leonard and Skipper 1971 : 271). The former use of 'theory' is to make 'rationalizations' of behaviour after it has occurred. In this case actions are considered to determine thoughts and hence theories are seen to be rationalizations for past actions. The other use represents the 'rational process of using thought or theory to guide social action.

Whatever the particular relationship between 'theory' and 'action', for social work *both* the utility of theory for influencing actions as well as its intrinsic value are relevant. This being the case raises a concern with the nomenclature 'social work practice theory'.

'Practice theory' is often used to differentiate theory which has immediate relevance to the *practice* (i.e. the 'action component') of social work, rather than contextual, background, or subsidiary material. For example, the theory and skills of interviewing would be seen as centrally relevant to the *practice* of social work, whereas information on demography and parliamentary procedures, for example, could be seen as important subsidiary or contextual material (Berreen and Browne 1986).

The term 'practice theory' is also used to refer to the writing about conceptualizations of social work, regardless of how explicitly this has been linked to observable practice behaviours. This is a characteristic of the work of Bartlett (1970), for example. However, given the relationship between social work 'thinking' and 'action', and the primacy of its purpose in interventions rather than discoveries and understanding in and of themselves, it can be questioned whether 'social work practice theory' has any legitimate distinction to make from 'social work theory'. To speak about 'social work practice' theory is to (i) imply there is a 'social work non-practice theory', or (ii) to be repetitious in order to emphasize that social work theory is related to a practice or action component.

To assume that there is a 'non-practice' theory would be to attribute a different historical characteristic to social work, that is, to use the term to refer to a discipline or pure science rather than to use the term to refer to a professional pursuit which implies an interventive or action component. Hence it adds nothing to 'social work theory' to say it is *practice* theory.

The ways whereby 'theory' and 'action' can be linked in social work remain problematic. Sheldon (1978a) observes that the 'linkage' between theory and practice in social work 'is a powerfully sanctioned if vaguely defined expectation of social workers . . . a belief in the superiority of theoretically informed practice and the amendment of theory at the point of use has always been an important test of the professional faith.' Sheldon argues, however, that 'the insistence that theory and practice are complementary aspects of the same thing is part of a verbal rather than a real tradition in social work' (Sheldon 1978a : 1).

The differentiation of 'deciding what to do' and 'doing the decided' (Compton and Galaway 1979) illustrates the different processes involved in 'thinking about' or 'theoretizing' on the one hand, and 'acting' or operationalizing a set of skills or behaviours in order to put that thinking into action, on the other. However, the logical connection between these two processes is rarely presented in a way where the integration or relationship of the 'theory' to 'action' is linked explicitly.

One of the causes of this gap between theory and practice is the presence of two 'cultures' in social work (Leonard and Skipper 1971 : 269ff. and Sheldon 1978a). On the one hand there are the 'thinkers in the ivory tower' (Leonard and Skipper 1971 : 272) or the 'theoretical sub-culture' (Sheldon 1978a : 2) and on the other hand, the 'doers' of the practising professions (Leonard and Skipper 1971 : 272) or the 'practice sub-culture' (Sheldon 1978a : 2). For the academic the highest value and rewards are seen in 'pure' research; where practical implications matter little; immediate benefits for society are given a low priority; and where the primary consideration is seen to be an increase in knowledge (Leonard and Skipper 1971 : 273). Sheldon (1978a : 2) remarks that this group is 'increasingly preoccupied with the discipline of social work and associated questions of evidence and validity; perhaps in some danger of forgetting its *raison d'être* in its quest for academic respectability.' For the practitioner, however, action is valued over 'contemplation', and 'practical' research (i.e. what can be seen to have immediate relevance to practice) valued over 'theoretical' research.

The presence of these two groups or 'sub-cultures' has had a divisive effect on attempts at integration between theory and practice. Sheldon (1978a : 3–5) outlines the 'products' of each group. 'The theoretical sub-culture typically offers as its best product the large-scale controlled study.' Often the results have little effect on the practice sub-culture, particularly where the findings are critical of established practice. For the practice sub-culture the emphasis . . . is on the individuality and uniqueness of the subject matter rather than on general patterns and degrees of uniformity. The favoured product is the impressionistic case study or report, which is often (mistakenly) seen as an atheoretical statement – and all the better for it.

(Sheldon 1978a : 3)

These two sub-cultures are delineated by Lecomte (1975) in his differentiation of the 'research–theorist' approach in contrast to the 'practitioner–research–theorist' approach. The former is characterized by an 'applied science' view of social work practice with its dichotomy between practice and theory-building; its 'normatively neutral' stance and commitment to 'formal modes of theory construction'; and its 'professionalist' style in research and practice (Lecomte 1975 : 225–6). The 'practitioner–research–theorist' approach is character-ized by its 'interventive science' view of social work practice with its assumptions concerning theory generation *within* social work; its 'value-laden' stance and commitment to 'informal modes' of theory construction and an 'occupationalist' orientation to research, theory, and practice (Lecomte 1975 : 242).

The gap between the two sub-cultures is maintained because of the attitudes towards the research efforts of the other. Often the results of research by the 'academic' sub-culture are seen to be of little practical relevance to the practitioner. Furthermore, research undertaken by the 'practice' sub-culture is not usually thought of as sufficiently 'hard' for academic use.

They may be regarded as interesting or creative accounts of a process, but they serve neither to confirm nor to deny the kinds of hypothesis about outcome which are the working currency of the theoretical sub-culture. Therefore theory is not amended by practice feedback because by and large it lacks certain qualities.

(Sheldon 1978a : 4)

Further, Brennan (1973 : 7) points out that social workers are more accustomed to using theory as a means of providing services to clients rather than using practice as a device to test the efficacy of any one theory or group of concepts. This situation arises not only because of the influence of the different sub-cultures of the 'academic' and 'prac-titioner' and practical considerations on the part of practitioners such as heavy workloads, but because of a 'fundamental incongruity' between universal type social science propositions about group and mass behaviour and individualized diagnosis and treatment of specific situations (see Gyarfas 1969 : 295–73).

Carew's (1979) evidence lends support to the gap between 'theory' and 'action' by demonstrating that social workers' use of theoretical knowledge as a basis for practice is minimal. But because of his small sample, Carew cautions against the generalization of these findings to the whole social work population at this stage.

A similar position, however, is taken by Howe (1980 : 321) who notes that 'Social workers . . . seem to do many things which make no conscious recourse to the advice given by theory and its method.' He suggests that if this is in fact the case, then it can mean two things: (i) that because there is an absence of theory in practice, this can result in bad uninformed practice, or (ii) the absence of theory in practice is something to do with the irrelevance of most social work theories to the things which social workers actually do. Whatever the case, this has not prevented both the burgeoning of theories on a wide canvas of concerns, and secondly, the continuation and growth of social work, despite its critics' claims that it has been unable to change behaviour and attitudes (Howe 1980 : 321, refers to Fischer 1976; Folkhard et al. 1976).

Compton and Galaway give the following analysis of the problem the division of 'theorist/practitioner' creates for theory construction:

> It is as though the profession had purchased an unfinished foundation in which different types of construction blocks were put together in different ways. We cannot proceed to build on this foundation until we have found some way to complete it so that the blocks not only fit together but can bear the weight of the structure we want to put on top of it. Social workers are having great difficulty in finding what kind of construction can bring very diverse foundation walls together in such a way that we can build on them. Or perhaps we may have to tear down the walls already built and, using blocks of knowledge from the walls, construct them differently.
>
> (Compton and Galaway 1979 : 44)

Lecomte (1975 : 244) argues that this analogy highlights the dilemma confronting the 'research–theorist' and the 'practitioner–research–theorist'. Social work has often relied on 'outside' architects (the 'research–theorist') to build and organize the blocks of knowledge for practice. However, Wooldridge (1971 : 88) notes that the 'research–theorist' is more likely to be interested in developing theories *about* social work practice than developing practice theory *per se*. But the 'practitioner–research–theorist' position contains its own set of problems, not the least of which is the need to combine skills of the practitioner, theorist and researcher in the one person or team (Lecomte 1975 : 246–8).

In order to bridge the gap between 'theory' and 'action', various other remedies have been suggested. The first is a willingness to face the issue by studying the behaviour of social workers. Despite its limitations, Carew's study (1979) attempts to describe actual social work behaviour and to account for the results. Few studies of this kind have been carried out, despite pleas for this kind of research dating back to at least the Milford Conference in 1929.[2]

In contrast to this type of investigation which endeavours to confront some realities of practice, Brennan (1973 : 5) presents the ideal, on the assumption that it is real: 'Most social work practitioners are very much aware of the important role that theory plays in helping them provide more effective service to their clients.' He then assumes that this *ideal* is an accurate description of reality. Such an assumption is of questionable validity, and provides an example of an attitude which has hindered the proper investigation of the explicit linkage between theory and practice.

A second remedy to bridge the gap between theory and practice is the suggestion that knowledge be developed within practice contexts. This position is strongly argued by Rein and White:

> knowledge that social work seeks cannot all be made in
> Universities by individuals who presumptively seek timeless,
> contextless truths about human nature, societies, institutions, and
> policy. The knowledge *must* be developed in the living situations
> that are confronted by the contemporary episodes in the field. . . .
> [T]he basic movement of knowledge gathering is to provide for
> contexts in transition. The knowledge that is gathered – the
> perceived utility or relevance of the knowledge – is bounded in
> time, place and person.
>
> (Rein and White 1981 : 37)

This position is a reinforcement of Briar's position some years earlier: 'By far the most important trend for the future of the practice–research relationship is . . . the reduction of the separation between research and practice activities . . . . The concept of the practitioner–scientist symbolizes the trend' (Briar 1978 : 10).

The importance of developing knowledge in context *in situ* is also reflected in Leonard and Skipper's (1971) proposal for action-oriented research in programmes which have the following characteristics: (i) they are academically respectable, i.e. basic research meeting all our best scholarly standards; (ii) they are done by fully qualified academics; (iii) they are practical, i.e. usable and acceptable by the practitioner in his or her natural habitat; and (iv) they are done by fully-qualified practitioners who meet all legal, professional and/or bureaucratic criteria for appointment within the work organization (Leonard and Skipper 1971 : 270). Research carried out under such conditions is both 'basic' *and* 'applied', with no compromise in either academic standards or in practical support (Leonard and Skipper 1971 : 287).

Given the effects of socialization within the 'ivory tower' and 'practical world' (Leonard and Skipper 1971 : 272), research which meets Leonard and Skipper's suggested standards is itself idealistic. However, as an incremental step the further generation of 'grounded theory' (Glasser and Strauss 1967), in contrast to theories generated by the process of logical-deduction, ensures that these are explicitly linked to some of the realities of practice, rather than relating only to the ideals of the 'social work' philosopher.

Using a different approach to study the gap between theory and action, Pilalis (1986), after establishing a need to re-examine the problematic nature of the *relationship* between theory and practice in social work, develops a model around the processes of 'thought' and 'action'. For her, 'theory' and 'practice' are not separate entities to be combined or integrated or related to each other. She argues:

> 'Practice' cannot be devoid of theory. Similarly, it is difficult to conceive of 'theory' which is 'purely' descriptive and devoid of a reference to purposeful action. The attempt to understand in social work has an action goal (or is practice) in itself.
>
> (Pilalis 1986 : 92)

Instead of 'theory', Pilalis substitutes 'reflective thought', and for 'practice', substitutes 'purposeful action'. She then examines the degree any behaviour emphasizes either 'thought' or 'action'. For her, the importance rests not in the integration or lack of it (given that there will always be some distance between theory and practice),

41

but rather 'what factors increase and decrease this distance?' She concludes:

> this reconceptualization focuses our attention on the integral part played by the general social context and specific agency context of social work in any consideration of the 'integration' of 'theory and practice'. . . . [This implies] that the specific institutional and specific social context of practice must be built *into* practice models. . . . [Further] the requirement that students 'integrate' theory and practice needs to be redefined as a requirement that they develop a more critical stance toward the nature of theory *and* theory in practice and to constantly analyse out factors which increase or decrease the distance between them.
>
> (Pilalis 1986 :94)

'PRACTICE THEORY' AND 'THEORY FOR PRACTICE'

The distinction between 'practice theory' and 'theory for practice' has been made because social work is a heavy 'borrower' of knowledge, theories, and concepts from other disciplines and the 'pure' sciences. 'Theory for practice' (or similar nomenclature) is used to describe the knowledge, concepts, and theories 'borrowed' from other disciplines and the 'pure' sciences, which are relevant to social work's aims and areas of interest. 'Practice theory', on the other hand, is the theory developed by social workers for their own use for the purposes of carrying out their thinking and doing within a social work frame of reference (Baker 1980 :32; Siporin 1975 : 105ff. and 118ff.).

Because social work is concerned with the 'person-in-society' frame of reference, it will depend for its 'theoretical sustenance' on concepts drawn from a variety of sources (Sheldon 1978a : 9; Loewenberg 1984 : 316–20). This complexity and magnitude has been increased by the wide scope of social work's interests. Thus the social worker 'borrows' material from a large number of disciplines and it is assumed that the purposes and *modus operandi* of professional practice will influence the selection of material. Failure to relate the selection and use of this 'borrowed' material to the purposes of social work is to risk the 'borrowed' material itself dictating the purposes of practice (Bartlett 1970 : 71). Further, it would fail to take account of the effects which specific contexts and sanctions have upon social work in practice (Howe 1980 : 323–7). As Stevenson (1971 : 230) asserts, 'we must be the masters of theory for practice, that is, in the selection and use of theory for a professional purpose.' She notes further that 'in the long run we will do much more for the profession if we seek to identify the distinctive contributions of various disciplines, the points of overlap and the points of conflict' (Stevenson 1971 : 230) in relation to social work. Stevenson warns against building 'a social-work house on shifting sands of social science theory. . . . Social work should probably concentrate on erecting strong, portable, flexible tents rather than houses' (Stevenson 1971 : 226; see also Epstein 1986). She suggests that rather than looking for a 'premature consensus' and 'false integration', frames of reference be devised which can recognize complementarity and conflict (Stevenson 1971 : 226–31). Then 'we can move from the separate frames of reference provided by different disciplines in the social sciences, to the use of *principles and concepts of our own for our own particular purposes*' (Stevenson 1971 : 234).

The dangers of not keeping the distinction between 'practice theory' and 'theory for practice' are recognized by Bartlett (1970) and Baker (1980), resulting principally in social work action being seduced into abandoning its own *raison d'être* and its own *modus operandi* for those of more powerful disciplines. The 'psychiatric deluge' (Field 1980) is a powerful example of this.

However, the separation of 'practice theory' and 'theory for practice' is not without problems. The differences in approach to theory-building between the 'practitioner–research–theorist' and the 're-search–theorist' (Lecomte 1975 : 217ff.) have already been noted. While Lecomte is referring to the relationship between practice, research, and theory, a similar argument can be developed in relation to 'practice theory' and 'theory for practice'. The latter is often seen to be developed by 'outsiders', that is, social scientists who are not necessarily identified with the same professional commitments as social work practitioners. Lecomte (1975 : 245) argues that social work has often relied on 'outside' architects 'to build and organize the blocks of knowledge for practice.' This has often put the 'research–theorist' in a 'messianic' role. The 'research–theorist', argues Lecomte, may study a given practice, but he seldom does so for the prime purpose of advancing practice theory. The position of the 'practitioner–research–theorist', while bringing a professional practice perspective and commitment, has its own problems, because it requires the rare ability to combine practice, theory, and research.

A further problem related to 'practice theory' and 'theory for practice' involves the different assumptions underpinning the development of these two types of theory. Our dependence on non-social workers for what is seen to be relevant 'theory for practice' (see Epstein 1986) has often been misleading since it is not the role of the social scientist or members of other disciplines to prescribe goals for social work. But social work practice is essentially a normative activity. Hence the assumptions made by the social scientist may be at odds with those being made by the social worker.

This failure to recognize that 'practice theory' and 'theory for practice' may have been generated under different assumptions and for different purposes has contributed to the difficulties in linking these two types of theories and in selecting 'theories for practice' which are compatible with a 'practice theory'.

The desirability of recognizing the difference between these types of theory can be acknowledged. However, there remains a series of problems which need to be addressed, prior to such a distinction acquiring *operational* value. These problems will be outlined.

Are these two groups of theory of essentially the same kind, with their difference lying in their being generated for different purposes? Theories generated in the 'pure' sciences are generally regarded as having intrinsic value, whereas theories generated in the 'applied' sciences are regarded as having greater instrumental value. This raises the question of what will be included in 'theories for practice': is it 'theories', 'knowledge', and 'concepts' from the pure sciences alone, or does it also include material from other professional disciplines? If the latter case, one can ask how much 'transformation' or 'reinterpretation' has occurred already to material being borrowed from other professional disciplines.

Evans (1976 : 179), while supporting the desirability of making a distinction between these two types of theory, raises an epistemological problem that 'theories of (for) practice' can be *known* simply because they are codified and written down (Evans 1976 : 180). 'Practice theory', on the other hand, is often implicit. 'Practice theories . . . are the "commonsense" or "home-made" theories which social workers carry around in their heads and which are implicit in their day-to-day activities' (Evans 1976 : 179).

To accept this distinction is to relegate 'practice theory' to the unknowable, in that it remains implicit. However, attempts to explicate practice theory immediately take it into the 'knowable', hence the distinction between the two types of theories is not one of being

either explicit or implicit, but rather one where the theoretical explication is seen to have a different status.

This relates to a second problematic, and that is the need to
acknowledge the assumptions these two types of theory make. This
acknowledgement will make explicit what conflicting and incompatible assumptions are being made within each of these two types
of theory. If conflicting and incompatible assumptions are found,
then a further problem to be addressed will be *how* can these theories,
which have incompatible assumptions, be linked or related to each
other?

Furthermore, a lack of attention given to the assumptions of these
two types of theory can lead to 'false' distinctions being made between
'science' and 'art' and 'theory for practice' and 'practice wisdom'
(Fay 1975; England 1986). Because the influence of positivism on
social work has been strong, 'science' and 'theory for practice', where
they conform to the standards for evidence and knowledge generation
within the positivist paradigm, are often given a superior value to the
'art', 'practice wisdom', 'practice theory' part of the dialectic. These
latter are seen as depending only upon 'unqualifiable' and 'unobserv-
able' phenomena which do not meet the dictates of positivism.

However, where a non-positivist frame of reference is used (see
Leonard 1975; Burrell and Morgan 1979), the substance of the 'art',
'practice wisdom', and 'practice theory' components can be given a
different status. This is because the assumptions about what shall
count as evidence are different. Hence these aspects of practice
do not have to be relegated as ancillary, but can take an equally
important place alongside the 'theories for practice', 'scientific' part
of the dialectic.

It is the failure to acknowledge and to give credence to the different
social science paradigms in which knowledge and theory are created
which gives rise to this 'artificial' delineation between 'art' and
'science', and hence a failure to give what is called 'practice wisdom'
any status alongside so-called 'facts' derived by the hypothetico–
deductive methods of 'science'. This represents a failure to give
credence to subjectivism over objectivism and hence recognition
of interpretive theory over functionalist. This accounts in part
for the pre-eminence given to 'scientific knowledge' created by the
hypothetico–deductive method, rather than giving due recognition to
the 'experiential/phenomenological' part.

Wilkes (1978) argues that social work theorists will have to decide what is most important: the 'hard scientific' approach to theory development represented by positivism, or the more subjective, yet more elusive phenomenological approach. While conclusions to these debates are not capable of solution at the present time, the different components of the arguments and their implications need acknowledgement.

A third problematic relating to the distinction between 'practice theory' and 'theory for practice' concerns the use of eclecticism. Given social work's broad concerns and different perspectives to practice, it can be characterized as eclectic in its approach to theory selection (Loewenberg 1984; Sheldon 1978a).

The selection of practice insights and theories from a range of disciplines can help prevent social workers distorting practice realities by an 'overcommitment' (Brennan 1973 : 6) to what Wrong (1961 : 183–93) refers to as 'unreal abstractions' such as 'economic man, the gain seeker of the classical economists; the political man, the power seeker of the machiavellian tradition in political science; self preserving man, the security seeker of Hobbes and Darwin; sexual or libidinal man, the pleasure seeker of doctrinaire Freudianism . . . socialized man, the status seeker of our contemporary sociologists.'

In addition, a selection of theories and concepts can be made from a range of other sources in order to help meet the goals defined by the social worker. In this way the social worker does not have to become 'overcommitted' to any one of these. Thus Baker argues there is a need to reinterpret 'theories for practice' for use within a social work frame of reference. If this fails to occur then:

> there is a tendency for the worker to identify with particular
> theories or concepts for practice, such as transactional analysis,
> behaviour modification, existentialism or Marxism . . . . The
> result is a form of practice which is not social work, and
> practitioners who use the title 'social worker', but sound and
> behave more like a latter day Freud, Marx, Berne or Sartre.
>
> (Baker 1980 : 32)

However, Lecomte (1975 : 30) argues that one does not select any or all theories indiscriminately under the 'pretense' of 'eclecticism'. 'Eclecticism' does not mean inconsistency, nor the combination of opposing orientations but, rather the mixing of different theories within a consistent orientation' (Lecomte 1975 : 30). While an eclectic tradition in social work might be justified on the grounds of the diversity of the profession's concerns and the *emerging* nature of its theory, such justification cannot of itself solve problems created by this type of theory selection. Simons and Aigner (1979 : 208) remark 'it is a large step from demonstrating that social work demands an eclectic use of practice theory to showing how this eclecticism is to be accomplished.'

A fourth problematic relates to the 'transformation' or 'translation' of 'theories for practice' for use within social work 'practice theory'. This problem is accentuated by the fact that 'theories for practice' are formulated within different contexts: within different social science paradigms and/or different professional and occupational contexts. The assumptions of these different contexts are not always made explicit and hence the risk of theory incompatibility is usually present.

Given the relationship between 'theory' and 'action' in social work, any 'theory' must have an explicit relationship to a set of behaviours and action on the part of the practitioner. These actions must be related both to a context of practice as well as a set of operational skills to achieve explicit purposes. Thus theory can be expected to deal with a set of components, both philosophical and professional, and the relationships between those components, as well as the linkage between these and a detailed set of instructions for action, in order to achieve the purposes of any kind of practice.

A useful analogy used by Rein and White (1981 : 3) relates to what they call the 'power' and 'precision' grips. The 'power grip' relates to the normative purposes, power arrangements, myths of the profession as well as prescribed client and problematic situations, certain value positions, and certain legitimate authorizations. In other words, this component would itemize contextual purposes, possibilities and constraints, overall professional goals, and the collective *modus operandi* of the profession.

The 'precision grip' attends to the 'fine tuning'. It relates to a basis upon which specific skills may be brought to bear on any particular situation; the skills of the profession to do its work following a different order of rules and definitions; moment-to-moment practical activities.

Using this analogy in relation to types of theory, it can be seen that any theory in its ideal form should link behaviours of both the 'power' and 'precision' grips – that is the relationship between the aims of the profession, the sanctions, both prescriptive and pro-

47

scriptive, the socio-economic contexts of practice, and parameters with the sets of behaviours and skills necessary to operationalize practice.

To the extent that these two aspects are not linked, the theory is deficient. This can be the result of the way that the theory was developed. These components can be left unlinked because the development of the theory can be too much skewed to either an empirical, positivist position at the expense of a normative position, or vice versa. Or, the operational procedures of the practitioner are not linked to the contexts and specifically the power arrangements of a particular arena of practice.

CONCLUSIONS

This chapter has highlighted some of the problems in developing social work theory given the need to explicitly link theory with the behaviours of social work practitioners. The extent to which explicit links are not made will adversely affect the accuracy of the theory developed. That is why it is argued that there should be no substantive distinction between 'social work theory' and 'social work practice theory'.

While a distinction between two classes of theory, 'theory for practice' and 'practice theory', can be useful in helping social work remain distinct from the social sciences and other occupations whose theories are relevant for use within social work, a series of problems has been outlined both in delineating these two classes of theory, and how they might be integrated in order to have operational value. In evaluating any social work theory, it is important to observe whether such a distinction has been made, and if so, how the two types of theory are related.

Chapter Four

META-THEORY: 'ENDS' AND 'MEANS', AND THE CONTEXT OF PRACTICE

SOCIAL WORK META-THEORY

We noted in Chapter 2 that theories are constructed using both explicit and 'background' assumptions. These assumptions help to locate a theory within a particular paradigm. We have noted Kuhn's position in relation to paradigm shifts. The career of a particular theory will depend more upon the paradigm in which it is located than through a 'rational empirical' examination of it (Gouldner 1970 : 29; Haworth 1984).

Because the work of particular disciplines is carried out within paradigms, one or more paradigms can be chosen as the most popular for a discipline's work, including theory construction. But despite the effects of 'background assumptions' and paradigms on a theory's construction and its 'career', few attempts have been made to study meta-theory in social work. Yet failure to acknowledge meta-theory leads to such dubious differentiations as 'practice theory'/'theory for practice' and 'art/science/practice wisdom'. It also results in a lack of examination of the range of contextual variables affecting theory construction, which in turn has resulted in an emphasis on theory relating to the 'individual' and the neglect of theory relating to 'society'. Furthermore, it often leads to cross-paradigm criticism with a failure to appreciate the sets of assumptions which underlie each paradigm.

When considering social work meta-theory it is necessary to study sets of assumptions related to three major concerns: (i) the philosophical assumptions related to the nature of the social sciences; (ii) the assumptions related to the nature of society; and (iii) the assumptions related to the nature of the social work profession. These particular sets of assumptions are justified on the grounds that social work is concerned with the interaction of 'person-in-environment'; it is concerned to intervene in order to bring about change in one or both of these systems, and social work practitioners act as members of a recognized occupation or profession, within a particular societal context. They possess influence and work within sanctions which play a significant part in influencing their intervention.

Two significant and detailed studies of meta-theory which will provide useful direction to future work in this area will be described: one from a social work perspective (Lecomte 1975), and one from an organizational perspective (Burrell and Morgan 1979). A related, but less detailed paper by Leonard (1975) also studies some effects of meta-theory on social work theory construction.

Taken together, these writings provide a useful treatment of meta-theory in that they address the three major variables covering philosophical issues of social sciences, the nature of society and professional assumptions of social work. What is now required is a synthesis and development of this material.

1. *The Burrell and Morgan study*

While the Burrell and Morgan (1979) framework was developed to study the meta-theory underpinning studies of organizational structures, it provides two of the key sets of meta-theory which also affect social work theory, that is, the nature of social science, and the nature of society. Their framework develops four basic paradigms by using two intersecting axes. Each axis is a continuum representing different views on the nature of social science (from the objective dimension through to the subjective dimension) and the nature of society (from the sociology of regulation through to the sociology of radical change).

On the axis representing the nature of social science, the authors examine the major debates of ontology, epistemology, human nature, and methodology. They argue that on the continuum representing the subjective dimension to the objective dimension, the debates of social science can be characterized as follows:

ontology: nominalism to realism

epistemology: anti-positivism to positivism
human nature: voluntarism to determinism
methodology: ideographic to nomothetic

On the nature of society axis the authors characterize the sociology of regulation or order in terms of commitment, cohesion, solidarity, consensus, reciprocity, co-operation, integration, stability, and persistence. The sociology of radical change (or conflict) is characterized by coercion, division, hostility, dissensus, conflict, malintegration, and change.

This enables the authors to develop four paradigms, each underpinned by different assumptions relating to the nature of both social science and society. These paradigms are characterized as 'interpretive', 'functionalist', 'radical structuralist', and 'radical humanist'.

This model is represented in Figure 4.1:

Figure 4.1

Sociology of radical change

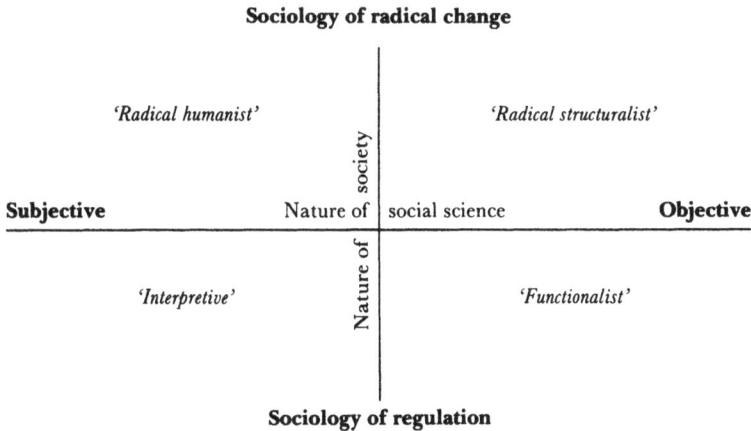

Source: Adapted from Burrell and Morgan (1979 : 22)

Burrell and Morgan note:

Our proposition is that social theory can usefully be conceived in terms of four key paradigms based upon different sets of meta-theoretical assumptions about the nature of social science and the nature of society. The four paradigms are founded upon mutually

51

exclusive views of the social world. Each stands in its own right and generates its own distinctive analyses of social life.

(Burrell and Morgan 1979 : *x*)

These authors explicate the influences such paradigms have in determining the way social scientists perceive the world and hence the effects this has upon the generation of social theory and research.

They note that in relation to organizational studies a vast proportion of theory and research is located within the bounds of only one of the four paradigms, thus leading to their conclusion that the 'socio-scientific enterprise in general is built upon an extremely narrow set of meta-theoretical assumptions' (Burrell and Morgan 1979 : *x–xi*). This situation reinforces what is then regarded as the dominant orthodoxy within a discipline. Because this is usually strong within a discipline its adherents take it for granted as right and self-evident. Rivals to this orthodoxy are seldom strong enough to establish themselves as anything more than a deviant set of approaches; thus, their possibilities are seldom explored (Burrell and Morgan 1979 : *xi*).

2. *The Lecomte study*

The work of Lecomte (1975) is complementary to that of Burrell and Morgan (1979). Lecomte's work is related specifically to social work meta-theory and, significantly, develops arguments related to the 'professional' assumptions of social work. His work does not, however, take into account the effects of different assumptions related to the nature of society, as does the work of Burrell and Morgan.

Lecomte divides his analysis into a consideration of the philosophical assumptions and professional assumptions of social work. He divides each of these two sets of assumptions into their normative and empirical components and examines each using a descriptive as well as dialectical process. The philosophical assumptions of a normative type are characterized by holism, idealism, subjectivism, introspectionism, and informalism. The philosophical assumptions of an empirical type are elementalism, realism, objectivism, extrospectionism, and formalism.

The professional assumptions of a normative type are the 'interventive science' view and the 'practitioner–research–theorist' view. The professional assumptions of an empirical type are characterized by the 'applied science' view and the 'research–theorist' view.

Thus in order to analyse social work theory, Lecomte (1975 : 69) argues, one must review five basic sets of philosophical issues in terms of their normative and empirical aspects. These are set out in Figure 4.2.

In addition, two basic sets of professional issues need to be examined. These are set out in Figure 4.3.

In noting the poverty of criteria to analyse theories amidst an abundance of different types of theory, Lecomte (1975 :28–9) believes it is necessary to develop greater sophistication in theory evaluation and criticism. He concludes (1975 : 254):

> there has been far too facile an acceptance and adoption of 'theories', 'approaches', and 'models' without a critical awareness of their limitations with respect to the kinds of assumptions on which they are based, and the kinds of questions to which they are applicable.
>
> (Lecomte 1975 : 254)

There is 'an unhealthy preoccupation with methodological tools and the "verification logic" at the expense of analysis' (Lecomte 1975 : 255). Lecomte exhorts social work to re-examine its commitment to a narrowly defined 'scientific' method, noting there is not only *one* philosophy of science, but *many* (Lecomte 1975 : 75 and 255–6).

Lecomte cautions social work against aligning with only one philosophy of social science, especially one related closely to the methodology of the physical sciences. He relies on Deutscher:

> In attempting to assume the stance of a physical science, we have necessarily assumed its epistemology, its assumptions about the nature of knowledge and the appropriate means of knowing, including the rules of scientific evidence . . . [one of the consequences of using the natural science model] was to break down human behaviour in a way that was not only artificial but which did not jibe with the manner in which the behaviour was observed.
>
> (Deutscher 1966 : 241)

An inappropriate allegiance with so-called 'scientific' theories has often been misleading, he argues:

> since it is not the role of the scientist to prescribe goals and since

Figure 4.2 Framework for the analysis of philosophical issues involved in the analysis of social work theory

Philosophical assumptions in theory construction	Philosophical issues of choice in the normative and the empirical orientations
A. Assumptions *re*: level of abstractions of theory construction	Holism versus elementalism
B. Assumptions *re*: views of reality and location of values in theory construction	Idealism versus realism
C. Assumptions *re*: extent of generalization of theory construction	Subjectivism versus objectivism
D. Assumptions *re*: theorist's perspective in theory construction	Introspectionism versus extrospectionism
E. Assumptions *re*: modes of theory construction	Informalism versus formalism

Source: Adapted from Lecomte (1975 : 71)

Figure 4.3 Framework for the analysis of professional issues involved in the analysis of social work theory

Professional assumptions	Professional issues involved in the normative and the empirical orientations		
A. Assumptions *re*: relation between theory and practice	'Interventive science' view	*versus*	'Applied science' view
B. Assumptions *re*: relation between theory and research	'Practitioner–research–theorist' approach	*versus*	'Research–theorist' approach

Source: Adapted from Lecomte (1975 : 188).

theories of social work practice are essentially normative rather than empirical, they are outside the province of scientist as scientist.

(Lecomte 1975 : 257)

The confusion in social work of presenting normative formulations as empirical results partly from its attempt to 'cast contradictory role requirements in a single mould' (Lecomte 1975 : 257). His study emphasizes the need to change the emphasis and direction in the generation of social work theory as a result of considering alternative frames of reference.

3. *The Leonard study*

Leonard's (1975) model is confined to an explication of four essentially different paradigms for the development of theory within the physical and human sciences. He argues that not only is there a need to consider rival and conflicting explanations of human behaviour and social structure, but also that:

many of these different perspectives are based on different *criteria* of explanation itself. In other words, the answer to the question 'What shall we count as evidence?' is itself subject to dispute and demands the exploration of a number of different philosophical approaches to the bases of explanation.

(Leonard 1975 : 325)

This author develops a 'device' in order to help 'develop in social workers a more critical stance towards social science inputs into practice' (Leonard 1975 : 326). This is illustrated in Figure 4.4.

These studies clearly demonstrate the importance of meta-theory, yet very little has been written on this in social work. This in part may be the result of the complexity of the undertaking, especially given that so many sets of variables need to be taken into account when teasing out the underlying assumptions of a professional discipline operating within a variety of contexts and taking for itself a very broad subject matter. However, in assessing the contribution of any theory or genre of theory, it is necessary to take into account the meta-theoretical assumptions being made, and the degree to which these have been made explicit by their authors.

Figure 4.4

Physical sciences paradigm

Position A:

Social sciences should aspire
   to status of physical
   sciences
Importance of measurement and
   objectivity
Public knowledge is determined
   by sensory data

Position B:

General similarity of physical and
   social sciences in objectives
   and methods
Stress on inexactness of the
   physical sciences
Importance of probability in both
   sciences

Human sciences paradigm

Position C:

Subjective understanding
   crucial to the social
   sciences
Questions are value-laden:
   answers can be relatively
   value-free

Position D:

Social sciences are socially determined
Ideological influences are central
Importance of studying socio-
   economic context of theories

Source: Leonard (1975 : 327)

'ENDS' AND 'MEANS' IN SOCIAL WORK

Social work intervenes in the lives of people. Thus it is a moral activity, and as such needs to consider the purposes and consequences of its actions. It is a normative activity which is open to empirical observation, but a description of current observations can in no way be used as a justification for what *ought* to be the case.[1] Thus for social work, teleological explanations are necessary in order to discern a connection between 'ends' and 'means'.

> [Teleology is] the study of ends, goals or purposes; more specifically, the theory that events can only be explained, and that evaluation of anything . . . can only be justified, by consideration of the ends toward which they are directed. Teleologists contend that living organisms can only be explained in a forward-looking way and that mechanistic explanation in terms of efficient causes is inadequate. As an ethical doctrine . . . teleology argues . . . that the rightness is not an intrinsic property of actions but is dependent on the goodness or badness of the consequences, whether actual, predictable, or expected, to which they give rise.
> (Bullock and Stallybrass 1977 : 626)

56

While it can be argued that within ethics more generally the justification of 'means-type' behaviour is possible and desirable, within the context of a profession the actions of practitioners require justification not only in terms of 'means' but in terms of certain ends, that is, professional behaviour is teleological. Removed from an explicit end state, related to both professional ethics on the one hand and knowledge and purposes on the other, the 'means' used by practitioners of themselves cannot be justified, except as choices of private and individual persons.[2]

It follows that if the purpose of a social work theory is absent or obscure, then it will be impossible to know what actions ('means') need to be undertaken. Furthermore, a justification of the actions will be difficult if not impossible to make.

A positivist view of social sciences differentiates 'ends-means' considerations in order to treat 'the best means to a presented end' as a factual question and therefore able to be decided 'scientifically' through a policy science. This view is strongly repudiated by Fay (1975 : 49–57), who argues that any 'means'-type behaviour is value based.

> For all political decisions, even those which are seen as means to an end, are social policies, and as such they embody a notion of what people ought to be required or permitted to do to others. No social policy's worth can be solely instrumental because any such policy will require that people interact with one another in certain definite ways, and for this reason it must have a moral value *in itself*.
>
> (Fay 1975 : 52)

And again,

> Questions as to the best means necessarily involve and express certain basic values on the part of the policy scientist, and it is for this reason that the demand for such a science is in principle unrealisable.
>
> (Fay 1975 : 56)

However, the acceptance of this argument does not invalidate the differentiation of 'ends' and 'means' but rather highlights the necessity of justifying both the ends *and* the means of achieving them. Thus while teleological and deontological arguments can be seen in opposition to each other from an interpretive social science perspective, *both* types of behaviours and outcomes need to be justified. For the professional social worker, unless there is an explicitly stated purpose or purposes, the use of any technique of intervention cannot be justified, because the social worker will not know why such a technique is being employed.

The explication of purpose in social work therefore is crucial. Given that resources are limited (time, number of agencies, financial and material goods and services, and so on), without a particular stated social work goal to be achieved within a stated ideological framework, the direction which choices should take remains unclear. This can be clearly illustrated in the eligibility for social work service. Should the service be directed to a certain group of people with particular needs, particular social problems or circumstances in life, or should social work services be available for everyone? Should all groups of recipients of social work service get what they want? Or if not, if a choice has to be made, on what grounds is the choice justified? How does the social worker deal with a conflict of interests? Without explicit purposes these issues can never be properly justified. While all behaviour ultimately needs justification, in the presence of limited resources, and therefore choices, criteria for these choices related to professional decision making must be related to stated 'ends': it cannot be limited to a justification which deals with 'means-type' behaviour alone.

This problem can be illustrated by considering *who* are the clients for social work. In much of the social work literature, 'client' has not been defined and the implication seems to be that anyone can be a client. If no attempt is made to define the status of people with whom the social worker deals then this leaves completely open the possibility of the social worker being caught up with two groups of clients with conflicting interests. For example, there are many instances in practice where both landlord and tenant, patient and doctor, beneficiary and administrator, each could be potential clients. By using Pincus and Minahan's (1973 : 56–8) definition of 'client', for example, a doctor might request a social worker's help in making more beds available for acute patients by removing rehabilitation-type patients to another facility. The doctor makes this request, he/she forms an agreement with the social worker about how this will be done, and he/she is one of the expected beneficiaries because more beds will result for acute patient care. In this scenario does the 'person in the bed soon to be removed elsewhere' have any status with the social worker except as a 'target' for the social worker's actions? No matter what 'means' the social worker employs (humane or otherwise), the 'person in the bed' is being removed, not necessarily because of his/her own wishes, but because of the needs of others. The interventive behaviours of the social worker cannot be justified except by reference to some defined goals, purposes, ideology, and 'ends' of practice. To the extent that these are not made explicit, this results in difficult and often unjustifiable decisions on the part of the social worker.

Further conflict can occur between the interests of two groups of people or between the interests of the individual versus the interests of the collectivity to which that individual belongs. In these cases reference to purpose is necessary to make justifiable choices.

Along with these questions is the need to examine interests of groups and individuals. The need to be explicit about a variety of interests and conflicts in interests is related to how conflict can be recognized and dealt with. The method often employed is one of mediation and conciliation. It is based on the premise that a meeting ground of interests can be found. It does not consider that a meeting ground might not be possible and thus one person or group winning and holding power over another.

At a technical level it is difficult to devise a methodology for acquiring a useful/accurate means of achieving something if one does not know the purposes or ends for its use. For example, the use of behaviour modification techniques including the rational–emotive therapies can be said to alter people's behaviours in one way or another. In a correctional institution they can be used to tailor behaviour towards particular norms, in a teaching situation a student might be desensitized to the emotional impact of emotive and taboo subjects. Without debating the efficacy of such techniques, it can be generally recognized that some behaviour change is possible. However, the more difficult question is the direction of that behaviour change and its justification.

Thus any practice framework utilizing technologies to bring about behavioural changes, such as in social work, needs to specify the purpose to which behaviour change can be directed. Otherwise, social workers could be simultaneously using and/or trying to find the means of increasing a person's assertiveness and aggressiveness on the one hand, and trying to foster more conforming and less aggressive behaviour on the other. For whose benefit is this? Whose interests is it serving? How does it relate to social work purposes?

The failure to come to terms with clearly explicating purpose or 'ends' for social work is closely tied with the need to clearly distinguish between description and prescription. In making a descriptive statement one is trying to communicate in the best possible way what is happening or what did happen. However, to prescribe some behaviour or action is to say that this *should* have occurred or *ought* to be the case. When one makes a prescriptive statement one expects a justification or a reason why something 'should' or 'ought' to be the case. It will be the plausibility of this reason which will convince others of the rightness of such an action.

Often, where no justification is given, prescriptive statements may appear as descriptive ones. For example, take the statement 'the social work profession commands great respect.' This appears to be a descriptive statement. But a check one can make is to enquire what is the basis for drawing such a conclusion, in other words, where is the evidence? If the person making such a statement can convince you that this statement accurately describes a particular state and can show you the evidence in the form of a data base, then you can accept this to be a description of some reality within the parameters of the methods used to collect the data. More likely, that person will not have the evidence, and furthermore when pressed will insist 'but social workers *ought* to command respect.' Now this is a prescriptive statement, and if you are to be convinced that this is so, you will ask for some reasoned arguments to support this. On the basis of these arguments you may or may not concur with this judgement.

This distinction is reasonably easy to maintain. The difficulty, however, occurs when prescriptive statements are couched in descriptive language (the use of 'is' rather than 'ought') or when the intent of the statement is unclear. In any particular writing, particularly involving normative behaviour such as in social work, a clear differentiation and intent is necessary to effectively communicate the intended meaning.

This very brief treatment of ends and means in social work indicates the necessity of considering moral criteria, along with observed behaviours and desired outcomes. In order to evaluate any theory in its accurate accounting for practice behaviours and its descriptive, prescriptive, and predictive capacities, it is necessary to consider the place given to an explication of both its 'means' and its 'ends', particularly the 'ends' desired by the profession.

In addition to the need to clearly articulate 'ends' and 'means' in social work, a further question relates to what constitutes justificatory criteria for both ends and means. It has been argued by Lawrence (1983) that justificatory criteria must be of a moral kind since social work deals with interactions between *people*. He thus argues for a central place for moral philosophy within social work (Lawrence 1983) (see also Siporin 1982). It will not be debated here what the precise nature of justificatory criteria is or ought to be. It is important to establish, however, that justification (of any variety) is crucial in providing a rationale as well as a direction for a social worker's actions.

THE CONTEXT OF THEORY CONSTRUCTION

The context in which theory construction takes place influences the theorist. Whatever the mode of theory construction, the amount of recognition given to the influence of the theorist and his or her context on the theory will depend upon the value placed on the different paradigms of 'science' by individual theorists, as well as the norms which operate in a particular discipline from time to time. These issues have already been discussed in Chapters 1 and 2. Particularly with informal modes of theory construction, the 'image of reality' which the theorist subscribes to will affect the kind of theory developed and hence an acknowledgement of an historical location is essential. While the proponents of formal modes of theory construction may not acknowledge the need for an explicit recognition of their historical location, nevertheless its influence can be observed.

The importance of an historical location and context for a theory has important implications for its universality – that is, whether theories generated within one particular context can be transferred and applied in another context.

It is argued by Rein and White (1981 : 2–4) that practice is always carried out within an organized social framework which provides a context in which social workers share purposes, power relationships and myths. However, these are not unitary entities: there is not simply one grand and shared purpose (Rein and White 1981 : 5): social workers are caught up in networks of solidarities and politics of purpose with every single professional action (Rein and White 1981 : 11). While professional dogma might help to maintain a set of shared purposes (characteristically context-free and consensual), 'of course, social workers never meet consensual values. They live amidst the pull of competing and conflicting solidarities. They construct various individual attitudes and studies to manage several tensions between abstract values and reality and among conflicting solidarities' (Rein and White 1981 : 33). The implication from this is that social work theory should reflect contextual diversity.

Rein and White (1981 : 37) further argue that if it is true that knowledge is bounded in time, place, and person, then knowledge *must* be developed in the living situations taking into account the contemporary 'episodes in the field'. Such a position, it is argued, leads to the possibilities that:

> (1) the 'applied' segments of the behavioural and social sciences, now generally regarded as secondary and peripheral aspects of the disciplines, may in fact be leading edges of knowledge developments in the fields; and (2) the social and behavioural sciences, now generally held to be unitary disciplines or disciplines that march toward a unity in the future, may be deeply and intrinsically pluralistic in their very nature.
>
> (Rein and White 1981 : 38)

The effects of contexts in promoting attitudes toward theory development and the predominance of some theories over others have been demonstrated (see Field (1980) on the 'psychiatric deluge', and Bakan (1966) on the rise of behaviourism). This reinforces the importance of taking into account the historical context of a theory's development as well as a specific socio-political context. However, whether such variables are taken into consideration will depend upon the scientific paradigm in which the theorist is working, as to whether such contextual variables will count as evidence.

Even this decision on the part of the theorist is not made in a vacuum, because the influence of the 'theorist–researcher' sub-culture or the 'practitioner' sub-culture, that is, the ideological and occupational location of the theorist, will influence that theorist in the choice he or she makes to operate within a particular paradigm.

A similar argument is developed by Howe (1980) that the nature of social work knowledge is not to be found in the literature, but *in situ*. Howe (1980 : 322) argues that it would be more profitable to look at social workers in action rather than dismiss them for not living up to the expectations created by their writings. He notes the increasing 'immodesty of purpose' of social work including the breadth of the enterprise exacerbated by a 'bout of generic thinking', the influence of sociology, professionalization, and the 'steady accumulation of unrelated relics' (1980 : 318–21). One of the suggested remedies in reaction to the critics of social work's ineffectiveness is to find and develop a theory to unify and integrate. Such a remedy, however, is challenged as being premature and spurious:

> To look for form and unity actually blinds us to the richness of social life and limits our ability to conceive other ways of acting. Social theories and social maps can only represent certain bits of the social world.
>
> (Howe 1980 : 322)

The remedy suggested by Howe is to

> try and understand the job less in terms of an applied social science, an instrument of personal and social change, but more as the exercise of concepts such as duty, responsibility and practical judgment in problems of everyday living.
>
> (Howe 1980 : 322–3)

His hope is that this kind of enquiry would wash 'away much of the profession's ornamentation, leaving something which, though less extravagant, would be smaller and more manageable.' However, he adds that 'it remains to be seen whether social work theory is yet prepared to leave the age of high baroque' (Howe 1980 : 323).

Such a remedy clearly dictates the need to study the differential effects of contexts upon theory development. Whether this will be possible will be centrally linked to the theorist's view of how theory should be developed, and what criteria will be used to decide upon relevant evidence, for example, the different positions taken to formal/ informal theory development, the view of the theorist towards his or her work as 'applied social science' or 'interventive science', and the view of himself as a 'research–theorist' or a 'practitioner–research–theorist'.

The need to take into account so many variables, including contextual variables, is challenging. Maybe social work theorists are not ready at this point in time to portray their thinking and practice by acknowledging so many influences. This raises the question of where to start. Does one begin with the 'broad canvas' of social work theory as a universal and contextless 'grand theory', or does one start with the narrower, time-limited, context-limited study? The genre of theory, which is the subject of this book, is representative of the former approach; at the other end of the scale the study of 'low key practice'

(Mispelblom 1985) makes an important contribution in terms of the *in situ* attributes to which Rein and White (1981) and Howe (1980) refer.

CONCLUSION TO PART 1

Prior to observing the genre of writing known as 'integrated', 'unitary', or 'generic', it has been necessary to review some general issues related to the development of social work theory. Chapters 2, 3, and 4, by way of an essay-review, highlight particular issues and problems for social work theory. These issues will be used as part of the evaluation of this genre of theory.

What we have noted so far can be summarized as follows:

1. Key terms used to depict theory and its construction do not have an uncontested meaning either in social work or other disciplines.
2. There are both 'formal' and 'informal' modes of constructing theory and the choice of the theorist often depends upon the particular social science paradigm to which that theorist is committed.
3. Social work theory, by its very nature and its history, needs to be explicitly linked to 'action' and 'intervention' in the lives of people and societies.
4. Because of the necessary linkage between 'theory' and 'action', there should be no distinction between 'social work theory' and 'social work practice theory'.
5. While it is necessary to differentiate social work 'practice theory' from 'theory for practice' borrowed from other disciplines and professions, such a distinction often denigrates 'social work theory' as subservient to the 'truths' of the 'sciences' because of a failure to recognize the legitimacy of a range of different paradigms in which knowledge and theory can be constructed, and what should count as evidence.
6. A study of meta-theory, while it has so far been neglected in social work, is a crucial part of evaluating a theory.
7. Because social work is a normative activity then its actions and interventions can only be justified when the purposes and 'ends' of social work are made as explicit as possible.
8. Where little work has been done on justifying both 'ends' and

'means' of behaviour then the risk of confusing description and prescription is great.

9. Because social workers practise under the sanctions, both proscriptive and prescriptive, of particular socio-economic-political regimes, then the context of their practice, and hence the context of theory construction for social work, has implications for the universality of that theory.

THE DATA

In Part 1 some general issues of theory construction in social work were examined. In Part 2 we shall examine some of the primary data which has been chosen to represent the genre of 'integrated' theory. In the initial study (Roberts 1987), eleven conceptual frameworks were analysed and critically evaluated. These were the frameworks of Bartlett (1970), Goldstein (1974), Pincus and Minahan (1973), Middleman and Goldberg (1974), Whittaker (1974), Siporin (1975), Haines (1975), Baker (1975 to 1982), Loewenberg (1977a), Compton and Galaway (1979) and Germain and Gitterman (1980).

For the purposes of this book, four frameworks will be discussed in detail: Bartlett, Goldstein, Pincus and Minahan, and Middleman and Goldberg. Each author's work will be briefly described, and a critique developed. This selection demonstrates some of the principle characteristics of 'integrated' theory and the method of analysis. The findings from all eleven frameworks will be used in evaluating the contribution of 'integrated' theory to social work developed in Parts 3 and 4.

In presenting this material, it is the expectation that the reader will make reference to the original works of the primary data. While every effort has been made to give a fair coverage of four frameworks, this should not be seen as a substitute for direct consultation of each of the author's works.

Chapter Five

EXPLICATION AND CRITIQUE OF FOUR CONCEPTUAL FRAMEWORKS

THE FRAMEWORK OF BARTLETT

Introduction

The framework developed by Bartlett (1970) was the first to draw attention to the need for social workers to establish a central point of reference in the form of a 'common base' for their thinking. She argued this is necessary for the further development of social work as a profession and in order to prevent social work being pulled away from its central focus towards that of a more powerful discipline or profession.

> Ego psychology, role theory, organization theory, and other clusters of knowledge are relevant for social work if they are appropriately integrated with its purpose and focus. If used separately, however, they tend to pull the practitioner away from the social work focus toward that of the other profession or discipline from which they are derived. . . .
>
> (Bartlett 1970 : 71)

Bartlett seeks to write *about* practice, and it is not her intention to provide a 'how to do it' manual. 'It is not a description of practice or an analysis of practice, but rather a consideration of social workers' *ways of thinking* about their practice' (Bartlett 1970 : 10). This last phrase could more accurately read '*Bartlett's* ways of thinking about practice', because it is based upon *her* practice and educational experience. She provides no empirical evidence of how widespread this form of thinking is amongst social workers.

The development of her model and her arguments against a conceptualization based on a particular agency or field or a particular method of practice accept social work as a profession. As such, she argues, it requires a high degree of generalized and systematic knowledge and an orientation to community interest rather than to individual self-interest. The major distinction between a *profession* and an *occupation*, she asserts, is the 'substantial body of knowledge' on which the former rests (Bartlett 1970 : 19). In treating social work as a profession, Bartlett accepts that not only does it have a substantial body of knowledge but this body of knowledge has to be conceptualized in such a way that it will provide a central reference point for *all* social work practice.

> when eventually defined, the central focus will appear as a single concept or constellation of concepts on which practice can be based and around which theory can be developed.
>
> (Bartlett 1970 : 17)

Bartlett provides the following reasons for developing a 'professional model'.

First, the result of a continued focus on method 'tends towards even greater technical precision and increasing narrowness of focus. Thus social workers worked at refining their own ideas but were prevented by the barriers between the methods from communicating easily with each other . . .' (Bartlett 1970 : 52).

Second, an approach based solely on methods or fields was inhibiting theory-building:

> because of the emphasis on 'the uniqueness of the individual', 'the case' and 'the specific situation', generalizations were not forthcoming from practice experience in any significant number. . . . Growth of theory was held back and the professional literature was not developing in a cumulative fashion.
>
> (Bartlett 1970 : 53)

Third, the establishment of the National Association of Social Workers in 1955 made it easier to deal with 'social work practice as a whole'.

Fourth, without a professional model, the method-and-skill model focused on the 'art' rather than the 'science' of the profession with a central concept of 'helping service', and a 'therapeutic' focus on 'treatment goals' and 'professional skill'. In isolation, 'method-and-skill' viewed practice from the perspective of the individual worker, rather than the profession as a whole.

Fifth, social workers have tended to be pulled away from a social work focus by being side-tracked into clusters of knowledge and theory from other disciplines.

Bartlett's central thesis

Bartlett's central thesis (1970 : 56) is the need to combine both a 'method-and-skill' approach and a broad 'professional model'.

> What is now needed for the profession's forward movement is not to discard the method-and-skill model as a whole, but to carry over from it those aspects that are contributing the strengths of social work and to include them in the *new* professional model. In this way, the concept of the skilled worker can take its proper place within a comprehensive concept of social work and its practice. The method-and-skill model needs greater breadth, while the overall professional model needs substance.

While the linkage between 'method-and-skill' and the new 'professional' model provides the basis for the development of the integrated approaches to social work in general, it must be noted there are fundamental difficulties which are not addressed by Bartlett.

The first of these is that the strengths of the method-and-skill model are not made explicit. Indeed, Bartlett has been highly critical of such an approach, yet she fails to outline what particular strengths such an approach might have. One might infer she is referring to the development of specific skills. Yet skills used within a profession need to be related to underpinning theory. So, is she thereby implying that the theory underpinning a 'method-and-skill' approach is compatible with the theory of the professional model? In any case the 'strengths' of 'method-and-skill' will depend upon the particular definition of social work being employed, and the effectiveness of these methods and skills in achieving these ends.

Second, Bartlett does not make clear whether she considers her conceptualization a more accurate description of what exists or whether she is advocating a 'new' kind of practice, that is, a prescription for the future. In the former case she might claim that her conceptualization of practice of the 'social worker in action' is a more accurate description of reality. On the other hand, she might be

72

suggesting a new form of practice which *ought* to be occurring. This confusion is evident throughout her work. Furthermore, it remains unclear whether Bartlett is critical of the way social work has been *conceptualized* in the past, or the manner in which it has been *practised*.

Third, in making reference to the 'skilled worker' it is not clear whether this concept refers to the skills of a particular method, or whether she means a wide range of general skills reflecting a comprehensive concept of social work. This difference is crucial in order to explicate what the social worker, utilizing the professional model, will be expected to do in practice – i.e. locate specific method skills in the professional model so that he or she has some idea of how they fit into a comprehensive framework, *or* have available a repertoire of skills which will enable the social worker to operationalize the professional model by utilizing a wide range of general and specific skills.

Fourth, Bartlett claims the 'method-and-skill' model needs greater breadth. Is she implying that the methods *per se* do not meet a particular conceptualization of social work practice? By stating that the 'professional model needs substance' is she implying that this model has nothing substantive in its own right? If it is totally dependent upon 'method-and-skill' for substance, what makes it different?

These basic confusions run through her work and have an impeding effect upon understanding it and its operationalization.

Developing a professional model

The starting point for Bartlett's professional model is the concept of 'social functioning' (Bartlett 1970 : 84ff.). It is this concept which best fits the central social work focus on 'person-in-the-environment'. It deals with people coping with life situations where the demands of the social environment and people's coping efforts are balanced. However, from the outset this cornerstone of her model is fraught with problems.

First, there is no indication *when* social work intervention is required. What sets of criteria need to operate before social work intervention is seen as appropriate? How are coping capacities and environmental demands evaluated? Bartlett seems to want to deny any kind of evaluation of this interaction when she asserts that 'the overall concept of social functioning . . . is to be regarded as neutral and not incorporating normative criteria. . . . Thus patterns of coping, patterns of environmental demand, and the relationships between them should be studied as *rigorously and objectively as possible'* (Bartlett 1970 : 110) (my italics). But how is this possible? The demands upon the individual by his environment and his response are evaluated, in order to determine patterns of need. Any definition of social work has to contain normative criteria if directions and goals are to be set. Rigour and objectivity alone will not provide these. Bartlett emphasizes her point:

> the purpose of studying social functioning is not to define certain types of functioning as good or desirable, but simply to *understand* the various components, their relationships, and the outcomes. As more adequate knowledge regarding social functioning is built up by the profession, practitioners will be better able to foresee the possible and probable consequences of the various patterns of exchange between people and environment.
>
> (Bartlett 1970 : 111)

As outlined, this sounds like a sociological exercise in making some interesting observations. Social work has always been identified with an interventive (action) orientation and this demands not only observing the exchange between person and environment but placing a *value* on the exchange. Bartlett's stance is thus untenable for practice, and hence highly limited for theory development.

Furthermore, by choosing 'life task', and 'coping', Bartlett is placing considerable emphasis on the individual. It is questionable whether the concept will provide a bridge between person and environment in spite of the interaction. Given that there is interdependence between the two, life tasks are often defined in terms of and are enhanced or hindered by the social structure in which the individual is located. Bartlett has virtually nothing to say about social structures: her theory development has stopped with the individual, thus she could rightly be criticized for her one-sidedness or narrow focus, a fault she finds in others.

Emanating from a central focus on 'social functioning', social work's orientation is then linked to a 'body of values' and a 'body of knowledge'. She states the need to clearly separate 'knowledge' and 'values'. She states that 'values' refer to what is regarded as good and desirable. These are qualitative judgements, they are not empirically demonstrable. They are imbued with emotion and represent a purpose or goal toward which the social worker's action will be directed. They refer to what is preferred. Knowledge propositions refer to verifiable experience and appear in the form of rigorous statements that are made as objective as possible. They refer to what is confirmed or confirmable.

She argues further that some statements which are identical in form can be taken either as knowledge or as value. In this case it is the *intention* regarding the proposition, rather than its actual substance, that makes the difference, e.g. 'home is the best place for a child.' This can be taken as preferred, or as an hypothesis for investigation.

Bartlett claims that the oldest and most widely-held value in social work asserts the worth and dignity of every human being. This in turn has led to the importance of self-determination in social work practice. This highly individualistic approach is seen by Bartlett as consistent with democratic ideals of the state. However, such a position is asserted rather than argued.

In terms of Bartlett's 'professional model', a number of problems arise. First, it is not clear whether it is the substantive content of 'knowledge' and 'values' which defines the parameters of the social worker or just the (abstract) concepts themselves. One can study how knowledge and values can be defined, that is, the development of these concepts; but to have any utility in guiding practice, a choice of substantive content has to be made. Bartlett attempts this only by way of example and illustration. She provides no guidance as to how the substance of 'knowledge' and 'values' can be known.

A second problem is her insistence that a clear differentiation in knowledge and values exists. She asserts that this is necessary in guiding practice: the practitioner needs to be aware if he or she is invoking a value or a piece of knowledge, and that in conflicting situations, knowledge should take precedence. This view places her within a *positivist* school of thought. Thus there is no recognition of the influence values, particularly cultural values, exert on the development of knowledge nor is there serious recognition of the conflict which exists between competing and opposing sets of values. Nowhere does Bartlett argue why knowledge *should* take precedence over values.

A third problem is the emphasis on sets of values based around the individual and his or her rights to self-actualization and self-determination, with little recognition of collective values and the tensions which exist in the individual/collective interface. Even more problematic in her treatment of values is her assumption that there is agreement and consensus amongst social workers about the core social work values. In this way values are being divorced from behaviour.

A fourth problem is Bartlett's assumption that a 'common base' exists. Yet she makes no effort to provide empirical support for this.

Operationalization

Bartlett remarks (1970 : 83) that when practitioners use this common base, 'the whole scene shifts'. The practitioner 'now becomes a *social worker*, broadly engaged, who develops *competence* in *all the essentials of the profession*' (my italics).

But one can ask, what are 'all the essentials'? Does this refer to essentials in 'understanding', or 'essentials in skills'? This remains ambiguous, although Bartlett gives the qualification:

> it does not mean that practitioners must acquire competence in all the techniques . . . social workers will be aware of the full range of interventive measures. . . .
>
> (Bartlett 1970 : 80)

Bartlett might claim she is not writing a manual *on* practice but *about* practice, and hence there is no reason to address the questions I have raised. But unless her framework can be seen to relate to a range of substantive theory, it provides no focus at all for either practitioner or theoretician.

Bartlett (1970 : 85–6) recognizes the need for substantive theories, both for the strength of the profession and for social workers' effectiveness. The 'helping process' she claims depends upon an understanding of the nature of influencing social behaviour and conditions. Professional knowledge-building requires identifying particular phenomena as well as concepts for organizing thinking around these. However, nowhere has she attempted to spell out what particular theories or concepts are relevant in influencing social behaviour and conditions.

She (1970 : 86) exhorts us to 'work as intensively on understanding social phenomena and social situations as on understanding processes, methods and action.' Her rhetoric becomes even more emotive in advocating an 'integrative thinking' which

will draw from social work's past the ideas that are relevant, combine them with new ideas, and link the essential components into powerful comprehensive concepts regarding the profession's focus, which will demonstrate convincingly to its members and to society where the profession stands and what it has to offer.

(Bartlett 1970 : 86)

But this emotive call is no more than saying, 'it would be a good thing if . . . .' In other words, Bartlett is not making clear the *purpose* of her model development. Is it to ask and test empirical questions? (What are common substantive matters of social work which can be observed? Does it make social work practice achieve particular ends more effectively? Does it cause the social work profession to become strengthened? etc.) Is it a value of hers (it would be 'good' if everyone had a common identity)? Is it merely an emotive rah-rah? ('Let's get together: things are sure to be better if we do!')

Bartlett recognizes the dual commitment of social work, but it is by no means clear what she means when she refers (1970 : 124) to the people 'being served'. Does she refer to people who have become *clients* of the social worker, and if so how is this status reached? There seems to be an assumption that social workers will indeed be able to 'serve' the interests of various client groups. Without a definition of the latter, there is an implicit assumption that the needs and rights of persons so defined will be able to be met and that these will take precedence over the needs and rights of non-clients. This illustrates the author's failure to recognize and make suggestions for dealing with conflicts of interests.

Where conflict is recognized, a solution of 'mediation' is suggested. In conflict situations,

the social worker moves back and forth between the individual who is receiving the service and those on the agency staff who are giving the service. . . . While there must be a temporary shift in identification with either the individual or staff, . . . the social worker never relinquishes his basic identification with the individual or his place on the staff that is giving the service.

(Bartlett 1970 : 123)

This essentially 'mediating' position assumes that conflicts of interests can be resolved, but there is no substantial treatment of the value preference which the social worker invokes, nor of the techniques used in resolving the difference or upholding one side against the other. To be fair, Bartlett does recognize (1970 : 124) that 'so much attention' has been given to the 'direct working relationship with those being served' and to the 'enabling process' that 'there has been insufficient analysis of this particular capacity of social workers for managing simultaneously a variety of orientations, often conflicting, with clients and others'. While recognizing this bias she provides little in the way of redressing this imbalance.

Bartlett reiterates (1970 : 123) on a number of occasions that the 'common base' model is not about the *techniques* of practice, but is what underlies them. But if the base is going to have any meaning *in reality*, there has to be a mesh between the operationalization of the elements of practice with their underlying theoretical development. To ignore the reality of practice and to confine one's discussion to issues 'about' practice techniques in the absence of concomitant operationalization of these techniques, is a reification of the first order.

To this seeming confusion, Bartlett (1970 : 135) then tries to develop an operationalization of the common base by resorting back to a 'method-and-skill' perspective. However, she does not address the explicit nature of the relationship between these approaches other than stating it. Is the common base perspective operationalized by a method-and-skill perspective? If this is the case, is a separation between social work *assessment* and *intervention* implied? Should a common base perspective be used to make an assessment to be followed by the application of particular methods and skills?

Professional judgement

The use of the social worker's professional judgement (Bartlett 1970 : 139) is a crucial factor in the assessment of social situations, and the selection of basic and specialized concepts for social work intervention. 'It is through the professional judgement and skill of the practitioner' that the professional values and knowledge are applied. It is the use of professional judgement which distinguishes occupations from professions. The social worker 'must be able to select the relevant principles from his profession's body of knowledge and values and apply them appropriately in assessing the situation' (Bartlett 1970 : 149). Such an application of professional judgement to assessment is important, 'so that they can bring about *social change* effectively' (Bartlett 1970 : 146) (my italics).

Given this purpose it is curious that Bartlett gives no treatment to the concept of social change and any substantive theories relied upon in either the assessment of a situation or activities likely to bring about social change.

Bartlett (1970 : 150ff.) is elusive about the selection of knowledge used in making assessments. Practitioners do not have to encompass 'the whole mass of knowledge' but 'they must command the major generalizations and theoretical propositions so that they will be able to find what is relevant for their use at any one time'. . . . 'Practitioners must be able to judge when knowledge used by all social workers – that which is common for the profession – is sufficient to guide them in assessing situations and when additional knowledge is needed.' However, no criteria are offered upon which such choice can take place, except the 'clues' (unspecified) (Bartlett 1970 : 151) of knowledge related to (i) human behaviour and social environment and (ii) social welfare and services. There is no attempt to be more specific about *base* knowledge and *special* knowledge to be utilized in assessing situation.

Interventive action

'Because the elements are not sufficiently defined . . . it is not possible at this time to show the use of the common base' (Bartlett 1970 : 161). This quotation highlights two important issues. First, the common base formulation is tentative, and it needs testing to establish its reality. These issues are further reinforced by Bartlett's footnote (1970 : 161) on stressing that this monograph does not represent a 'survey of practice' but rather 'an analysis of social workers' thinking about their practice, based upon the writer's experience in practice and education. . .'. It is not envisaged by the author as an 'inclusive' or definitive statement, but rather to point directions for further thinking.

Second, this quote highlights the dilemma of whether a 'common base' of social work *does* or *should* exist: 'It is the thesis of this discussion that in order to have a significant impact on society, social workers *must and should operate on a strong, consistent common base*' (my italics). It is the consistent invoking of this *must and should* which can lead one to the conclusion that, despite the inconsistency throughout the monograph, this framework is not a description of practice, or even *thinking about* practice as it exists, but rather this author's viewpoint (preference) for the future development of practice and the future development of practice theory. As such, it is not a matter for testing to see if this is an accurate description of existing practice, but rather it is a prescription for how practice *ought* to be. If so, such a case needs justifying.

It is interesting, however, to contrast this position with Bartlett's earlier stance (1961 : 159). 'Social work has now arrived at a point as a *unified profession* where the relation between the whole and its parts can be understood clearly.'

Conclusions

Bartlett's framework was the first to give explicit recognition to the need for social work to have its own central reference point. This she developed as a 'common base' consisting of a constellation of elements of knowledge, values, purpose, and method.

She outlines the need for 'integrative thinking' both for the consolidation of the professional organization of social work, as well as an aid to theory development. However, while recognizing the importance of this work in setting a new way of conceptualizing social work, a number of significant criticisms need to be kept in mind.

Although the author develops a 'common base' of social work in a way which could be verified empirically, she does not undertake this, but relies upon her own experience in education and practice. There is confusion throughout the work because one is never certain whether Bartlett intends this as a description or prescription. So the assumption that a common base exists is confused with the need to establish one.

There is little or no substance given to the components of the constellation. These terms remain vacuous.

In identifying the components of value, purpose, knowledge, and method of the working definition, Bartlett fails to deal with a number of problems. First, she recognizes that both values and available knowledge influence the purposes of the profession. However, she appears to take the position that there is *one* set of values accepted by the profession and that there is consistency within this set of values. She does not recognize the potential conflicts which exist in accommodating the wishes of individuals *vis-à-vis* collectivities. She makes no attempt to establish the ontology of these values and whether there may be discrepancies between stated or aspired-to values and the realities of practice. She takes a monolithic view of 'society' rather than recognizing disparate and conflicting interests within 'a society'. Further she takes no account of societal context and the effects differences in setting may have upon values and purposes.

Second, Bartlett notes that the concept of *sanction* in the original Working Party definition was used to cover the auspices under which practice is carried on. It was later omitted, as the NASW subcommittee suggested it was not a basic definer of social work practice; Bartlett therefore excludes it. This would appear to contradict Bartlett's explicit assumption that social work is a profession, and allude to its being seen as a 'social science'. This then poses difficulties for its right to intervene, its historic *raison d'être*.

Third, she does not clarify her use of the word 'method'. As used in the Working Party definition, 'method' 'is already moving away from the particular connotation given to it in the three-methods concept. It is presented as a basic concept in social work practice and is not tied to or divided among the three methods' (Bartlett 1970 : 60). Yet the Working Party definition of '*method*' is 'an orderly systematic mode of procedure. As used here, the term encompasses social casework, social group work, and community organization' (see Bartlett 1970 : 223). If it is a *procedure*, as distinct from a *technique* or *skill*, in what way does it encompass social casework, social group work, and community organization? Assigning a different meaning to the term only adds to the confusion; it gives no indication of the particular matrix of interrelationship or interdependence of these three traditional methods.

Fourth, Bartlett (1970 : 60) believes there is a need for 'integrative thinking . . . at this time'; thus she has chosen to emphasize that 'the basic elements are common and shared'. But this is a hypothesis which could be tested, rather than treating it as if it were a value. In this kind of argument it is crucial to know *why* Bartlett is placing so much emphasis or value on the need for 'integrative thinking'. Is it for the consolidation of the profession, and if so to what end? Is it for the benefit of the individual practitioner to enable help in the more effective achievement of particular goals?

Finally, Bartlett does not consider the influence of the particular context in which her framework is developed and the effects of this on her thinking. The implication of not addressing this matter is that this framework applies to social work universally. This implies that social work theory is not affected by the socio-political context, that it is neutral. This position thus sidesteps the influence of 'sanction' on its development, and sidesteps the role of social work within any society in maintaining or changing power relationships.

THE FRAMEWORK OF GOLDSTEIN

Introduction

Goldstein[1] has developed a framework of practice which has attempted not to use the traditional boundaries of the 'methods' approaches, and which has attempted to systematize the knowledge drawn upon by the practitioner. Such an approach is based upon the premise that there is a common knowledge base, and an agreed purpose for social work.

The issue, he argues (1973 : *xi*), is not about the availability of relevant knowledge for use in social work, 'but how this knowledge can be systematized and ordered so as to afford the profession a coherent foundation for practice.' The systematization presupposes that a rational selection of knowledge can be made in the first place.

Goldstein's 1973 book attempts 'a synthesis of concepts drawn from the behavioural and social sciences that best explain inter-personal and interactional processes, that are germane to practice with a broad array of social units and that are denotable and identi-fiable for application to the requirements of assessment, planning and action' (Goldstein 1973 : *xiii*). The importance of the individ-ual practitioner's style and purpose is also a theme to be repeated throughout Goldstein's writings, and the practitioner's own ideology is also shown to account for the *particular* selection of guiding theory and knowledge.

At the outset the author's objective is

> not to bestow upon the practitioner a set of methods or techniques, but to offer a knowledge support, a groundwork for practice upon which the individual practitioner can build his own model and style of action in accord with his own predilections, skill, and person attributes. For excellence in practice is construed here as an art that is evident in the unique fusion of ingenuity, versatility, knowledge, skill, and learning.
>
> (Goldstein 1973 : *xii*)

The conceptual content is organized around three major frame-works (Goldstein 1973 : *xiii*):

1. a social systems model which depicts the structure of practice and helps to locate and identify the salient problem or task and the key social units relevant to it;
2. a social learning or problem-solving model which illustrates the logical and episodic nature of learning; and
3. a process model which captures the sequence and components of practice through the consideration of the variables of strategy, phase, and target in the interaction.

While aspiring to cross the boundaries of traditional practice, Goldstein adopts an 'individual-oriented tone.' This is because of the 'experience and inclination' of the author, and also because

> a person-oriented construct underscores the belief that, irrespective of the design and objective, whether practice is aimed at grand schemes for social change or the resolution of a common place problem, social work practice is ultimately concerned with persons as distinct individuals – their plans, hopes, ideals, needs, and the way they go about living them out. The final worth of the professional act can only be found in the meaning it holds for certain persons individually or in association.
>
> (Goldstein 1973 : *xiii*)

Thus, from the outset a paradox emerges: the setting of broad parameters of social work practice within a social systems framework, yet at the same time restricting this to the personal ideology of the practitioner and an individual perspective.

A reason for looking beyond the traditional methods' approaches (1974 : 61) was to avoid the 'cloistered' nature of the relationship to clients with its concentration on intrapsychic processes and no or little account of social conditions. Such dissatisfactions led to changes of focus which emphasized the importance of the present rather than the past, and social interactions. This involved greater utilization of knowledge from the socio-behavioural sciences, particularly relating to motivation, communication theory, social systems theory, and a problem-solving approach (Goldstein 1974 : 63–6).

Social work practice: a definition

Goldstein (1973 : 3–4) argues that any measure of a profession is observed in its actions, thus *intervention* is the goal around which an identity can be formed. The central purpose of social work:

is its capability for providing the *means* and the *opportunity* by which persons can work out, find alternatives for, organize about, contend with, or, in otherwise autonomous ways, deal with conditions (internal, inter-personal, or environmental) which interfere with productive social living. This purpose is in accord with and in response to individual needs, individual means, individual ends, and individual experiences expressed singly or collectively.

(Goldstein 1973 : 5)

To this end social work is 'the *management of social learning*, a process which develops within the context and as a consequence of a purposeful human relationship comprising and involving the social worker and the individuals (singly or collectively) relevant to the objectives' (Goldstein 1973 : 5). It is the influence of the social worker which guides this process and includes his 'technical, cognitive, affective, and personal resources derived from a system of knowledge, belief, and value' (Goldstein 1973 : 5).

Social work intervention is seen as a *means* rather than an end in itself. This means is provided by the *objectives* of practice: 'to provide a context in which the possibilities of improved social learning may be maximized' (Goldstein 1973 : 8). This new learning helps the person to increase his or her knowledge and form new perceptions of self and others. It is the medium of the *relationship* with the social worker and the forces of socialization within this medium that bring about the required changes (Goldstein 1973 : 10). Again, one can observe the *individual* focus and the importance of the social worker's personal involvement with individuals.

Reliance on such personal characteristics in order to fulfil the social worker's objectives therefore requires particular attention to be given to *qualities* as well as *competencies* of the social worker. Indeed, Goldstein remarks, 'the social worker *is* no less significant than what he does' (Goldstein 1973 : 56), and he is seen 'more as a *person* exerting *personal* influence rather than as an expert applying techniques' (Goldstein 1973 : 58).

The social philosophy of both the profession and the professional are considered important in order to identify the essential aims and directions of practice and to lend meaning and substance to the theories and techniques selected (Goldstein 1973 : 64–5). However, while alerting the reader to the necessity of taking such variables into consideration, Goldstein provides little substantive assistance. In a later chapter, he raises, but does not answer, the question of what *ends* should be aimed towards: 'Does the social worker or a member of any of the other helping professions have the moral right to participate in, if not to actually influence the decision to strive for one outcome or another that will affect another person's life situation?' (Goldstein 1973: 155). The ideal or principle of self-determination is invoked in an attempt to answer this question, but then this ideal may only be an 'illusion of autonomy', given that people are 'more often than not victims of some profound social problem,' or when they themselves 'perpetuate these aberrant conditions or bear the symptoms of inequalities in our society' (Goldstein 1973 : 155).

Goldstein, in his attempts to take account of personal ideologies, and to show how these affect relationships and the selection of knowledge to shape social work intervention, does not deal with the effects that conflicting ideologies are likely to have on his theoretical framework, nor for the implications such conflicts might have for the 'common base' of social work knowledge which is an underlying tenet of his framework.

The goals and means of change are arrived at by 'objective study, evaluation, and planning' (Goldstein 1973 : 157). However, he says these procedures only have validity 'when it is assumed that what each practitioner studies and evaluates is limited and governed by his own range of perceptions. These are guided by personal predilections, beliefs, identifications, and his own experiential history' (Goldstein 1973 : 157). This may well be so; however, it does raise serious implications for establishing commonalities within the profession.

The client – in and as a system

The term 'client' is 'used in its most extensive meaning to include any individual or collectivity of individuals who benefits from the use of the profession's services either directly or indirectly through the participation of others acting on their behalf' (Goldstein 1973 : 117). Elsewhere the author remarks that professional services are not reserved only for those who seek them but also include 'self-initiated preventive attempts to identify those conditions which impair social living' (Goldstein 1973 : 6).

85

This failure to more accurately define 'client' leads to two unfortunate consequences. First, the term could be used to include 'everybody' in that an individual, family, group, organization, or community sub-structure who uses social work services could cover 'anything from a problem family to the local authority which was defining problem families' (Seed 1975 : 229). A common fault of frameworks which inadequately define client status is to implicitly convey that *all* persons or collectivities are 'clients' or 'potential clients'. The implication of this, in terms of social work intervention, is to make the assumption that the same repertoire of skills is appropriate for all persons the social worker has contact with, regardless of their status.

This forms the second criticism, and often leads to the inappropriate use of influence and authority on the part of the social worker, as well as problems in advocacy, when conflicts arise between different people and groups. The lack of criteria in defining 'client' also means it is impossible to ascertain when a person or group with whom the social worker has contact, ceases to be a 'client' and moves into another status, and hence requires the redefinition of role relationships with the social worker. This is the case with an agency itself which at the different times could be seen in terms of 'client', 'target', or 'advocate' status, as well as the employer of the social worker.

Goldstein deals with clients in systems terms:

> we are concerned with matters of relatedness and coherence as we attempt to understand and treat the conditions attendant to a man's relationships with other men, with his various groups, and with society as well as their reciprocal effects.
>
> (Goldstein 1973 : 105)

He uses social systems concepts to help organize the structure and functional properties of the social worker–client configuration.

In keeping with a social systems orientation, Goldstein (1973 : 120) outlines the 'change system' which provides the context for the social worker and client. The agency is renamed the 'change environment' (1973 : 121) which Goldstein uses as a generic term 'for the setting which hosts, sanctions, or establishes the purposes and parameters of social work practice.'

After making an organizational analysis of the 'change environment' Goldstein (1973 : 122–7) emphasizes the individual practitioner's influence on and through this environment. How he identifies himself as part of the change environment and how he relates to the social problem and its victims will affect how he makes his purpose, plan and programme operational.

Such an approach further reinforces the individualistic nature of Goldstein's framework and the importance of personal ideology affecting the practitioner's relationship to the agency and his/her interpretation of the social problem. While this individualistic bias is reinforced from time to time in the framework, Goldstein does not elaborate on the parameters of the individual's *modus operandi vis-à-vis* the agency, or the sanctions under which the practitioner operates. It is as if the author is saying that the practitioner uses his or her own ideology to interpret and relate to the operation of the agency, yet does not recognize or develop the ramifications emanating from this position.

While Goldstein's (1975) development of the use of systems theory in social work leaves a more utilitarian impression than his case demonstration with 'Mr Able' (1973 : 106–9 and 118), nevertheless, he does not address the more problematic issues related to systems theory itself raised by Roberts (1981) and developed in Chapter 10.

Relationship

The individualistic focus is further emphasized by the author's treatment of 'relationship' through which the social worker's goals are achieved. The first task of the social worker is to provide the means and opportunity for the client system to learn how to become a member of the change system. This is done by successful role induction which 'is the building of a cohesive system that comprises a set of hierarchical roles' (Goldstein 1973 : 134). In order to reduce inequality and imbalance of the change system, the casework principles of 'self-determination' and 'acceptance' are invoked (Goldstein 1973 : 135).

Goldstein emphasizes the existential and elusive quality of 'relationship'. He says it is:

a somewhat amorphous concept which eludes definition in that it refers to a human phenomenon marked by affective and attitudinal characteristics. We may categorize the relationship by such labels as 'good', 'dependent', or 'intense', but these do not capture its experiential meaning. Its pivotal significance is in its potentiality for providing a climate for change, growth, and confirmation. Perhaps a major measure of the depth and meaning of any relationship is the extent to which it authenticates those who are part of it.

(Goldstein 1973 : 10)

Specht (1974 : 247) finds that Goldstein 'provides the reader with a rich understanding of the empirical knowledge available about "relationship" as well as an appreciation of the mysteries of and the gaps in understanding the concept' and contrasts it to Pincus and Minahan's more concrete and specific, though 'less favourable', handling of it. What Goldstein does not do, which the Pincus and Minahan framework does, however, is clearly differentiate 'client' and 'non-client' systems and the different *types* of relationships which may be appropriate with these different systems.

Social learning and social change

Within Goldstein's framework of practice, 'social learning' is the substantive theory which has a pervasive influence. For Goldstein (1973 : 154) social learning is not a method of practice or technique in itself, 'instead it is the means for constructing a conceptual framework within which specific methods or orientations can be ordered, studied or explained.'

Social adjustment and change 'are products of a logical series of learning experiences irrespective of the modes, techniques, or schools of practice employed to achieve these changes' (Goldstein 1973 : 154). Again, the individualistic orientation is emphasized in that he sees change taking place in *persons.*

The assertion that change is ultimately lodged in persons is not incongruent with more sweeping or expansive emendations of larger systems – for instance, social legislation, economic innovations, racial integration, or modifications in a community's structure and institutions. . . . They are, in reality, human endeavors brought about *by* persons who are committed to the need for change, reform, or modification. They are, in the final analysis, change events only as they have some significant meanings *for* the life patterns of certain persons, individually or in concert.

(Goldstein 1973 : 159)

Given the basic premise of a common or unitary knowledge base, and a form of practice designed to address various levels of change, it would appear rather too simple to reduce all collectivities to relationships between two people. The validity of such an emphasis on individuality must be questioned given our knowledge on small and large group behaviour and our appreciation of *gestalt* characteristics.

From an application of social learning theory (1973 : 166–7) and a Dewey problem-solving model (1973 : 170–3), Goldstein has created a model to demonstrate (i) the stages of problem solving in social work; (ii) the accompanying learning processes; and (iii) the role of the social worker at each stage. The generic character of this model allows its application to the various types as well as to the particular schools of social work practice (Goldstein 1973 : 173). The social worker's role activities are pertinent to practice with two-persons as well as group or larger systems.

Goldstein notes, however, that:

> this structure can only be used as a model within which practice can be organized and explicated and not as a technique in itself. It explains rather than prescribes the elements of technique and therefore intends to make the professional enterprise more comprehensible.
>
> (Goldstein 1973 : 174)

While presenting a complex process model, showing various stages of problem solving, learning, and social work role input, Goldstein does not address the more complex question of theory choice underpinning the various learning and role inputs. The model, on the surface, appears too complex to suit the pragmatics of the practitioner yet too simple to explain and prescribe the more complex decision choices which have to be made.

In 'Strategies and negotiations of social work practice' (Goldstein 1973 : 188), the development and explication of another process model is presented. This three-dimensional model addresses *strategy* (study and evaluation, intention and intervention, appraisal); *target* (individual, family/group, organization/community); and *phases* (induction, core, ending). Here Goldstein's (1973 : 185) aim is to 'integrate the disparate elements of practice into a comprehensive model that relates to the practical experience.' The complexity of this task is acknowledged by the author, and cannot be fully achieved 'due to the many facets, levels, and motives that are integral to this human event. Any model can fit only certain aspects of the practical situation as a multilevel, interactional phenomenon' (Goldstein 1973 : 185). This is an early forecast to the reader: that what is attempted will not succeed.

Goldstein fails to integrate the mass of material he attempts to use in this practice model. Throughout this section, both the organization and listing of diverse content areas as well as practice techniques creates problems in integration. This leads one to question the utility of the model for the practitioner. The author misses an excellent opportunity to demonstrate the utility of integration by failing to make any connections whatsoever in the two process models developed (Goldstein 1973 : 174 and 188).

Conclusions

The extent of what Goldstein attempts in his writings can be understood from the analogy he draws with the photographer, who on using telephoto *and* wide-angle lenses finds that he requires another kind of optical system, 'one that captures the figure and the ground at once, in so doing, accomplishes this end without loss to either' (Goldstein 1974).

> The counterpart of this need, for our purposes, would be a type of vision and understanding that takes in the whole of a social situation, delineates its significant parts and, most important, shows how these parts interact in a way that gives the whole its unique quality and character. This form of vision would achieve increased coherence among the strategies and techniques of the profession and place them in the service of the worker in response to his holistic appraisal of the problem or event.
>
> (Goldstein 1974 : 181)

This ambition is commendable, given the historical and contemporary press for integration. However, it is argued that while this purpose is reinforced throughout the writings, it is not explicated in a form that is likely to produce integration at either the theoretical or practical levels. As shown already, the author makes few explicit links between the purposes and goals of practice and selection of practice techniques. He stresses the importance of the practitioner's own ideology, but then does not develop the implications of this in terms of technique selection or how it relates to social policy or agency contexts, particularly relating to sanctions for practice. The author creates two seemingly different models of *process*, but makes no attempt to link one to the other. On the cataloguing of parts of the social work process, no rationale is given for theory or technique. The implicit assumption is that these are congruent with the worker's own style and preferences.

After reviewing several contemporary commentators on the nature of social work practice theory, and the problems associated with integration, Goldstein remarks that 'a straightforward process of integration of theory and practice would be very difficult to achieve' (Goldstein 1983a : 7).

Given this acknowledgement, perhaps a less ambitious task would now be undertaken by the author in approaching practice from a 'unitary' perspective. Indeed, one can observe a more individualistic focus (Goldstein 1981, 1982, 1982a, 1983) in recent writings, to support this claim.

Given the discrepancies between the claimed advancement in social work theory development and what eventuates, it is unlikely that a reader will concur that the author affords 'the reality of a common or unitary base for professional practice' (Goldstein 1973 : xi), nor that the book 'is not addressed to the traditional methods of social work' (Goldstein 1973 : xiii). Indeed, the individualistic perspective is endemic, both in terms of how the worker views the client and how social workers themselves are seen.

Even when collectivities are dealt with, the special qualities of *individual* relationships are emphasized over and above group or *gestalt* characteristics. This emphasis does not help to bridge gaps between methods which are primarily differentiated by the size of the client system as well as interventive technology. His position of a 'ground upward' rather than a 'top downward' orientation, 'so as to link the theory more relevantly to the real nature of the human experience' (Goldstein 1975 : 23), does little to justify the failure to include theories of society, justifications in terms of collectivities, and intervention strategies reflective of group processes, for example, team work and collective agency approaches. His lack of any social context in terms of social policy and social planning goals also stultifies attempts at linking the 'personal' with the 'public' and vice versa.

Goldstein's model of social learning, particularly when linked to cognitive therapies, again emphasizes the nature of change as vested in the individual, and certainly at face value neglects the importance of the effects of group membership. It is reductionistic to think only of an 'individual encounter' no matter what size of system one might wish to deal with. In addition, while reducing the number of variables to be considered, this hardly increases the validity of such an approach.

Goldstein assumes that the knowledge and technology related to a client or client group is sufficient for social work practice in general. The absence of information on relevant non-client systems which need to be engaged in order to achieve the goals agreed by the client, is an important omission.

This omission may be related to the unacknowledged fact that this is a consensus-oriented model of social work practice. The role of conflict, either at a general level of goal and purpose formation, or at a more specific level related to technologies and skills, is not addressed. The implicit assumption, therefore, is that conflict does not exist at either the general or specific levels of practice; that there is agreement surrounding ends and means of practice. A review of non-consensual models and conflict in ideologies reveals this is not the case. Lack of attention to technologies involving conflict, involving assertive and contentious debating skills, for example, will not only ill equip a practitioner to advocate on behalf of his or her client group, but also implies a homogeneity of skills undifferentiated by relationship. This is a strikingly peculiar position, given Goldstein's attention to 'relationship'.

Given Goldstein's conceptualization of practice, and the historical perspective outlined in Chapter 2 of his book, it is interesting that no contextual variables are considered in their influence on practice. This raises the question of the universality of the framework for use in other cultures and other western urbanized societies.

In terms of the techniques and practice principles presented there is no attempt at hierarchical ordering of data (Nelson 1975). For the student or practitioner attempting to consolidate this approach into his or her practice, the quantity of apparently unordered materials presents a real handicap.

THE FRAMEWORK OF PINCUS AND MINAHAN

Introduction

This framework is substantially built on the seminal work of Bartlett

(1970), particularly the use of her conception of 'life tasks', and the need to develop a theoretical framework clearly differentiated from a range of other substantive theory used to underpin practice. Their framework arose out of the authors' experiences in developing and teaching social work practice to first year graduate students (Pincus and Minahan 1973 : *xi*).

A basic assumption of the authors is that:

> regardless of the many forms social work practice can take, there is a common core of concepts, skills, tasks and activities which are essential to the practice of social work and represent a base from which the practitioner can build.
>
> (Pincus and Minahan 1973 : *xi*)

From their experiences using a traditional methods approach, the authors became increasingly aware of the similarities in the knowledge, skills and values underlying these methods. Their criticisms of the traditional methods approach led them to formulate the following criteria to be used in the formulation of their framework (1973 : *xii–xiii*):

● A model should avoid conceptualizing social work practice in dichotomous terms as person/environment, clinical practice/ social action and microsystems/macrosystems.

● A model should account for the fact that the social worker has tasks to perform and relationships to maintain with a variety of people. Work with 'other than the client' should be seen as deliberate and purposeful activity.

● A worker often has to work with and through many different sizes and types of systems in helping a client: the appropriate size and type of system(s) should be determined by the nature of the task at hand.

● A model should not be based on one substantive theory but should allow for the selective incorporation of theoretical orientations in working with specific situations. The social work model of practice should be clearly differentiated from any substantive theoretical orientations being used.

● The model should be applicable to analysing social work in a wide variety of settings and situations.

In constructing their framework the authors were guided by a view of social work practice as a goal-oriented planned change process. They also switched their focus

> from searching for a palatable way of combining existing definitions of the three methods and devising general principles that would fit them, to examining the tasks of the social worker in action and isolating and identifying the basic elements of social work practice reflected in these tasks.
>
> (Pincus and Minahan 1969 : 37)

The authors do not propose a 'supramethod' (1973 : *xiii* and 1969 : 37), but rather their framework represents a reformulation of the base of social work practice in order to give social work a clear place among the human service professions. It can set the foundation for either the generalist practitioner or specialist (1973 : *xiii*).

Their framework can be divided into three major parts:

- The nature of social work and its frame of reference
- Practice concepts (values, four systems, relationships, process)
- Skills

The nature of social work practice

The social work frame of reference focuses on three aspects: the performing of life tasks; interacting with resource systems; and relating private troubles to public issues. In discussing the nature of social work practice, the authors take an interactionist perspective between people and systems in the social environment. 'People are dependent on systems for help in obtaining the material, emotional, or spiritual resources and the services and opportunities they need to realize their aspirations and to help them cope with their life tasks' (1973 : 3).

In dealing with life tasks, Pincus and Minahan maintain that people find help from informal or natural, formal, and societal systems. However, these resource systems may fail to provide resources, services and opportunities, because the needed resource system may not exist or may not provide appropriate help when people need it; people may not know it exists or are reluctant to turn to it for help; policies of the resource system may create new problems; and several resource systems may be working at cross-purposes.

94

It is through a further development of an interactionist perspective that the authors develop a *purpose* for social work as they see it:

Social work is concerned with the interactions between people and their social environment which affect the ability of people to accomplish their life tasks, alleviate distress, and realize their aspirations and values. The purpose of social work therefore is to (1) enhance the problem-solving and coping capacities of people, (2) link people with systems that provide them with resources, services, and opportunities, (3) promote the effective and humane operation of these systems, and (4) contribute to the development and improvement of social policy.

(Pincus and Minahan 1973 : 9)

From their formulation of social work *purpose*, the authors develop seven major *functions* of social workers in carrying out this purpose. Intervention and tasks of social workers are designed to accomplish one or more of the following: (i) to help people enhance and more effectively utilize their own problem-solving and coping capacities; (ii) to establish initial linkages between people and societal resource systems; (iii) to facilitate interaction and modify and build new relationships between people and societal resource systems; (iv) to facilitate interaction and modify and build relationships between people within resource systems; (v) to contribute to the development and modification of social policy; (vi) to dispense material resources; and (vii) to serve as agents of social control (1973 : 15).

The following points are of interest. First, in trying to enhance people's problem-solving capacities, the authors point to the need for social work services to be easily accessible to those people who need them but who do not make an initial request. Social workers 'may aggressively seek potential applicants who might become clients' (1973 : 16). The social worker also 'helps identify and locate people who are in need of certain resources or entitled to certain benefits but who are not aware of their eligibility to receive them' (1973 : 18).

While recognizing the link between private troubles and public issues and the contribution which can be made by social workers to the development and modification of social policy, Pincus and Minahan differentiate between 'basic fundamental changes in social policy and middle-range levels of policy change.' Fundamental changes in social policy involve 'changes in the basic structure of

95

societal institutions, such as changes of national priority in the allocation and distribution of the resources of a society' (1973 : 26). While recognizing the connections between people's problems and basic social policies in terms of poverty, ill health, unemployment, etc., and while agreeing that 'social workers can and should work toward bringing about some of these changes' (1973 : 29), they outline severe limitations in this regard:

> One limitation is the fact that fundamental social change is brought about in the political area through political processes. The force that a profession can bring to bear on a problem is technical know-how and expertise. Battles in the political area, however, depend on political power, which in this society means mobilization of a powerful constituency. Such activity is more suited to social reform movements and political parties than to a profession.
>
> (Pincus and Minahan 1973 : 27)

The authors further maintain that issues of basic social policy changes are too important to be left solely in the hands of any profession, and that social work is dependent on society for its sanction and support.

> Awareness of these limitations should not be used as an excuse for ignoring fundamental policy issues; indeed social workers may support fundamental changes in basic social policy. Rather, this awareness should caution social workers against promising more than it is possible to deliver.
>
> (Pincus and Minahan 1973 : 27)

Practice concepts

Value dimensions and dilemmas

The authors recognize the central importance of values for any form of planned change, and propose to 'make the practitioner aware of the value dimensions which permeate his practice and the ethical dilemmas within which he must operate' (1973 : 37–8).

Pincus and Minahan clearly differentiate between values and knowledge. 'Values are beliefs, preferences, or assumptions about what is desirable or good for man. . . . They are not assertions about how the world is and what we know about it, but how it *should* be.

... [V]alue statements cannot be subjected to scientific investigation, they must be accepted on faith.' Knowledge statements, on the other hand, 'are observations about the world and man which have been verified or are capable of verification' (1973 : 38).

Values and knowledge act as guides to practice, but the authors point to frequent confusions between the two, where technical matters are stated in ethical terms and vice versa (1973 : 40). The need to differentiate knowledge and values has several implications. Acceptance of unconfirmed (but confirmable) knowledge statements as values inhibits the development of a valid knowledge base. Practitioners come to believe in a certain thing, rather than putting the proposition up for investigation. Furthermore, the 'separation of knowledge and values would help social workers avoid tacitly incorporating as value assumptions certain cultural norms whose effectiveness in providing the greatest satisfaction for individuals or groups should be regarded as problematic rather than confirmed' (1973 : 41).

> If a value is used as a guide when knowledge is called for, the resulting action is apt to be ineffective. If knowledge is called upon when a value is needed, the resulting action may be unpurposeful or even harmful.
>
> (Pincus and Minahan 1973 : 41–2)

The authors note a range of value dilemmas confronting a social worker. An example of some of these difficulties is demonstrated by a review of the principle of client self-determination and its limitations (1973 : 45–6). In order to deal with value dilemmas the authors suggest that practitioners must be aware of its existence through their own 'self awareness' by differentiating between *personal* views of values and the *professional* task; and by building into the change process procedures that will provide protection and resistance against behaviour manipulation (1973 : 47–8).

In another exhortation the authors say, 'Self-awareness, technical expertise, and a tolerance for ambiguity will help in this task. But the worker also needs to set some "bedrock" values that establish the outer boundaries of his flexibility' (1973 : 52). Despite this rhetoric, this acknowledged important area of practice is given very cursory consideration. Their example (1973 : 50) where the social worker shifts the issue from a consideration of the values around racial discrimination to a technical problem ('the best way to keep peace and order') highlights the problem these authors have in dealing with the effects of values upon practice beyond a superficial level.

In making a clear differentiation between values and knowledge, the authors present a positivist view of knowledge. There is no acknowledgement that there are other positions, or indeed of the effects values can have on the process of knowledge-building. More serious is the complete neglect of the issues surrounding value conflict in which different groups within a society seek different ends, often by different means. The suggested solutions of turning value issues into technical ones (as well as self-awareness and flexibility), do not address the more significant ideological question of the social worker's and the profession's value commitment, and the conflicts arising in this regard.

Four basic systems in social work practice

A major part of the Pincus and Minahan framework is their delineation of four basic systems of practice. This represents an innovation in conceptualization, particularly in the recognition of the significance of 'non-client' systems.

The delineation of four systems, namely the change agent system, the client system, the target system, and the action system, has several significant implications for the practitioner. First, it requires social workers to be clear of their relationships and responsibilities to various people. The social worker cannot continue to treat everyone as a client. The authors suggest this is achieved by three criteria by which client status can be evaluated. It is also achieved by considering *potential* as well as actual clients. Where the social worker has been sanctioned to intervene by the agency (and eventually the community) with a group of recalcitrant individuals, then these are to be seen as potential clients, and hence also seen as one target for change, that is, assisting them to see the value of achieving client status. This is related to the issue of *sanction* for social work intervention. This is of two kinds: (i) from the profession, and in some cases statute, which gives social workers the right or opportunity to make their services available to the public and certifies competence; (ii) from the clients themselves when the services of the social worker are voluntarily contracted.

Second, in considering how the goal of intervention might best be achieved a specific target (or targets) needs to be formulated, and the client may or may not be one of the areas of needed change. This is in contrast to the orthodox position which implicitly assumed that a client was also a target for intervention. The social worker may work with or on behalf of the client system in order to influence some other system (e.g. a housing authority), and indeed the change agent system (agency) itself is potentially a target for change (e.g. the ward of a treatment facility) (1973 : 67 and 300–8), where its operation is contributing to the client's need or problem. The social worker is required to consider the *multiple* targets for influence or change, in order to reach the desired goals of intervention.

Third, the variety of people utilized in an action system could include the client system, e.g. where a client was instrumental in the organization of a lobby or pressure group to fulfil a specific purpose.

Fourth, the social worker is forced to consider the wide variety of relationships with non-client as well as client groups. The authors point out that in all cases social workers 'are working to change people, not vague abstractions such as "the community", "the organization", or "the system"' (1973 : 63).

And fifth, no assumption can be made that any type or size of action system is the most appropriate to deal with the presented problem. 'Only after the purpose and goal of the change efforts have been established can a worker determine if a one-to-one relationship, a face-to-face group, or another type of action system is most appropriate' (1973 : 65).

Worker relationships

> A relationship can be thought of as an affective bond between the
> worker and the other systems operating within a major posture
> or atmosphere of collaboration, bargaining, or conflict.
>
> (Pincus and Minahan 1977 : 84)

These relationships the worker forms with the people in each of the four systems. Because of the sanctioning involved, social work relationships can be characterized as *professional*, in contrast to *personal*, in that they are *purposeful, client focused,* and *objective* (1973 : 69–70 and 1977 : 84ff.).

A significant contribution of these authors is their recognition of the variety of relationships social workers have with different people, in particular non-clients. The focus of many orthodox frameworks is on the client, and hence relationships are seen primarily in terms of collaboration. Such a relationship is based upon feelings of trust, genuineness, and honesty, and indeed is possible only when there is agreement upon the goals and methods of achieving them. When there is some disagreement over the goals and methods of achieving them, then bargaining and conflict more accurately characterize the nature of the relationship.

Process

In order to achieve a piece of planned change a *process* is undertaken. This is 'a systematic series of actions directed towards some purpose' (1973 : 85). The worker needs to have a purpose for each activity undertaken, as well as for the whole planned change effort. The authors outline the seven phases through which most change processes pass (1973 : 90–1). These are: development of a need for change; establishment of a change relationship; clarification or diagnosis of the client system's problem; examination of alternative routes and goals; establishing goals and intention of action; transformation of intentions into actual change efforts; generalization and stabilization of change; and achievement of a terminal relationship.

Such models are useful in assisting the worker think through what needs to be done in any planned change effort, however, any linear sequencing of events oversimplifies the actual process as the worker may be operating in more than one phase at any one point and with different types of systems. Three successive points can be identified. These are *contact, contract,* and *termination.* As well as these the system maintenance requirements of the action system must also be taken into account in order to achieve the specified goals.

Practice skill areas

Whatever the tasks of practice, there are a number of core skills common to a range of practice. These are assessing problems, collecting data, making initial contacts, negotiating contracts, forming action systems, maintaining and co-ordinating action systems, exercising influence, and terminating the change effort (1973 : 101–285).

Conclusions

Perhaps the most outstanding contribution of the Pincus and

Minahan framework is their development of a model and method of social work practice which attempts to reformulate practice, unhindered by traditional methodological, problem, field, and agency boundaries; attempts to shift the focus from an individualistic, case-based form of practice, to an interactionist one; develops a variety of systems, in addition to the client system, whose interactions with the social worker are crucial to the achievement of social work goals; recognizes work with both 'clients' and 'non-clients' without confining discussion to the essentially consensus orientation of the worker–client relationship; makes no prior assumptions about the kind or size of system intervention which needs to take place in order to achieve the goals reached with the client; and provides criteria for assessing *client* status, and differentiates this from other significant relationships in any piece of planned change.

Their framework can be seen as a further attempt to create and develop a social work practice theory and to differentiate this from other substantive theory. Their model, they claim, can be used in such a way to draw on a wide range of other theory, yet at the same time, they do not see it as a 'supra' method, but rather one which can set the basis of either generalist or specialist practice.

Having stated their intention to reformulate practice to more accurately describe what the social worker does, the authors proceed to develop a framework which contains both implicit and explicit flaws. These include a failure to explicate how the social context of practice might be better understood in terms of sociological theory; an implicit assumption that the model is one primarily of consensus which allows little analysis of conflict, either in terms of technical strategies or in terms of conflicting ideologies forming the base of practice; a failure to consider more adequately social work's relationship to the state; their 'monolithic' use of the concept of society without an explicit recognition of its heterogeneous and conflicting elements, such as class, power, decision-making processes, etc.; their failure to adequately consider the implicit as well as explicit political nature of social work enterprises and their relevance in defining and addressing both the means and ends of social work intervention; the inability of the framework to adequately deal with an ideology of practice, and hence to provide some direction for practice intervention; and failure to provide an explanatory theory to account for the nature of interdependence between the individual and his or her social location, and hence to provide some degree of prescription when dealing with aetiology and intervention choices.

Each of these positive and negative issues will now be developed more fully.

The influence of this framework has been widespread. In referring to the 'integrated' or 'unitary' model, and referring specifically to the Pincus and Minahan and Goldstein frameworks, Evans asserts:

> I do not think it is exaggerating the situation to suggest that if this model were to become widely accepted as the basis for practice we would be witnessing a revolution both in the knowledge base of social work and in the conceptual model of the social work enterprise that underpins practice.
>
> (Evans 1976 : 177–8)

The predominant feature of the model is the shift from a predominately 'individualistic' model to an 'interactionist' one (Evans 1976 : 178). This interactionist perspective is evidenced in both the purposes and process of social work practice which emphasize the interaction between people and the informal, formal, and societal resource systems; the life tasks confronting people within a variety of social contexts; and the relationship between private ills and public issues. The authors point to the need to look for interdependence between and within systems. Hence, their framework develops the four systems and encourages the practitioner to examine his or her role and relationships with each of these systems.

The effects of this are to encourage the practitioner to look for problems and needs arising from this interaction, rather than to locate the problems/needs solely within the person requesting assistance. This helps to 'depathologize' the 'client' and to assess appropriate 'targets' for change either in addition to the 'client', or excluding the client. The practical effect of this is to change the focus of practice from being 'case-based' to 'problem- or issue-based'. This provides for a wider range of intervention strategies utilizing a variety of relationship stances; it permits the client to become part of an action system in order to help influence another person, group, or organization; it implies that either the social worker or a social work team address the wider issues relating to social problems which are identified by individual cases.

This means that in confronting a 'case' in the first instance, no prior assumption can be made as to the particular method of intervention, the system or size of the systems to be worked with, or the necessary targets of intervention. These decisions can only be taken after an initial assessment, in which the applicant for service plays a major role in helping to shape the focus for attention.

The framework attempts to be explicit in delineating both the nature and purposes of social work practice utilizing the 'person-in-environment' concept. In this regard it is far more explicit than other practice frameworks.

It is of interest to note modifications to the seven functions of practice when they appear as 'five objectives' in a later paper (Minahan and Pincus 1977). Of particular note is the reverse ordering of functions 1 and 5. They make no comment on this apparent shift of emphasis from the *person* to the *social* aspect of the social work perspective. This apparent shift in emphasis does not represent a substantial shift in their overall position as they retain their original priority listing in their chapter in Specht and Vickery (1977). They also drop two of the controversial functions ('dispense material resources' and 'serve as agents of social control').

Such an explicit delineation of function assists in the listing of social work tasks and activities although as they point out such a list is illustrative rather than comprehensive (Minahan and Pincus 1977) and the tasks are global rather than specifically related to the purposes. The second use, which the authors do not point out, is its explicative value in moving from the *nature* to the *purposes* to the *tasks* of practice, and showing the connections in this process, although the latter is not as clear as it might be.

One of the useful features is the provision of criteria for defining a client in contrast to clientele or potential client or applicant for service. 'Clients', according to the authors, are those who have sanctioned or asked for the change agent's services, are the expected beneficiaries of service, and who have a working agreement or contract with the change agent (1973 : 63). It is with such people that a collaborative relationship is formed in order to help them achieve their goals.

While the use of these criteria to define client status is a step forward in differentiating that group of people who benefit from requesting a service, it does not account for those who benefit from social work intervention at the broader level when an individual problem is converted into a public issue. The group would be those represented by quadrant B of the Middleman and Goldberg paradigm (Middleman and Goldberg 1974 : 19–23). Lippitt, Watson, and Westley (1958), on whom Pincus and Minahan base some of their work, use the term client 'to signify the specific system that is being helped.' This broadened definition incorporates the idea of the social worker's intervention on behalf of people who may be disadvantaged or at risk, without their having to enter into an explicit contract with the worker. McInerney (1981 : 24) uses the term clientele to cover such people.

Pincus and Minahan recognize potential clients, those people the change agent tries to influence to become actual clients. This often happens in settings where the social worker's services are forced upon a group of people by agency mandate or law. It is useful to see this group of potential clients as targets for change, because often the social worker, in bringing influence to bear in order to change the status to client, uses bargaining and conflictual strategies. The patient in an acute hospital, for example, who is now convalescing, whose bed is required by an acute case, and who does not want to move to a nursing home, is clearly a target for influence, until that patient has entered into a working agreement with the social worker. Until this is achieved the social worker is designing strategies to 'clear the bed', and seeing the client in this instance as the agency (hospital/discharging doctor).

An important contribution of this framework is the authors' attempt to differentiate the development of social work practice theory from a range of substantive theory from other disciplines. This clearly relates to Bartlett's concern that the two often become confused, and hence practice moves away from the stated social work purpose (Bartlett 1970 : 71).

However, the authors do not address the following issues:

● criteria for selection of substantive theories from other disciplines to achieve social work goals;
● problems arising from possible incompatibility of selected theories;
● problems associated with eclecticism (see Sheldon 1978);
● the relationship between models and theories, and whether a model purporting to integrate concepts should itself be underpinned by an integrated theory (see Evans 1976);
● confusion whether the framework is a description of, or a

prescription for practice. The authors claim the framework more accurately accounts for what social workers do in practice (i.e. has some empirical basis). On the other hand, if few practitioners actually work in the way outlined, one could say that having developed the nature and purpose of social work, the authors have designed their framework around how practice *ought* to be carried out, i.e. the framework has been derived in a logical deductive fashion.

A major weakness of this framework, despite its claims, is its failure to adequately address the social context of practice including a consideration of the sociology of social problems, the implicit political nature of all social intervention, and the merits and demerits of utilizing a professional or technical model to address certain problems and needs without locating this within a clearly defined ideology of practice.

The authors make it clear they are not concerned with problems as an attribute of people, but 'rather we see people's problems as an attribute of their social situation' (Pincus and Minahan 1973 : 11). They are concerned about the adequacy of resource systems and people's linkage to them. They are also concerned about social work's contribution to social policy and its social control functions.

Given these concerns, and their stated purpose of the framework to work with the *connections* between person and environment; clinical, practice, and social action; microsystems and macrosystems, it is surprising to find no treatment given to the social context in terms of theories of society and social problems. In this regard it is hard not to agree with Mowbray (1977) when he comments that 'social problems' are

> persistently presented in clinical terms as if they were irrational disfunctions of, or blemishes on, the overall social system. This notion is directly counter to the established view in, even, liberal social science that social problems are functional for system maintenance.
>
> (Mowbray 1977 : 6)

Pincus and Minahan recognize the link between practice strategies and social problems:

> the problem of poverty requires a more equitable distribution of money; the answer to unemployment lies in the creation or

105

availability of jobs. Problems of inadequate medical care require new forms of health-care delivery systems, and those of inadequate housing in urban slums require a greater proportion of resources to be allocated to the rehabilitation of housing and building of new housing.

(Pincus and Minahan 1973 : 26–7)

However, they do not provide an adequate theoretical examination of the relationship of these social problems to the nature of society, and second they limit the intervention of social work by treating it as a technical process and ignoring both its explicit and implicit political nature (1973 : 27).

The authors separate technical and political behaviour. However, a more pervasive definition of politics relates to the whole social structuring of power (Mowbray 1977 : 4). If one accepts this view of political behaviour, then clearly the role of any technician in bringing about change can be seen to be political. Of crucial importance then is the *direction* of that change, and the *means* used to effect change. Mowbray comments:

With the broader sense of the term 'political', the drawing of such a line between political and non political acts (as Pincus and Minahan do between 'technical expertise' and 'political power'), is itself political. As such the distinction is a manifestly conservative one for it works to render certain behaviour aimed at social change, illegitimate. It attempts to free the 'technical process' of social work from political valuation, allegiance, or accountability.

(Mowbray 1977 : 4)

While accepting the logic of this proposition, the argument cannot be fully sustained when examining the work more closely. The authors do recognize the connection between private troubles and public issues (including social problems); they do seek to deal with aetiology not solely in terms of personal pathology; they do acknowledge the 'change agent system' or agency as a legitimate target for social work intervention; and they do see appropriate social work tasks and activities in the following:

● collecting and analysing information on problems and conditions;
● encouraging societal resource systems and formal

organizations, including the social worker's own agency, to take public positions on issues;
● forming new systems and coalitions to work for changes in social policy;
● providing information and advocating for changes to the makers of social policy;
● offering to advocate directly with policy makers for changes;
● designing services and programmes and draft legislation;
● co-operating with others to test existing laws and administrative policies in the courts and through appeal procedures.

(Pincus and Minahan 1973 : 28–30)

All of these possibilities and directions of practice indicate the awareness by the authors of the political nature of social work activities. The authors' difficulty is not so much recognizing the endemic nature of political activity, but rather incorporating such activity into a model which at the same time is incorporating 'technical expertise', in having to deal with the issue of an organized occupation requiring sanction in order to be publicly accountable for its activities, and in having to find a direction with no clearly explicated ideology.

Of fundamental importance to an examination of this issue is how the concept of *society* is regarded. Leonard (1975 : 51–2) criticizes the authors for their 'sociological naïvety and conservative ideology' in their use of society in a 'monolithic way': 'their lack of a class analysis of society reveals itself throughout their work and accounts for the poverty of their explanations at the macro-sociological level' (Leonard 1975a : 52). Leonard (1975a : 51) accuses the authors of having a reified view of society because their description of the concept fails to include a heterogeneous notion of complementing and conflicting elements. To refer to society without the explicit recognition of conflict within it and the implication of this for practice is to use this term in an uncritical way, devoid of accurate description.

The problem of the authors' consensus orientation is not only manifested in their inadequate treatment of the concept of society, but also in their treatment of the value dilemmas facing social work. In view of their failure to present a clear ideology of practice, the reader is forced to depend on the authors' treatment of values for operationalizing the principles of practice. 'If social workers lay claim to some expertise in effecting change, they must assume some responsibility for the nature and consequences of such change' (1973 : 37). As previously noted, the authors take a positivist position with regard to the creation of knowledge and the separation they make between values and knowledge. They also recognize the importance of values in affecting both the ends and means of practice, (1973 : 40–2) and the value dilemmas faced by the practitioner.

In view therefore of the importance accorded to this part of the framework, one might have expected a more thorough treatment in order to achieve some integration of this part of the framework with the rest.

The treatment of values (1973 : 38–9) reveals an inadequate consideration of the diverse nature of society and the different functions which social work can be seen to perform (from maintenance of the status quo to structural change) within that society. Mowbray remarks:

> these statements do not accord with the current reality of a great many people. . . . Since this society does not guarantee such rights to all people, such formulations are wholly ambiguous. On the one hand they might be taken to mean that social workers should act as if the rights, nevertheless, do exist, without necessary consideration of any effort directed at relevant social change. Alternatively, the formulations could be taken to prescribe action directed at social change in the social work context. However, we know that Pincus and Minahan, elsewhere, proscribe political activity as part of social work. Such confusion and mystification can only serve to undermine the serious concern of social workers to help bring about societal change.
>
> (Mowbray 1977 : 6)

Indeed the confusion between prescription and description is endemic, and detracts from both the validity and utility of such frameworks. The authors' treatment of the issues surrounding 'client self-determination' and the words of comfort do little to clarify the problem.

> To cope with the ethical ambiguities of the change agent role, the social worker must maintain a balance between flexibility and integrity. Self-awareness, technical expertise, and a tolerance for ambiguity will help with this task.
>
> (Pincus and Minahan 1973 : 52)

It is this confusion, and the lack of linkage to other parts of the framework, which has led critics to link the consensus orientation of the framework not to the use of systems analysis, but to the particular values invoked (Evans 1976 : 189–90; and Leonard 1975a : 51–3).

The effect of limiting the analysis to the individual and his or her immediate environment is the result of a restricted view of social work reality. This is evidenced by the authors' bias towards personal rather than societal interventions and their reduction of problems to individual relationships. This bias is evidenced in the explication of skills and also in relation to their notion of professional relationships. In the latter regard they say, 'in professional relationships the worker devotes himself to the interests of his clients and the needs and aspirations of other people, rather than his own interests' (Pincus and Minahan 1973 : 69–70). This assumes that the interests of his clients can be achieved, and can be accommodated with other clients' or people's needs which may of course be in conflict with those of other clients. It also disregards the transactions in relationships and the interests of or represented by the social worker.

Another problematic feature of this framework is the use of its own jargon to replace orthodox social work nomenclature and the uncritical use of terms and concepts.

The use of terms like *change agent, change agent system, target system,* and so on, while seeking to disassociate with a traditional form of practice, create their own set of problems. The term *change agent* is critiqued by Bisno (1982) who argues that when the term is used as a synonym for 'social worker', '[one] makes the basic error of confusing means with ends.'

> The relevant point for social workers is the need to be clear that the professional commitment is to various personal/social *goals,* and that while the attainment of some of these objectives requires change as a *means* others necessitate sustaining action. By talking about social workers as *change agents, per se,* an intellectual and psychological set is created that elevates change *as such* to the level of a constant goal without a linkage to the specified substantive or procedural reforms in question.
>
> (Bisno 1982)

Similarly one can question if there is any real advantage to be gained by changing 'agency' to 'change agent system'. The term 'system' does imply that there is a collectivity to be taken account of, and in this regard one needs to look at the interdependencies both within the system, and between that system and significant others. However, these authors do not refer explicitly to the use of social systems analysis (Roberts 1981) and hence leave it to the reader to decide how essential social systems analysis is to the understanding and operationalization of their framework. As already noted, the danger of not being explicit about their use of social systems analysis has made it easy for critics to lump the major defects of systems theory on to the framework itself without being sure how dependent the two were meant to be (Watts 1978). Evans refers to such a situation where because the authors have not made clear whether they are using an 'open' or 'closed' form of systems analysis, critics have pointed to a

> logical contradiction between the idea of social workers acting as agents of social change within the system and the system's tendency to maintain equilibrium. This seems to result from an imposition of the closed system model on their analysis where in fact they are far from clear themselves about what type of model they are using, if any.
>
> (Evans 1976 : 191)

Such a failure to address this aspect of their framework has led to criticism on the grounds of omission, rather than inconsistency.

THE FRAMEWORK OF MIDDLEMAN AND GOLDBERG

Introduction

This framework emphasizes the structural changes which the social worker must initiate in order to adequately carry out social work's responsibility. The framework has been designed to describe 'a new microlevel practice model consistent with the emerging social welfare-through-social-change philosophy' (Middleman and Goldberg 1974 : 6).

The authors' assumptions are first that people's problems are not viewed as individual pathology but as a manifestation of social disorganization; and second the response of the social work profession to the need for social change is the *obligation* of the social worker. They maintain that social change cannot be separated from social work in being relegated to specialists. It is to be pursued at every level of a social worker's assignment.

A major premise underlying the framework is that any therapeutic endeavour cannot be isolated from the social context in which the practice is carried out or the social location of the people social work seeks to serve.

> The book was written for the social worker who questions the systematic inequalities surrounding the disbursement of society's resources. . . . It was not written for the social worker who wants to be a therapist . . . . [It] furthers the continued interest of social workers in matters of social justice, particularly their interest in how unjust social conditions are experienced by individuals in their everyday lives, and how a difference can be made.
>
> (Middleman and Goldberg 1974 : 6)

The structural approach 'aims to adjust the environment to the needs of the individuals' (Middleman and Goldberg 1974 : 9).

The framework is divided into three major sections. First, a frame of reference based around the social worker's locus of concern and the persons engaged. The basic assumptions, principles, and roles are dealt with in this section. Second, a section on skills which are needed to operationalize this conceptualization of social work practice. Third, the organizational context and social science base of social work practice are discussed.

While no reference is made to Bartlett (1970) or Goldstein (1973), it is clear their framework is an attempt to view social work outside of the traditional boundaries of methods, settings, and fields.

> The book is for the microlevel practitioner . . . who wants to assume a social worker orientation rather than a method-based orientation, who wants to deliver services through a social work methodology equally applicable to a one-to-one, group, or community context. That is, the book is directed to the social worker who wants to work with the client wherever he is met and be free to pursue what needs to be done according to the tasks worked out together.
>
> (Middleman and Goldberg 1974 : 6-7)

There appears to be a curious contradiction between this last sentence based upon mutuality between worker and client and the authors' explicitly-stated position that their framework is not meant for 'the therapist' but rather focuses on structural change. The degree to which social problems are caused by the interaction of individuals and the social structures in which they live, or are caused solely by those structures themselves, is not clearly addressed. Hence it is not clear in what ways the authors see the mission for social work generally, as opposed to the mission of a social worker utilizing this particular framework of social work practice. This then makes it difficult for the reader to appreciate in what ways the authors view social work boundaries and specializations.

This ambiguity is reinforced by Goldberg when she asserts:

> the structural model should not be used with clients seeking
> services designed to change their behaviour, e.g. eliminating a
> phobia. The worker using the structural model would never
> undertake such a task. Rather, he would take the role of broker
> and connect the client with, for example, a specialist in behaviour
> modification.
>
> (Goldberg 1974: 155)

This position raises a number of questions. Is Goldberg prescribing that social work is not about individual needs, like phobias? A phobia is the result of an interactional process between individual and environment. Intervention *by whatever means* could improve the quality of that interaction. Goldberg, in referring to behaviour modification, is prescribing one kind of treatment which is making particular assumptions about the aetiology of phobias. She does not argue with evidence here. In any case she is confusing a treatment of choice with a particular assessment of a problem situation. Hypothetically, if the social worker assessed the environmental context as a significant cause of the phobia, what gives him or her the right to decide that his 'client' should be changed, regardless of whether he does the changing or refers the 'client' to someone else?

This raises a fundamental flaw in Goldberg's argument, that the locus of intervention needs to be argued on particular grounds both preferentially in terms of a value position and preferentially in terms of available knowledge about efficacy of various forms of intervention. Goldberg provides no substantive arguments about this at all. On the basis of a decision to intervene solely with an individual, the social worker absolves himself of the responsibility (because structural intervention is not indicated!) and makes a referral.

Goldberg (1974 : 155) alerts the practitioner that people often blame themselves for problems that cannot be alleviated by changing behaviour, and hence presumably request the social worker to change them. In this instance the social worker has to make a decision to (i) intervene in the structures which may be causing the problem, or (ii) acknowledge that the structures cannot or ought not to be changed and thus refer the person to another practitioner. This social work decision is at odds with Goldberg's assumptions about the client's ability to participate in his responsibility in making a 'service contract' (Goldberg 1974 : 151).

The authors recognize the diversity of practice which characterized social work in the past, viz. division by fields, methods, schools of thought, and purpose. They recognize the concerns expressed about the apparent lack of professional identity caused by these divisions and the attempts to find the 'generic', that is 'to find some underlying something that bridges the diversity and attests to the fact that there is a single social work profession' (Middleman and Goldberg 1974 : 18).

Furthermore, these authors note that the similarities which have emerged in social work have been largely in terms of values but go on to observe that a more accurate picture is gained by studying the activities of practitioners. 'If a profession *is* what it *does*, that is, if it is defined by its actions, then we must look to the activities of the social work practitioners for the data from which to define our boundaries' (Middleman and Goldberg 1974 : 18). They leave unstated, however, the observation that if values can be inferred from activities, and that if substantially different activities imply different value bases, then there might be very little that social work has in common values, whatever its rhetoric.

While a reliance upon observation will give an indication of what social workers do, that is, it will provide an accurate *description* of the activities of social work practice, it does not address the prescriptive questions of what *ought* social workers to be doing based upon certain other criteria, e.g. justification in terms of a particular value stance or statement of practice.

The authors are not clear about the relationship between their framework and the divisions of practice already observed, that is, whether their framework supersedes, encompasses, or complements these, or whether it is designed to completely replace these former conceptualizations in the form of a 'supramethod'.

An organizing framework

The authors develop a four quadrant organizing framework which is organized around two axes: a 'locus of concern' and 'persons engaged' (Middleman and Goldberg 1974 : 19–23). This organizing framework can be used to track the activities of a given social worker at work in a particular instance or to compare his activities across instances and, holding the situation constant, can be used to map differential social worker activity as a function of (i) school of thought, (ii) field of practice, and (iii) methodology.

From this perspective, it is clear that the authors see theirs as an *organizing framework*. They are clearly recognizing the use of 'specialist modes' depending on field of practice, methodology, and setting. They are also proposing that despite these differences there is a boundary which is able to differentiate social work activity from non-social work activity, i.e. it is a way of conceptualizing the whole.

While this conceptualization can provide a framework for mapping social work activities, the dichotomization into 'social service delivery' and 'social policy and planning' takes us back to a division along the lines of 'direct service' versus 'indirect service', and hence reinforces orthodox boundaries within the whole. Having formulated a model with a particular purpose in mind, one has to be careful how it is used, otherwise one's primary purpose may be defeated.

A structural approach

Middleman and Goldberg state their preference for intervention in terms of structural change. Their understanding of this is not clearly explicated, although from their justification one might assume it means changing social structures in which individuals are located. The authors recognize the futility of confusing the aetiology of problems with methodologies for intervention:

> While it is obviously ridiculous to define a psychological problem such as a fear of heights in social terms (e.g. buildings are too tall), the tendency to define social problems in psychological terms is a subtler version of the same mistake. And it is just such a fallacy of the latter type that has made some social workers unwilling parties to the mounting conspiracy against the poor.
>
> (Middleman and Goldberg 1974 : 24)

A similar sentiment is expressed by Butrym in her discussion of 'social functioning':

Inherent in the concept of *social functioning* is that as problems
reside in both the environment and the people, solutions to these
problems need to come from both the environment and the people.
To attempt to deal with a problem of homelessness exclusively by
means of psychological support is as futile as trying to provide
tempting tidbits to a person suffering from anorexia nervosa.

(Butrym 1976 : 8–9)

However, in Butrym's argument she is clearly indicating that
solutions need to be found in both individual *and* environment. While
Middleman and Goldberg's conceptualization is in terms of individuals within social contexts it is by no means clear why they prefer the
social environment as the primary target for change.

Their model 'presupposes that large segments of the population
– the poor, the aged, the minority groups – are neither the cause of,
nor the appropriate locus for change efforts aimed at lessening the
problems they are facing' (Middleman and Goldberg 1974 : 26). The
recognition of this fact does not of itself justify a *preference* for structural
change especially as the authors recognize that 'every instance of
social work involves an intervention into the *relationship*' (my italics).
One can question why the authors give a preference to this particular
mode of intervention. They may wish to redress the imbalance up
until now in favour of 'individual treatment', however, a preference
solely in the other direction is not justified by the authors.

An 'ideal type' description of such a position is outlined by Cowger:

The singular role of social work is to change elements of the
existing society. An assumption of this position is that social and
personal problems are the result of malformed social structures.
Therefore the primary concern of the profession should be to
change or destroy those social structures that are responsible for
the malfunctioning.

(Cowger 1977 : 26)

This rather simplistic view fails to take into account that these same
structures are serving the interests of particular groups of people, and
thus fails to consider the implications of the conflict between social
groups and hence the structures which serve to meet the needs of one
group while at the same time creating problems and needs for another
group. On this juxtaposition, a consideration of the concept of *sanction*
is imperative with its concomitant discussion of both its source

115

and justification. Unfortunately such a discussion is lacking in Middleman and Goldberg's framework.

This major weakness of the framework is exacerbated by the authors' failure to give any sociological consideration of the concept of 'society'. In their discussion of relevant social science concepts (in Chapter 12) and their list of relevant propositions for practice (1974 : 193–8) the emphasis is clearly upon individual behaviour. This is curious given their preference for structural change, and their discussion of the value components underlying the development of knowledge and the politics of concept formation. In this latter discussion they exhort the practitioner to exercise caution in the selection and use of explanatory theory. Their position is that every set of human phenomena can be interpreted in many different ways, and that each interpretation is political both in content and consequence. Given their position one might have expected more explicit treatment of the social contexts in which these 'relevant propositions' were to be applied.

A further apparent contradiction in the model occurs when the authors explicate its principles (1974 : 32ff.), viz. the worker should be accountable to the client(s), the worker should follow the demands of the client task, the worker should maximize the potential supports in the client's(s') environment, and the worker should proceed from an assumption of least contest.

These 'principles' represent a highly individualized form of intervention. Again, this is a curious position to take given their preference for structural forms of intervention. They take no cognizance of competing and conflicting interests of different client groups, and nor do they provide any justification, either empirical or value-based, for their injunction to exert the least pressure necessary to accomplish the client task.

Middleman and Goldberg recognize that the practitioner requires more than abstract principles:

> To specify a professional assignment and designate areas of
> specialization in terms of activity provides an orientation to
> practice, but it does not define practice itself . . . such a
> formulation, while essential to a coherent, systematic practice, is
> too abstract to guide intervention. Elaboration of a practice
> requires specification of a set of principles, operational definition
> of the principles, the functional roles that derive from those

116

operationally defined principles and the explicit acts which the worker should perform in order to implement his professional assignment in accord with the operational definition of those principles.

(Middleman and Goldberg 1974 : 31)

While one must applaud their rhetoric, they unfortunately commit the sin they are behoving others to avoid! As I have already mentioned the four major principles of their model do not make an easy fit with the authors' underlying assumptions. The delineation of the roles of *broker, mediator, advocate,* and *conferee* (in Chapter 5), is made without apparent justification for these four roles, nor with any attempt at looking at the practice implications for utilizing particular roles in specific situations.

The metawork and the organizational context

The authors do stress the importance of work directly connected with client goals, but which does not directly involve the client: 'all . . . work that may be once removed from direct engagement with the client task is the metawork – the activities that may enhance the work but are aside from the work itself' (1974 : 154–5).

In view of their emphasis on structural change, it is not surprising that the authors place weight on an understanding of the organizational context in which the client, and client-worker, find themselves:

Our central thesis is that service deliverers must know as much about their interrelatedness with others within the system, to the ways organizations move and shift or stick and stay, as they need to know about their own roles with clients.

(Middleman and Goldberg 1974 : 169)

The authors draw on some empirical evidence available in their discussion of metawork – recording of interviews: its efficacy and necessity, supervision, conflicts for competing scarce resources within organizations, means becoming ends, competition between vested interest groups within the agency, professional autonomy versus administrative control.

There is nothing new being raised in the discussion of these issues. Again, because of their position in relation to structures one might have expected less separation of practice functions directed towards

117

clients and those practice functions involving the 'metawork'. Indeed as one moves through the book a very contradictory picture emerges – on the one hand the authors opt for a position which emphasizes the necessity of structural or contextual change, yet on the other there is little discussion of the specific skills of 'metawork' and organizational context of practice. Indeed there is a curious disassociation from social work's responsibility in this regard.

> It is beyond the scope of this book to dwell at length on the organizational arrangements. Our major aim is to suggest that the future of the welfare system demands organizations that dispense social services, possess stability, an aura of legitimacy, and value to the larger society . . . so that the administrators can concentrate upon deploying necessary talent and resources to making the work place an exciting environment. . . .
>
> (Middleman and Goldberg 1974 : 178)

But one can ask how is this to be achieved, and what is social work's role (and the skills involved) in obtaining this objective?

Social science and social work practice

The authors give an introduction to explicating what theory is, and then move on to a discussion of the politics of theory development and concept formation. It is pointed out that the selection of some theory over other theory is a political decision. 'Concepts' do not exist in the real world, thus concept formation is political in that we invent concepts to make sense of the world of people and events and the concepts we invent are largely determined by the interests and occupations of our culture and language. The authors point to the necessity of considering 'the theorist in the theory' (1974 : 186) particularly if the social worker is going to exercise caution in the selection and use of explanatory theory. Given that social science theory is neither precise nor objective, every set of human phenomena can be interpreted in many different ways – and each interpretation is political both in content and consequence. Before any selection of theory is made and any single explanation of a particular event is accepted, the relative merit of alternative explanations should be weighed: the theory's *predictive value* ('is it useful?') and its *philosophic compatibility* ('should I use it?').

Middleman and Goldberg (1974 : 193) assert that the social worker should view social science theories as tools and 'should select the one that best fits the particular problem which confronts him at a given moment, and discard it when it no longer implements his task.' However, this position neglects what theory, either explicit or implicit, the social worker is using to define the problem in the first place; and to set the goals, in the second.

> This book is one effort to specify a mission and a set of tasks, and to suggest some of the many pieces of social science theory relevant to that mission and that set of tasks. Until the profession accomplishes this, however, eclecticism guided by the two criteria of predictive value and philosophical compatibility may be in order.
>
> (Middleman and Goldberg 1974 : 192)

This statement, however, is a tautology, because the stated mission and set of tasks itself arises out of theory (implicit or explicit) which if it is to be considered 'good' theory ought to be able to specify the relevant other theories with which it is compatible. To speak about a set of substantive theories relating to a stated mission without acknowledging the explicit or implicit theory upon which the mission is conceptualized, would appear to be setting an impossible task for any person seeking to make rational choices to guide his or her practice. Indeed, the authors pluck several pages (1974 : 193–8) of 'relevant propositions' from somewhere. While each proposition is adequately documented, there is no attempt to look at the assumptions upon which these propositions are based, nor attempt, in even a crude way, to give an account of why these particular propositions have been chosen over others.

Admittedly this is the theoretical homework of social work for some time to come, but one might have expected the authors to develop some rationale, particularly in the light of their preference for structural change as one choice for social work intervention.

Likewise, the authors can be challenged to explicate what particular goals *ought* to be pursued and whether we have the means of effectively realizing those goals or not. They say,

> Given that an instance of social work practice can be labelled 'effective', if, and only if, the act or set of acts performed by the worker produces the desired outcome, it follows that the desired

outcome must be clearly specified and stated in behavioural terms with observable referents.

(Middleman and Goldberg 1974 : 201)

What their set of propositions is attempting to answer is whether a particular outcome is possible. Neither these propositions nor any other part of this framework in any way attempts to justify what the 'desired' outcome (or goals) *ought* to be. It seems a bit like *Alice in Wonderland* when Alice says, 'I don't know where I want to go' and the Hare replies, 'Then any road will take you there.'

Use of terminology

Although Middleman and Goldberg (1972) speak about 'generic social work concepts', it is not until Middleman writes in 1977 that a definition is actually provided. 'Generic' and 'generalist' are defined: 'A generalist practitioner . . . can handle several different skills, fields, or aptitudes. One becomes a generalist by learning and doing practice one plus practice two plus practice three, and so forth' (Middleman 1977 : 143). This approach is additive, so that the differences as well as the likenesses of practice are blanketted in.

The generic refers to what is left over after adding together diverse processes, skills, and the like, when you *take away* all the differences. It is a subtractive process. Perhaps it should be termed distilling. Through a distilling process we may hope to approach what is basic or core, but we have lost some of the special flavour of the components in the process. . . .

(Middleman 1977 : 143)

It is speculation to ask if these are the definitions assumed in their earlier works. However, it is apparent that Middleman (1977) does not regard generic formulation to be sufficient of itself, but rather something to give coherence to an incorporation of specializations. She advocates the knowing of our social work history in order to be in a position to appreciate the duality of the profession.

For only out of appreciation of the duality of the profession can we face the immense difficulty of teasing out the generic or determine for ourselves . . . what specialized knowledge and skills we should have, and what goals and means to achieve the goals

120

are still worthy of being considered 'professional' even if different from our own precise values/means preferences. . . .

(Middleman 1977 : 143)

This 1977 position would appear to be a departure from the 1974 position of Middleman and Goldberg where they give a clear preference for structural intervention. In this discussion Middleman is giving a more balanced weight to the duality of intervention with individuals and with the environment.

Conclusions

There are many useful features in this framework. Assuming that social work concerns the assessment of and intervention in problems which arise at the interface of person and environment, this framework attempts to develop a frame of reference in which the person as well as his or her structural location is taken into account. The development of the four quadrant frame of reference means that interventions with the identified client as well as work on his behalf with 'non-sufferers' is considered and given its due weight. Further, this frame of reference has the advantage of highlighting the public issues arising out of private troubles of individuals.

The authors conceptualize the principles of practice being operationalized by sets of skills, that is, specific behaviours which are used under specified conditions thus achieving particular goals. These skills are not located within particular methodologies, schools, fields, or settings of practice. Rather they arise from relevant propositions which are chosen in order to reach particular goals of intervention.

The authors' preference is for structural change; thus there is, at least in theory, some redressing of the imbalance in favour of the individual/psychological variables of intervention which has occurred in the past and a concurrent restoration of social/environmental variables.

Significantly, the authors give attention to the nature of social science theory and demonstrate the importance of the role of the theorist in theory development.

The authors opt for a framework where the preferred intervention is in structures in which individuals are located, rather than the individuals themselves. But this framework is developed in a complete vacuum as no attention is given to particular substantive economic or social theories about the society in which the framework could be operationalized. There may be an implicit assumption on the part of the authors that this framework is relevant for a present-day capitalist and/or urban-industrial and/or American context. However, this is not made explicit. It may be implicit that this framework is sufficiently general that it could be applied in any societal context given that social work is an international activity. On the other hand it seems almost inconceivable that a practitioner would embark on any change, whether individual or structural, without first discussing relevant social theories. The authors appear content to encourage a practitioner to embark on structural change without first considering relevant substantive theories. Needless to say there is no discussion of the *process* of choice related to these substantive theories. There is a short discussion of consumerism and accountability but this is not integrated with other sections of the framework.

Social work activities are not linked explicitly to possible or desirable outcomes apart from those related to individual client goals. Thus no treatment is given to situations where these individual goals are competing and conflicting. While a practitioner may have been content to enable individual clients to realize their potentials and aspirations, the heterogeneity of client populations surely points to at least the possibility of a conflict of interest in the goals of competing client groups, and certainly between client groups and the rest of society. Hence any social work intervention which embarks on individual goals without considering these within the wider societal context is short-sighted and predictably will run into fundamental conflict.

While the authors delineate activities based within the four quadrants of their model, there is no discussion of priorities. What criteria enable the individual practitioner to choose between different types of social work? This difficulty is exacerbated by the lack of substantial discussion on 'who is the client?' Furthermore, there is an implicit assumption that clients are always able to express their needs.

Part 3

THE FINDINGS

Chapter Six

PURPOSES OF 'INTEGRATED' THEORY

The ways the frameworks articulate their purpose will be dealt with under six headings: (i) rejection of orthodox boundaries for conceptualizing practice, (ii) the relationship of the frameworks to 'methods', (iii) the development of a 'common base' and the problems in conceptualizing this, (iv) the universality of the claims, (v) the relationship between education and practice, and (vi) operationalization.

REJECTION OF ORTHODOX BOUNDARIES

All eleven frameworks reject the orthodox manner of categorizing social work practice activities in terms of 'methods', settings, fields of practice, or bound to particular techniques, theories, problem areas or particular groups of clients. Their aim is to capture the 'realities of practice' unhindered by these artificial boundaries. The 'interventive repertoire' (Bartlett 1970) is potentially relevant to *all* social work situations: the frameworks are designed for the practitioner who wants to assume a 'social worker orientation' rather than have that limited by artificial parameters.

Each framework acknowledges that the boundaries created by methods, fields, settings, particular problem and client groups, artificially constrain an assessment and can prematurely prejudice the way in which a problem situation is viewed. Those boundaries can affect the practitioner's thinking about aetiology and possible types of intervention. This in turn may cause the practitioner to limit assessment and intervention to either an individual *or* his/her social context without considering their interdependence. These are the major claims put forward by the authors rejecting the orthodox boundaries of practice.

A similar position was argued by Bisno highlighting the inadequacies of a methods conceptualization:

> The present conceptualization of social work methods seems to be gravely misleading. It is probably not too intemperate to say that both social work education and practice have been confused and distorted by an inappropriate methodological framework. . . . The reality . . . is that social workers *professionally* employ a wide range of one-to-one methods and techniques in a whole host of transactional relationships (by no means just with clients) in all fields of social work activity. . . . Yet, the training in one-to-one methodological skills (other than in just one variant, casework) is extremely limited, with almost no systematic conceptual base.
>
> (Bisno 1969 : 5)

It is argued by the writers of the frameworks under consideration that the experience of practitioners supports the proposition that social work activity, when accurately delineated, cannot be fitted into the orthodox boundaries. The processes and skills involved in dealing with the client are only one part of the social work task. To view a problem situation through a framework primarily developed around a particular methodology of intervention is to run the risk of imposing a solution or making the problem situation fit the available intervention techniques rather than suspending judgement about appropriate forms of intervention until the 'broad canvas' of data has been assessed in a more open way.

RELATIONSHIP TO 'METHODS'

Given that all the eleven frameworks reject the 'artificial' boundaries imposed by an orthodox methods approach, it is surprising that more detailed attention is not given to the actual relationship between this 'new' conceptualization and the 'methods'. In all frameworks the specific nature of this relationship is quite unclear. Siporin does claim his framework provides 'bridges' between clinical work and social action. Middleman and Goldberg claim their framework is for the 'microlevel practitioner' taking into account the need for structural change. These authors do include 'methods' material, but there is no specific treatment of how the two very

126

dissimilar types of practice conceptualizations are linked. Bartlett, Loewenberg, and Whittaker make reference to the 'methods' approaches, but the nature of the relationship between these and their conceptualizations is not developed.

In the frameworks of Baker, Compton and Galaway, and Middleman and Goldberg, it could be assumed that these authors believe their 'new' conceptualizations render the 'methods' approaches obsolete, given their comments on the defects presented by a 'methods' approach.

Bartlett claims that her professional model provides breadth and needs to be linked to a 'method-and-skill' approach for 'substance'. She further claims that both the 'method-and-skill' model (viewed from the individual worker) and the professional model (viewed from the profession) depict the 'social worker in action'. It remains unclear, however, whether she means that the 'professional model' can never be operationalized by the practitioner but only 'thought about' and 'studied' by the 'profession'. Further, it is unclear whether her model depends upon 'method-and-skill' for its operationalization.

Loewenberg notes that his framework provides a common professional base upon which specializations can be built. Whittaker claims his framework is a conceptual 'coat-rack' on which to place various methods and strategies of helping. Pincus and Minahan claim that their framework can set the foundation for both the generalist and the specialist depending how the practitioner incorporates his/her own special knowledge regarding social problems, client groups, resource systems, theoretical orientations, and social science knowledge. However, the nature of the relationship between these frameworks and other conceptualizations of practice is not enunciated.

Put in historical context, the failure to make definitive statements about the relationships between orthodox methods and 'integrated' approaches is a serious omission, especially given that a 'methods' approach still remains a popular choice for practitioners.

THE 'COMMON BASE' AND ITS CONCEPTUALIZATION

Bartlett, Goldstein, Haines, Baker, Compton and Galaway, and Loewenberg, all refer to a 'common base' or 'common core of elements' to which practice can or should be related. Bartlett, Haines, and Baker use this common base to underpin all social work practice claiming that these 'generic elements' are common to *all* social work practice. Goldstein is more modest in that he aims to show what is common to a 'unitary model' of social work practice. Compton and Galaway and Loewenberg do not specify the extent covered by this common core of elements, but both maintain this core forms the foundation upon which specializations can be built. Pincus and Minahan claim their model is for use both in its own right as well as providing a foundation to which specialist approaches can be linked. These authors, together with Siporin, regard their models as mechanisms by which one can link the purposes and functions of social work with the particular techniques, skills, and relationships necessary to practise social work.

The notion of a 'common base' was developed as part of the Working Definition (1958). However, for whatever purpose the conceptualization of a 'common base' was intended, the particular elements constituting this 'common base' present problems because of the lack of agreement about what these should be and the actual substantive content of these elements.

The Working Definition of 1958, for example, maintained:

> Social work practice, like the practice of all professions, is recognized by a constellation of value, purpose, sanction, knowledge and method. No part alone is characteristic of social work practice nor is any part described here unique to social work. It is the particular content and configuration of this constellation which makes social work practice and distinguishes it from the practice of other professions.
>
> (Bartlett 1970 : 221)

However, Bartlett omits 'sanction' from her 'common base' on the grounds that this element was 'not a basic definer of social work practice in the same sense as the other essential elements and operates differently from them' (Bartlett 1970 : 59). She further states that 'sanction' does not operate 'within social work practice but is an outside influence' (Bartlett 1970 : 192). However, this differentiation is a moot point, given that a substantial knowledge and value component is also an external influence. Furthermore, no evidence is provided that 'sanction' does not influence the very form and nature of practice. The author may consider it desirable that social work practice should be independent of its various sanctions (society, the law, agency or programme, professional association)

(Bartlett 1970 : 59), but it is not possible to make an a priori claim that such *is* the case.

Baker identifies seven elements of his common base: 'knowledge', 'values', 'process', 'purposes', and 'roles, tasks, and action strategies'. Other writers refer to this 'common base' but are less specific about what elements constitute it, e.g. Haines, Siporin, and Loewenberg.

A further crucial issue is not *what* elements constitute the 'common base' but rather the *substantive content* of the elements. In order for such a constellation to provide direction to the practitioner, the propositions presented under each of the 'elements' need to be explicit.

In none of the writings which utilize such a 'constellation of elements' is the substantive content fully explicated and justified. The statements used by Bartlett and taken from the Working Definition are very general and consensus-oriented. Baker's discussion is a narrative of what he believes to be important drawing on a range of ideas from other writings. However, this choice is not justified. In referring to the 'purpose' of social work, Baker (1980 : 18) refers to Cowger's (1977) four stances of the relationship between social work and society. Baker claims that *all* four stances, which represent conflicting views, can be used at different times. Such treatment of the purpose of social work thus fails to provide proper directions for the framework's operationalization.

Furthermore, writers proposing a 'constellation of elements' of a 'common base' for practice write *as if* there was agreement both on the type of elements as well as their content. This relates to the problem of confusing prescription with description. A description of practice, if only based on the writings available rather than actual observation of practice itself, will confirm that there is *not* agreement about the purposes of social work practice at the present time. To fail to give recognition to this fact results in a distorted and inaccurate conceptualization of a 'common base'. Thus rather than having the potential to underpin social work practice generally, at best it can be seen as having the potential to underpin only a particular kind of practice.

UNIVERSALITY

A further significant aspect related to purpose is the author's view of the extent of application or universality of the framework: whether it is supposed to represent social work practice *in toto*, whether it represents just one of a number of approaches, and whether the context in which the framework was formulated plays any significant role in determining the particular nature of social work represented by the framework.

While the frameworks claim to address 'social work practice' they do not specify the importance of a context in terms of a particular country's socio-economic-political system or social welfare arrangements. The assumption therefore is that they are universally applicable. Baker (1980 : 13), for example, has linked the term 'unitary' with 'universal'. Bartlett has used the term 'generic' to apply to a common core of components which underpin *all* social work practice. This leaves open to debate what is common (if anything) about social work practice as it is operationalized in different cultural and sub-cultural contexts. What effects do 'sanctions', for example, have upon practice? How far do they modify or determine the particular *form* of practice? What effects do wealth or poverty, educational level, standard of housing, unemployment level, heterogeneity or homogeneity of ethnicity or race, have upon the practice of social work? Do these factors influence both the 'ends' and 'means' of social work?

The manner in which these frameworks are articulated would suggest that such factors as these are unimportant in the conceptualization of social work. However, this surely is a proposition to be examined.

The danger of universalism is in importing frameworks which have been designed in one particular socio-cultural context to an entirely different sphere of practice on the *assumption* that they will be appropriate. However, where the effects of a specific context are not made clear, the framework's efficacy must be limited until the influence of a context is shown to be irrelevant or its effects studied. In the meantime it will do well to note the danger of importing practice concepts and methods from one context and using them in another. Such disadvantages and adverse consequences have been well described (Midgley 1981).

Perhaps the frameworks of Baker and Haines implicitly make the greatest 'universal' claims of the frameworks being studied. The writings of Baker imply that his approach is superior to others. He delineates 'method', 'multi-method', and 'unitary', and then rejects the first two for various reasons. One could assume therefore that he intends his 'unitary' approach to replace other formulations especially given there is no provision to link his framework with other formulations.

Haines makes universal claims as well, although these are less explicit. He claims that his framework fits what social workers do, though they may only be aware of this intuitively. This rather high-handed comment, however, is not backed by empirical evidence (see Stevenson and Parsloe 1978). He further claims that this framework can be taken as representative of the state of social work in Britain in the 1970s. Such claims are all-encompassing. Even a cursory perusal of the social work literature of the 1970s will indicate that these claims are debatable.

It is rare for social work theory developed by North American writers to make reference to any literature outside that country. Thus one can question whether these writers assume that their products will be applicable only in their country of origin, or whether they assume a universal applicability.

RELATIONSHIP BETWEEN 'PRACTICE' AND 'EDUCATION'

Each of the eleven frameworks fails to make explicit its educational and practice purposes. There are crucial differences in writing an educational text book about social work on the one hand, and expli-cating a particular model for application in practice, on the other hand (Vickery 1977 : 40–1). The failure of authors to make clear their intentions has led to confusion.

An author aiming to present a conceptual framework for practice would be expected to develop internal consistency within the frame-work so that all the various components could be seen to form a whole. One might expect the author to demonstrate how this particular approach arises out of and links to other approaches. In addition an explicit set of operational guidelines would be expected to provide clear directives for the practitioner.

By contrast, a text for educational purposes, especially for begin-ning students, will probably take a developmental approach, intro-ducing rudimentary concepts and describing practice skills before attempting more difficult ones. A common pattern in texts for begin-ners is to present a loose framework in which to locate a range of practice approaches. However, there is no intent for this loose organizing framework *itself* to be used by the practitioner. In addition, a text would usually present the strengths and weaknesses of several approaches and place these in historical perspective. In presenting these possibilities, it leaves the ultimate choice to the practitioner and provides few, if any, criteria to assist the user to choose one approach over another. In other words, the primary aim in a text book is to aid the education of the student. The student uses the text, not to solve a specific social work problem, but to learn about a number of approaches and to evaluate the respective merits of each one.

With this brief outline of some issues relating to the aim of writing a text and in producing a conceptual framework for social work practice, it can be seen that a failure to be explicit about the *intent* of the author is likely to lead to confusion. This is in fact what has happened in the case of these eleven frameworks.

All frameworks, with the exception of Bartlett, Middleman and Goldberg, and Whittaker, claim to write both for education and for practice. Bartlett claims to write *about* practice in such a way that she is not necessarily suggesting a framework which *in toto* can be operationalized, but one which needs to be linked to 'method-and-skill' approaches for substance and hence operationalization. Middleman and Goldberg claim their aim is to teach a particular *kind* of social work practice, rather than write about it in a general way or write a text for all. Likewise, Whittaker makes no explicit claims for general education.

One of the real problems in not making one's aims explicit and realistic, within the scope of a book or set of papers, is the potential for confusion. A beginning text for students of social work practice is likely to include quite a different set of materials than one claiming to develop a conceptual framework for a type of social work practice.

In Goldstein, for example, there is a chapter on the history of social work practice. While this chapter is useful in an introductory text on social work practice, it has not been specifically related to the development of Goldstein's particular practice framework. Likewise, Compton and Galaway include a chapter on 'useful theoretical perspectives'. This provides an introduction to some 'foundation knowledge' for use by a social worker. However, the authors do not attempt to link it to their framework in such a way that it could be used for operationalization. Issues concerning theory compatibility and eclecticism are not properly addressed. The reader is thus left with questions about the author's contribution to the development of social work theory over and above the bringing together of a collection of writings and ideas from diverse sources.

OPERATIONALIZATION

The frameworks vary in their potential for operationalization. Bartlett's (1970) framework was designed to assist in the *conceptualization* of practice, and not as a model to direct practice activities. In view of the arguments connecting theory and action in social work, Bartlett's position is an untenable one. Conceptualizations which have been constructed in the absence of clear operational guidelines, are more in the nature of a 'study' of some phenomena, and thus can be characterized as belonging to a discipline rather than to a profession.

Each of the other frameworks addresses operationalization in some degree or another. However, in these frameworks there are clear gaps (if not chasms) between the theoretical conceptualization and the skills, techniques, and models to operationalize them. Part of the reason for this is the very wide brief depicting the nature of social work. To operationalize such a broadly-defined purpose for social work would require considerable instruction.

Given the broad purpose each of the frameworks claims for social work, the *viability* of this type of practice has been questioned. Of the applications so far published, the parameters have been considerably narrowed; for example, McInerney (1981) to a neo-natal intensive care ward; Coulshed (1977) to a psycho-geriatric ward; Vickery (1976) to a community half-way house; and the early study used in the Pincus and Minahan (1973) text by Foster (1965) to an oncology ward.

Furthermore, the ability of one practitioner to possess the skills and techniques necessary to operationalize such a broad approach, has led to the suggestion that its application requires a team approach (Currie and Parrott 1981; Evans 1978). The exact nature of how a team might co-operate in order to practise in this way has not been developed.

In terms of informing social work curricula in order that students can attempt this type of practice, the difficulties have been outlined (Roberts 1982; Roberts and Zulfacar 1986; Rosen 1983). The difficulties which can be observed at the level of application reinforce the gap which exists here between theory and action, the formulation

133

of theory in a way which is isolated from practice realities, and the development of concepts which are not ontologically committed. In much of this writing there is a sense that it is being written by scholars for other scholars: there is little intention, if any, on the part of the writers, to produce theory which will guide activities either of practitioners or educators.

Chapter Seven

PROBLEMS IN ACHIEVING AN 'INTEGRATED' SOCIAL WORK THEORY

AN IMMODEST DOMAIN

Perhaps the most difficult task faced by authors in constructing 'integrated' theory is the integration of social work purpose with the rest of the conceptual framework. This results primarily from their defining purpose in very broad, global, and immodest terms. While social work has a history of this immodesty of purpose (Howe 1980), nowhere is it highlighted as much as in the set of writings under consideration here. When it comes to translating rhetoric into action, the difficulties of grandiose purposes become very apparent.

Given the relatively global nature of this group of writings and their attempts to construct guidelines for practice, it would not be unreasonable to expect explicit delineation of the purposes of social work, as these writers see them, and how these purposes are derived. It is only through such an explicit delineation that one can judge whether in fact each framework has been able to achieve the purposes so outlined.

Given the importance of 'purpose' for this kind of evaluation, it is surprising to find how little attention is given to this matter by the authors. Prior to examining the attempts to define purpose in the different frameworks, some general problems will be considered.

First, in referring to the purposes of the profession, it is necessary to ask whether these are observable, whether there is general agreement about them, whether there is significant disagreement or alternatives, and what means have been used to establish these purposes. None of the frameworks looks at this issue in a critical manner. They present the purposes of social work *as if* there were general agreement and *as if* the purposes were known. In the absence of corroborating evidence and justification for the authors' assertions, one might argue that the purposes portrayed in each of the frameworks represent the authors' private views, rather than those of members of the profession or the purposes as perceived by other groups of people. If such acknowledgement were made, one could attempt an evaluation in a more confident manner, rather than having to rely on a consensus view which on face value at least has dubious validity. In a few instances, authors present the differing views, both complementary and conflicting, of other writers. At least this approach gives some recognition to the possibility of differences within the profession on this matter. However, the final decision on what to accept is left to the reader. This is the approach taken by Compton and Galaway, and Loewenberg. While this approach is more 'honest', and while it might be an entirely appropriate educational strategy in a text book, it is entirely unsatisfactory if the aim is to describe a major variable in a conceptual framework to provide guidelines for the practitioner.

Second, given the importance of explicating 'purpose' to which other variables in the conceptual framework of practice relate, it is surprising to find purpose stated in very general and global terms. Definitions include 'assisting people with problem solving and coping capacities', 'assisting individuals realize their potential', 'assisting the interaction of persons and environments', 'linking people with resource systems', and so on. No qualifications are placed upon these general statements. Being so general, they are wide open to different interpretations, which proves convenient for both writer and critic alike.

With the exception of Middleman and Goldberg, purposes are couched not only in global terms, but also in 'neutral terms'. Thus they fail to provide direction or the 'ends' to which practice activities might be directed. No consideration is given to how viable such purposes are in terms of available resources, power and authority, conflicts of interest, social work sanctions, and available skills and techniques.

The purpose of social work is defined by Pincus and Minahan as follows:

Social work is concerned with the interactions between people and their social environment which affect the ability of people to accomplish their life tasks, alleviate distress, and realize their aspirations and values. The purpose of social work therefore is to

136

(1) enhance the problem-solving and coping capacities of people, (2) link people with systems that provide them with resources, services and opportunities, (3) promote the effective and humane operation of these systems, and (4) contribute to the development and improvement of social policy.

(Pincus and Minahan 1973 : 9)

It is interesting to note that these authors see these 'purposes' as similar to the 'functions' of social work, with the addition of 'dispensing material resources' and 'serving as agents of social control' (Pincus and Minahan 1973 : 15).

However in these, and similar definitions, major difficulties arise. These relate to (i) confusion between prescription and description, (ii) inadequate consideration of teleological matters, (iii) failure to deal with the social control functions of social work, and (iv) failure to enunciate the concept 'person-in-environment'. Each of these will be dealt with in turn.

CONFUSION BETWEEN DESCRIPTION AND PRESCRIPTION

In all eleven frameworks, the authors do not make it clear whether their intention is to *describe* the present reality of social work, or whether they are providing a *prescription* which ought to be followed. While all definitions of social work purposes are consensus-oriented and expressed in a highly-generalized form, one is left again and again with the enquiry: is this statement of the 'is' or 'ought' variety? The authors provide neither the data base for a description nor a justification for a prescription.

With any prescription, one is entitled to expect a justification. However, this is not given (with the possible exception of Middleman and Goldberg) precisely because the authors, in confusing these two kinds of activity, provide a prescription *as if* it were a description, and therefore see no need for justification. Such a confusion is a fundamental error in this set of writings. The absence of a data base prevents the findings being replicated and hence authenticated. Furthermore, such a fundamental confusion makes it difficult, if not impossible, to evaluate these frameworks in terms of their role in assisting to achieve the purposes of social work.

137

INADEQUATE CONSIDERATION OF TELEOLOGICAL MATTERS

A serious problem is caused in all frameworks because of a confusion between 'ends' and 'means', and a confusion between technical processes and ideology. The frameworks of Bartlett, Pincus and Minahan, Compton and Galaway, and Germain and Gitterman make reference to 'enhancement of problem solving and coping capacities', and the 'enhancement of social functioning.' However, it is not clear whether these authors view these tasks as 'ends' or 'means' and whether they see them relating to 'outcomes' or 'processes'. For example, are 'improving problem solving and coping capacities' and 'enhancing social functioning' ends in themselves, or means to some other ends? If these tasks are treated as ends in themselves then the authors fail to explain why such ends are important. The social worker is not provided with any justification as to why such qualities are being developed, or whether by acquiring them their clients will be any better off. In addition, if this view is accepted, it follows that the social worker would not be interested in social problems as states which have to be changed, but rather in ensuring that certain qualities (i.e. improved problem-solving capacities, etc.) are developed in and for their own right.

The problem can be illustrated by reference to the Pincus and Minahan framework where the purposes can be seen to relate more to technical processes rather than describing hoped-for end products. In other words technical processes are substituted for a discussion of and a preference for a particular ideology. In neither the Pincus and Minahan nor the Compton and Galaway frameworks is a particular *direction* given for eventual hoped-for outcomes as a result of social work intervention. Instead, the frameworks concentrate on processes and procedures. The process of 'linking' does not of itself provide criteria which differentiate social work activities from any other kind of undertaking. For example, the purpose of 'linking' could apply equally well to linking an unemployed person with a job, a starving person with an agency to provide food, a robber with a bank, or a millionaire with a lucrative money market.

In each of these examples persons are being 'linked' with resources, services, and opportunities. One could argue that in each case these people are being assisted to enhance their problem-solving and coping capacities as well. Therefore would each of these examples be accepted as depicting social work purposes? If not, what criteria help the social worker to decide the legitimacy of working with the unemployed, the poor, the bank robber, or the millionaire? It is precisely a treatment of these issues which will provide some direction for the practitioner, rather than a description of technical processes which hopefully provide the means to some end.

By not clearly delineating ends for social work, the practitioner is given no criteria to use when deciding who has rights to social work service, and indeed what preference will be given to certain activities and *causes* over others, given that resources are usually limited. This problem is highlighted in the case study (The House on Sixth Street) quoted in Pincus and Minahan. In whatever way one uses their formulation, there are no indices available from the framework itself to make judgements about eligibility for social work intervention: the tenants or the landlords (they both had problems!) Nor are any directions provided for deciding whether a preference should be given to helping those who are defined as clients *cope* with their problems of inadequate housing or to *changing* the conditions which led to this problem in the first place.

Therefore, if the characteristics of 'improved social functioning and problem solving' are considered as 'means', then one must enquire as to what 'ends' these behaviours are being directed.

Siporin attempts to address this difficulty when outlining purpose. He attempts to define outcomes (ends) rather than processes (means), and then addresses how certain outcomes might be achieved. The purposes listed by Siporin (1975 : 13–14) are:

1. To develop, maintain, and strengthen the social welfare system, so that it can meet basic human needs. This general function is realized through social work efforts in the form of social intervention . . .: individualized social case services, social welfare policy planning, income maintenance, welfare administration, and social action.
2. To assure adequate standards of subsistence, health, and welfare for all.
3. To enable people to function optimally within their social institutional roles and statuses.
4. To support and improve the social order and the institutional structure of society.

Siporin (1975 : 19–25) lists ways by which these purposes might be achieved. However, the purposes, it will be noted, are so global and idealistic that one can legitimately enquire whether specific 'means' can be devised for their realization.

Goldstein (1973 : 5) takes the view that social work is a 'means' and *not* an 'end'. This 'means' is provided by the objectives of practice, i.e. provision of a context in which social learning can be maximized. This is connected with the other purposes which Goldstein sees for social work, viz. 'capability of providing the means and opportunity whereby individuals can deal with conditions which interfere with social living.' This is in accord with individuals' 'needs, means, ends and experiences.'

In considering the provision of 'means' as a purpose for social work, one might be able to invoke specified values in order to gain some direction. However, in reviewing the major values outlined by Goldstein, one finds that the major value centres on the individual. Goldstein refers to 'self-determination' and 'acceptance' in order to reduce the inequality and imbalance between client and worker. Invoking these values, however, does not resolve the dilemma of *which* person or cause is appropriate for social work action.

Apart from the question of whether in fact social work possesses techniques and skills which can provide a 'means' to achieve certain 'ends', more importantly the question: 'should social work provide the "means" for *any* "ends" as long as the person requesting social work assistance is "self-determining"?' is significant. In other words, without an ideology which includes a discussion on 'ends', the practitioner is given no guidance as to what 'ends' to put his or her technology, nor guidance about the allocation of resources of money, time and personnel. In order to make a choice between the bank robber, the millionaire, the poor, and the unemployed, for example, a social work purpose needs to specify an ideology which will guide choice among competing options. In other words, social work practitioners need to be able to make choices related to the appropriate use of available technologies.

It is this failure to be explicit about direction, preference, and choice, of competing and conflicting alternatives, which leads to major difficulties in trying to assess the ideological components of the frameworks. The ideology of most frameworks is not explicit. This is one reason why it is difficult to evaluate whether a framework has been successful in achieving its intended goals.

The Middleman and Goldberg (1974 : 609) framework is explicit about its preferred direction. Their preference rests with the poor and powerless, in attempting to change social and economic structures which they see as a significant part of the aetiology of social problems, rather than trying to change individuals through therapy. Their aims are to change the environment to meet the needs of the individual through an ideology of social justice. This is reflected in their treatment of values wherein they recognize the conflicts which exist, the recognition of the influence of values and politics on concept formation and the importance of the influence of social science paradigms in which concepts and knowledge are developed (Middleman and Goldberg 1974 : 184ff.). They limit their treatment of purpose, however, to a personal level, rather than attributing their ideas to the profession as a whole. Being explicit about an ideology provides a point of reference to which the practitioner can refer in trying to decide if his or her skills and techniques are appropriately employed with the robber, the poor, the unemployed, or the millionaire.

Where a preference has been stated, this helps in the decision of *who* is the client, because in addition to the technical criteria provided by Pincus and Minahan (1973 : 63), it provides *normative* guidance. Most commonly the question of 'who is the client' is not addressed: it is assumed that anyone can be a client. This issue is rarely considered within a context of limited financial, personnel, time, and expertise resources. Haines (1975 : 2 and 23) does acknowledge that the focus *should* be directed to the poor and disadvantaged, but then generalizes his framework to include 'everybody', because everyone is concerned in some way or another with the poor and needy. Such a treatment of client status provides no explicit guidelines for the practitioner.

NEGLECT OF THE SOCIAL CONTROL FUNCTIONS OF SOCIAL WORK

A further problem in achieving 'integrated' theory relates to a failure to be explicit about a *comprehensive* list of social work's purposes. This is highlighted in their failure to consider the regulatory and social control functions of social work (Day 1981). It is difficult to know whether this omission is deliberate or not. Certainly a study of the sociology of regulation and social control can locate at least certain aspects of social work fulfilling this purpose (see e.g. Simpkin 1979). Given the global claims made for these frameworks it is curious that this aspect is generally neglected. It is suggested that the failure to be explicit about description and prescription partly accounts for this situation.

Pincus and Minahan (1973 : 15) recognize the social control functions of social work; however, they fail to make mention of this in subsequent writings. Likewise, Haines recognizes that a central concern of social work is the provision of the necessities of life and the regulation of behaviour. However, beyond this initial recognition, the issue is not developed further.

It is suggested that authors may have difficulty in dealing with the question of explicit control and regulation because of their failure to make explicit their assumptions about human nature. While no framework makes this assumption explicit, because of their reference to 'self-determination', 'maximize each person's potential', 'identify, foster, maintain and enhance people's autonomy', it can be assumed that a preference for an optimistic rather than a pessimistic view of human nature is made. Thus to admit to the need to provide social control functions, is to have to admit to behaviour resting on opposing assumptions.

Furthermore, none of the frameworks gives adequate treatment to the question of *obligations* as well as rights, and the question of how the development of *one* person's potential affects the development of the potentials of others. There is the assumption that *all* potentials can be realized, and maximized! A cursory glance at blatant differences between the industrialized nations in contrast to the developing Third World, as well as the differences between the rich and the poor within a country, would indicate, at least on face value, that the potentiation of some people is clearly at the expense of others.

FAILURE TO ENUNCIATE THE CONCEPT 'PERSON-IN-ENVIRONMENT'

Another significant problem relating to the treatment of the purposes of social work is the use of the concept 'person-in-environment' without a clear enunciation of this concept. All frameworks assert that social work's main concern lies with the interaction of person and environment, and, at least in their rhetoric, single out social work's *primary* interest being at the *interface* of person and environment.

142

Having recognized that this is where social work's interest is (or where it ought to be), there is then, however, a marked discrepancy in the way the two components of this dialectic are treated. This difficulty arises primarily from a failure to adequately define 'environment'. This is not a term with a self-evident meaning, particularly when used to help clarify social work's main concerns. It can be used to refer to different realities, e.g. to all contextual variables such as family, friends, peers, social institutions, community and broader social, economic, and political structures. It can be used to refer to only some of these or a more restricted view of a person's immediate 'social milieu'. It can be limited to only specific organizational contexts or specific social welfare arrangements, without linking these to broader socio-economic-political arrangements.

To use the term 'environment' in an unexplicated form gives rise to the strong possibility of misinterpretation. This creates difficulties in understanding the realities of practice which are being referred to as well as making a critique of the framework within the claims of its parameters. To leave the concept 'environment' unexplicated runs the risk of confusing 'social milieu' with 'social structure' (Mills 1959 : 10–11), and the theories which are required to explain each one. Social psychology may explain 'social milieu', but structural sociology is required to explain 'social structure'.

In a similar way Haines recognizes there are difficulties with the abstract notion of the concept 'community'. Is it a geographical area, interest group, or need group? But he says it is the individuals with whom the social worker deals who comprise the community. This interpretation places sociological concepts in an inferior place to individual psychology.

It is clear, for example, that in the ecological model of Germain and Gitterman (1980), the influence of the wider social and economic structures and their effects on the individual are important. Yet this wider context is not developed within their current model. This work, they claim, needs to be undertaken in the future. Given the nature of their particular framework, it is curious that such a fundamental part can be disregarded 'until later'.

Middleman and Goldberg, while presenting their 'structural approach', limit it to 'microlevel' practice. Their model is consistent with a social welfare-through-social change philosophy, and is developed for the social worker who questions the systemic inequalities surrounding society's distribution of resources. However, while recognizing the importance of this and claiming this to be a significant part of their ideology, they limit the practice focus to the 'microlevel'. This is particularly evident in their treatment of practice skills.

Whittaker likewise limits his focus to 'interpersonal helping', for while he recognizes the influence of societal and structural contexts, he excludes these broader parameters for pragmatic convenience in order to maintain manageability of the large number of variables to be considered in assessment.

Loewenberg takes much the same position, claiming a rather spurious justification in that one has to learn individual skills first *before* being able to develop skills to use with larger collectivities. Furthermore, he claims that most beginning students work with individuals and small groups rather than larger collectivities, and as his is a text book for these students, then this justifies limiting the variables. This demonstrates the confusion which results in mixing the aims of developing a framework for both education and practice at the same time.

Pincus and Minahan and Haines recognize the impact of wider social structural variables, but believe that changes in these are ultimately effected by *political* processes. They further assert that these political processes which are required to effect these changes are too important to be left in the hands of professionals, such as social workers. Haines gives recognition to the role of politics in controlling the means by which social workers are able to attempt to bring about changes. However, these authors assert that if politics is the social worker's prime interest then it is doubtful if social work is the right career choice. This attempt to limit the scope of social work practice by these authors, seems to place a particular and limited construction on the meaning of 'political'. If social work has any ambitions of seeking to change even parts of social environments, then it seems axiomatic that this involves political behaviour.

Baker also fails to properly address issues related to environmental change. He makes universal claims for his framework but then totally omits substantial treatment of environmental issues whether in terms of small group and neighbourhood contexts or related to wider societal parameters. This omission is compounded by his process models which tend to reinforce an individualistic/psychologistic frame of reference.

As portrayed in these frameworks, one component of the person–environment dialectic is given preference, despite the rhetoric that social work's concern is at the interface of person and environment.

Most writers invoke a position enunciated by Schwartz (1969, 1976) who describes a 'symbiotic' relationship between the two components of this concept. However, such a position has a nebulous ontology. This failure to relate the concept to reality, and the failure to adequately define 'environment', can be considered partly to account for the ultimate focus on the individual.

INADEQUATE TREATMENT OF 'SOCIETY'

While each framework recognizes the importance of the environmental context, each one fails to give any substantive treatment to the concept of 'society'. It is curious to find an almost total neglect of theories, concepts, and knowledge from sociology in order to help understand the social location of both the practice of social work, and also the social location of clients.

Even in the framework of Middleman and Goldberg, where they explicitly elect to take a 'structural approach' and maintain that their aim is to change structures in order to meet the needs of people, there is a curious lack of sociological content. Thus the material on operationalization has a distinctly interpersonal bias.

Not one of these frameworks deals with a detailed treatment of 'society' or 'social change'. Given that each one asserts the need to draw on a range of theories and concepts from the behavioural sciences, it is indeed curious why more theoretical attention has not been afforded to sociological theories, particularly given that these 'new' conceptualizations claim to take into account the realities of practice.

It is trite to say that in order to understand the social context one must study the various theories that have been devised to help understand how society functions. Indeed, on the other side of the person–environment dialectic, numerous theories, concepts, and knowledge are invoked in order to help understand individuals.

The neglect of sociology of society and of social change raises a number of issues. First, the most obvious effect is to reinforce a clinical picture of practice. This is the case in the 'interpersonal process' model of Baker (1976). Here we see a wide range of psychological concepts invoked in order to explain a process of change in relationship over time. It has been argued by Van Krieken (1980) that this process model is no more than 'casework recycled'. While I believe this use of 'casework' to be too simplistic (casework does not fall into one homogeneous block fulfilling one purpose), nevertheless the claim that the Baker interpersonal process model relies heavily on individual psychologistic concepts and theory is valid. One can note the author's attempts to change some of the variables over time (e.g. in the bio-psychosocial model, the first version had at its centre 'the ego' (Baker 1975); in later versions this was replaced by 'person(s)'. In the earlier version of the purposes of social work the author stated: 'to identify, foster, maintain, and enhance the psychosocial autonomy and identity of the client unit'; in a later version this was changed to 'identify, foster, maintain, and enhance *people's* autonomy *as well as their civil, political, and human rights*' (Baker 1980c; author's emphasis).

A second problem occurs where 'society' is mentioned (whatever its specific meaning) and then treated in a monolithic and homogeneous way. This is evident in all writings. It is as if there is no conflict or competing interests in the environment. It is as if there are no competing interests between clients and client groups. There is no discussion of how social work is used by certain groups to assert their interests over other groups or to protect or change the status quo. Loewenberg, for example, recognizes the co-existence of particular values and their counter-values, as well as the fact that certain norms may only reflect the preferred behaviour of one dominant class in society. However, he does not develop this matter to the point of providing clear operational guidelines for the practitioner to deal with these conflicts.

Third, there is a failure to consider the sociology of social problems. Haines makes an attempt to link the welfare state, poverty, and social stress, but does not develop his analysis beyond assertion. No framework considers the aetiology of social problems in terms of the sociological context of modern urban industrial society. While some connections are made, for example by Haines and Middleman and Goldberg, between social problems and the social structures of modern urban industrial societies, such connections are ignored in the operational tasks of assessment and planning interventions.

The failure to consider the sociology of social problems has the effect of individualizing problems and thus reinforcing the use of psychological theory in preference to sociological theory. Thus the rhetoric advocating the importance of 'social location' remains empty because operational tools are not provided for the practitioner.

Fourth, none of the authors give due recognition to conflict in values and hence interests in 'society', especially conflict between the interests of various so-called client groups.

Baker advocates a multi-ideological, multi-disciplinary base to 'maximize flexibility'; but this is both naïve and unworkable. It has been pointed out (e.g. Bywaters 1978, 1982) that in operationalizing a 'unitary' approach, there needs to be basic agreement between team members on a philosophy of practice if there is to be any hope of effective operation. However, all authors write *as if* there were agreement about a philosophy of practice. In neglecting to place these frameworks in an historical as well as contemporary context, the question of incompatibilities arising from different ideological assumptions affecting practice is avoided. This has the effect of creating a conceptual framework in an ideological vacuum: a situation which is unrelated to the realities of practice. It is this artificial relationship to reality which is criticized by Armstrong and Gill (1978a : 22).

FAILURE TO RECOGNIZE PROFESSIONAL CONCERNS

In addition to the assumptions about the nature of the social sciences and the nature of 'society', it has been argued that assumptions about the social work profession affect theory construction (Lecomte 1975). The failure to acknowledge social work as a profession, or even an occupation sanctioned by society, rather than as an applied social science or discipline, has led to the neglect of several important aspects and their effects on social work theory.

Of fundamental importance to social work is the sanction it is given by various authorities. It has been noted that 'sanction' was excluded from Bartlett's (1970) framework, but this exclusion was not *adequately* justified. None of the other frameworks deal with the effects 'sanction' has upon social work, and thus the effects this variable will have upon social work theory. The failure to take this variable into consideration reinforces the view that practice, as portrayed in these frameworks, is contextless and universal. Recognition of different types of sanction (government, agency, professional, client) would at least alert the practitioner to the ways these authorities might affect practice in different contexts.

In addition to the non-recognition of 'sanction', none of the frameworks makes explicit the differential effects which power, authority, access to resources, and available skills and techniques, have upon social work practice. Even where these matters are dealt with, their treatment is undertaken separately so that their effects upon the framework itself are not made explicit. This gives the impression that social work is not affected by the differential operation of these factors.

The issue of 'sanction' is particularly important, because it relates to the issue of the 'right to intervene' (Irvine 1964) in a range of situations. None of the frameworks takes this up in terms of governmental, agency, or professional authority. Some frameworks address the question of 'client', and hence relate the authority to intervene to the agreement reached between client and worker alone.

Client sanction is perhaps the least problematic, when someone makes a request voluntarily for social work service with clearly-defined goals and clearly-articulated methods to achieve these goals. However, taking a wide spectrum of social work, it can be observed that social work intervention is carried on with those who do not necessarily request assistance and who do not necessarily form a co-operative contract with the social worker. Court orders, for example, often require social work intervention with people before the courts, or where the lives of third parties are at risk.

Furthermore, to restrict social work intervention solely to those situations where the social worker responds to a request, neglects a consideration of social work intervention in 'public issues' where social work intervention might be justified on the grounds of prevention.

What most of the frameworks fail to take into account is that social work activities are rarely restricted to work with 'clients'. If social work's concern is with the *interface* of person and environment, then social work activities will always include significant other non-clients. To achieve social work goals it is usually the case that significant others, who are not clients and who do not suffer from the problem themselves, will form an important part of the 'action system'.

Baker does not provide a definition of 'client', but he does acknowledge this significant other group in his definition of 'direct' and 'indirect' service. 'Direct' service is work with clients, and 'indirect' service is work with others on behalf of clients. Middleman and Goldberg do not define 'client' but they separate two major

148

groups of people: those who are 'sufferers' and those who are 'non-sufferers'. While this terminology may seem pejorative, nevertheless this dimension is important in giving recognition to the variety of people with whom the social worker has to deal in order to achieve social work goals.

It is this recognition which has led Pincus and Minahan to define a variety of relationships: consensual, bargaining, and conflict. Most authors neglect non-consensual relationships. While Middleman and Goldberg direct the practitioner to various 'public issues' arising out of 'personal troubles', there is no explicit treatment of how the social worker establishes the right to intervene at this 'public' level. The movement into public issues requires a public form of sanction.

Pincus and Minahan enunciate a position where the change agent system itself can be seen as a target for change. However, they do not consider the legitimacy of this in view of the social worker's authority.While an agency could terminate the social worker's services if a conflict of interest arose, there is also the need to consider the principle of self-determination as applied to an agency. While all frameworks uphold the right of self-determination for clients, it is unclear whether the same principle applies when the practitioner is intervening to change an organizational structure such as an agency, especially when there are strong forces to uphold the status quo. This has implications particularly where a social worker is employed by a company (e.g. an industrial organization), because the employer is not concerned only with the welfare of individual employees, but also with the welfare of the company as a viable, profit-making concern.

The failure to give adequate treatment to criteria for defining a client has led to many problems. Without some clear criteria there is often the implicit assumption that *everyone* is or can be a social work client.

There is often confusion over the exact person (or 'cause') the social worker is representing, or just who the social worker is trying to change and for what reason. Not everyone can be a 'client', if there is a voluntary connotation in this word. If everyone is given the title 'client', then this word loses its power of differentiation. It is suggested that a possible reason for the propensity of social workers to see everyone as a 'client' is the profession's roots in 'helping', and further its failure to recognize conflict of interests.

This has resulted in an attempt to use the 'helping relationship' with all people.

It is further suggested that social work's historical influence from psychology is partly the reason for emphasizing 'helping relationships' to the exclusion of other types of relationships. These, however, were designed with only individual clients in mind usually to achieve some intra-personal goals. The development of a range of other relationships to be utilized with non-clients or for use in situations which contain a high degree of dissensus or conflict has been neglected.

This in turn has led to a dearth of appropriate strategies and skills being developed for use with significant non-clients, particularly those who are uncooperative. Textbooks have a propensity to assume these skills are similar to the ones needed in work with clients.

In order for social work practice to have a legitimate place within an institutional view of social welfare it must be engaged in future planning to prevent or minimize social problems through changes to the social structures which cause and contribute to current and anticipated future problems. Thus its activation cannot rely solely upon an individual's request for assistance with a current problem. Yet the definitions of 'client' formulated by Pincus and Minahan, Compton and Galaway, Loewenberg, and Haines, all rely on a request coming from a person. Clearly this restricts social work to remedial assistance.

The failure to properly recognize issues relating to the profession, such as sanctions for practice, the right to intervene, and properly defining clients, brings into question the validity of theory which has been formulated *as if* social work were a social science. Such a view, whether intentional or not, neglects to take into account social work's historic function of active intervention into problems, rather than seeing these as interesting phenomena to be viewed from the sidelines.

UNCRITICAL DELINEATION OF 'SOCIAL WORK VALUES'

All the frameworks, with the exception of Germain and Gitterman, delineate major values which they assert are part of social work. The most common theme is the recognition of a set of values which it is assumed is accepted by the profession as a whole. Within this homogeneity of values there is a definite bias towards values of the individual, rather than values related to collectivities of one kind or another. This is particularly the case in Bartlett, Goldstein, Haines, Siporin, Baker, Compton and Galaway, and to a lesser extent in Germain and Gitterman.

The 'maximum realization of an individual's potential' is seen as an important value by Bartlett, Haines, and Baker. Linked to this is the recognition of the 'worth and dignity of the individual' (Bartlett, Haines, Siporin, Loewenberg). From these primary values emanate such principles as 'acceptance' and 'client self-determination'. The difficulties of operationalizing these values in practice (McDermott 1975) have been recognized for some time. Because these values are expressed at such a high level of generality they can be seen to support widely different behaviours. Only three frameworks (Middleman and Goldberg, Whittaker, and Loewenberg) give some recognition to the fact that there may be conflicts of interests and therefore conflicting values.

Both Pincus and Minahan and Loewenberg recognize society's responsibility to ensure certain things for an individual's welfare. Again, the responsibility of the society is seen in terms of meeting an individual's needs rather than being responsible for collective needs and goals. In neither Pincus and Minahan nor Loewenberg is 'society' treated in a sufficient way for the practitioner to know just which part or parts of society have this responsibility. As already noted, 'society' is represented as a monolithic structure, rather than being seen as heterogeneous with many differing and conflicting interests. If this latter position was recognized then the inadequacy of referring to 'society' as an entity would be realized.

Three frameworks recognize some conflict of interests and values in society. Middleman and Goldberg, Whittaker, and Loewenberg recognize this in one way or another, although Loewenberg asserts that there is very little disagreement about 'basic' social work values (i.e. worth of the individual, inherent dignity, society's responsibility for the individual's welfare, and the individual's responsibility to contribute to the common good). However, as already noted, what these values connote in behavioural terms is open to fairly wide interpretation.

Whittaker raises pertinent questions regarding conflict: when should the rights of society supersede the rights of individuals?; when do individual rights clash with sound ecological principles?; in recognizing a value base, do we assume limitless resources?; how do we bring goals for both large-scale and individual change into harmony? However, he makes no attempt to address these matters.

Outlining the 'major values' raises two crucial issues.

First, the assumption that there is agreement on basic social work values is treated as if it was a fact, yet no empirical evidence is advanced to support it. A distinction is often made between 'fundamental' and 'instrumental' values. It is claimed there is agreement on 'fundamental' or 'core' values, but the ways these are operationalized in practice varies. This seems to point to some conflict because it is generally agreed that values can only be inferred from observable behaviours. Thus if different behaviours are observed it is open to question whether these are reflecting different values. If the core values are expressed in such a global and undifferentiating way that they can be used to support fundamentally different instrumental values then the former are meaningless.

Second, the predominance of 'individualistic' values over 'societal' values can be challenged. Of all the authors, only Haines treats this as a substantial problem. He links this with a consideration that resources for social work are limited. By taking a solely individualistic approach, this leaves little room to consider needs in terms of available resources for collectivities and whole societies.

What happens when the provision of particular services to an individual jeopardizes the chances of a group of clients in similar need receiving them or a share of them? All other frameworks proceed as if resources were limitless and no conflict of interest between competing clients or groups of clients existed.

Furthermore, none of the frameworks give due recognition to conflicting and competing values and interest between social work clients and others. For example, the competing interests of the different parties in Pincus and Minahan's House on Sixth Street are not dealt with, nor is how the practitioner is going to direct his or her time, skills, and resources to each of these competing groups. The presentation of technical processes rather than a discussion of the value dilemmas and conflicts will not bring the practitioner any closer to resolution. In the absence of an explicit ideology of practice, such decision making is made extremely difficult.

RELATIONSHIP TO 'SOCIOLOGICAL POSITIVISM'

While it is difficult to locate these frameworks within a particular paradigm because of their failure to make explicit many of the assumptions upon which they depend, it can be argued that ten of the frameworks can be linked to 'sociological positivism'. The possible exception is the Middleman and Goldberg framework.

For the purposes of this analysis, Burrell and Morgan's characterization of 'sociological positivism' will be accepted. They state:

> in essence ['sociological positivism'] . . . reflects the attempt
> to apply models and methods derived from the natural sciences
> to the study of human affairs. It treats the social world as if it
> were the natural world, adopting a 'realist' approach to ontology.
> This is backed by a 'positivist' epistemology, relatively
> 'deterministic' views of human nature and the use of 'nomothetic'
> methodologies.

(Burrell and Morgan 1979 : 7)

While the relationship of the frameworks to reality (or their ontological commitment) is ambiguous, the writers *attempt* to present an ontology of 'realism' rather than one of 'nominalism' (see Burrell and Morgan 1979 : 4). This ambiguity results partly because of confusion as to whether the frameworks are *describing* an empirical reality or *prescribing* normative guidelines which social work ought to be following. It also occurs because of the way this social work 'grand theory' is constructed, that is, by means of logical deduction with little regard to the influence of practice contexts.

By far the most convincing evidence of its 'positivism' resides in its positivist epistemology. While all the frameworks at an explicit level take a simplistic view of the debates concerning the philosophy of the social sciences, the frameworks take an explicit stand in the sharp differentiation of 'knowledge' and 'values', thus affirming both a 'positivist' epistemology and a 'realist' ontology.

All of the authors, with the exception of Middleman and Goldberg, sharply differentiate 'knowledge' and 'values'. This position asserts that 'knowledge' can be discovered by the application of 'scientific' procedures like the hypothetico-deductive methods. It is restricted to observable behaviours, it is concrete, and it exists apart from its context. Values on the other hand are preferences, they are choices made by individuals, they are neither true nor false, right nor wrong, and they are not empirically demonstrable.

153

Bartlett (1970 : 69, 111–12, 153, 190) implies a clear preference for 'knowledge' over 'values'. However, she does not justify this position, thus providing further evidence of her positivist epistemology and her failure to recognize that her position is based merely upon another set of assumptions. The way Bartlett treats 'knowledge' as superior to 'values' seems to assert that there is something more profound, more important and fundamental which has been arrived at by the application of certain methodologies, without recognizing that the acceptance and use of these methodologies is itself based in certain values concerning the nature of knowledge and what should be accepted as evidence. Thus, whether knowingly or not, Bartlett is subscribing to a set of assumptions consistent with a 'functionalist' paradigm (see Burrell and Morgan 1979 : 22).

Most frameworks differentiate between the 'science' and 'art' components of social work. The science part includes knowledge derived from the application of scientific methodologies and the 'art' part includes values and 'practice wisdom'. This differentiation again highlights the influence of positivist thinking on social work, where 'knowledge' is apparently only discovered by application of methodologies like the hypothetico-deductive methods. But if an alternative paradigm was to be recognized then the subjectivist/phenomenological experiences of the researcher and practitioner, which include 'values' and 'art', could be seen as a legitimate part of knowledge creation.

An implication of the sharp division between 'knowledge' and 'values' is the need to study the criteria which have been used in determining what constitutes 'knowledge' or 'values'. If positivist criteria alone are used, this will have limited use in developing a social work theory because many of the actions of practitioners cannot be reduced to a form to meet such criteria. An important part of practice appears to be concerned with the quality of relationships, feelings, innovation, as well as ideologies of practice related to particular societal contexts. To arbitrarily put such matters in an inferior position to 'knowledge' developed by the employment of positivist criteria, is altering observations of practice to make them fit a particular methodology. Thus 'reality' is distorted (only certain things will be taken into account) to fit the method of investigation, rather than developing a methodology to accommodate the many and varied aspects of social work practice.

What is not recognized in most of this writing is that 'sociological

154

positivism' belongs to *one* paradigm of assumptions relating to the nature of social science. If this in itself was recognized and made explicit it would mean that at least the possibility of constructing theory within other paradigms, with different sets of assumptions, could be envisaged.

It is worth noting that, while maintaining a distinction between 'knowledge' and 'values', Haines and to a lesser extent Goldstein recognize the influence of values on the formation of knowledge. Haines asserts that the 'route to respectability' does not lie only in 'science'. He emphasizes the interactional nature of social work and its phenomenological components. Facts are dynamic elements but constantly subject to change and development. This is a far 'softer' approach to the recognition of 'knowledge' than the clear separation between 'knowledge' and 'values' asserted by Bartlett, Pincus and Minahan, Siporin, Compton and Galaway, and Loewenberg.

Middleman and Goldberg are the only authors who give recognition to the influence of values and ideology on the creation of knowledge, concepts, and theory. They recognize the influence of different social science paradigms and how they influence methodologies by which knowledge is recognized.

Finally a position of 'sociological positivism' is reinforced by an essentially nomothetic methodology. It is not being argued that the frameworks specifically place emphasis on the importance of basing research upon systematic scientific methodologies. Rather they *aspire* to have a scientific methodology which could result in the creation of generalized and *generalizable* propositions about social work reality.

The frameworks have not been constructed from an ideographic methodology as there is no evidence of a detailed study of individual cases, applications, and developments within an historical or social welfare context. There is little importance given to subjectivism and as already demonstrated, the peculiar aspects of social work represented by its 'art' and 'practice wisdom' are given a definite second place to 'science' and the search for *principles* of practice.

TYPE OF 'THEORY' AND ITS CONSTRUCTION

In Chapter 3 it was argued that theory can be developed as a means of rationalizing past actions as well as to give an explanation of current realities in order to guide practice in the future. Once theory has been developed it can act as a powerful filter through which current realities are observed and can serve merely to reinforce what one believes already. Given that each of us uses theory, both implicit and explicit, to make sense of the world, makes 'objective' observation of current reality difficult as a basis for constructing new and hopefully more accurate theory. The extent to which observations are influenced by current beliefs and theories, and the extent to which they influence the construction of new theory, is difficult to measure. This is so because observations are selective and the very nature of 'theory' requires interpretation.

Like many other theorists, the writers of the genre under consideration here do not shed much light on this issue, and furthermore, the confusion they make between description and prescription (already noted), does not help to elucidate this problem. The development of over-arching frameworks to take account of the whole of social work's practice including a broadly-defined mission, is an attempt to bring some order and coherence to a multitude of variables. Furthermore, it has been argued that for a profession the linkage between 'thought' and 'action' is crucial, thus one could expect from this theory not only a set of logically-related concepts, but some indication of what difference such a theory will make for practice. However, as already noted, there are few accounts of the operationalization of 'integrated' theory and hence no critical evaluation of the benefits of this theory to practice.

This may be the result of the way 'integrated' theory has been constructed. It seems that its construction proceeded by way of logical deduction, rather than by retroduction or with clearly devised links to practice. These frameworks attempt to devise general principles and propositions, but there is no evidence in any of the frameworks that individual accounts of descriptive aspects of practice have been used to reshape the general principles of practice. In this way the general principles can be seen to be remote from observable practice behaviours, and uninfluenced by them. The general principles are not linked to grounded empirical realities such as developed by Glasser and Strauss (1967), nor to case studies such as exemplified through studies of 'low key practice' (Mispelblom 1985). Given this level of removal from the day-to-day actions of the social worker, it is little wonder they are unable to prescribe practitioner behaviour beyond the broadest of generalities.

This may be related to the influence of the 'academic sub-culture' to which these theorists belong. Furthermore, because of the strong influence of positivism on their writing, there has been no attempt to consider the influence of the 'theorist in the theory'. Had this been recognized, then attempts might have been made to encourage greater practitioner input, more practice applications, and a greater attempt to amend this theory in the light of practice experience. Such a move, however, would have necessitated a different set of assumptions, that is the treatment of social work not as an 'applied social science' whose theory is developed by the 'research–theorist' but as a profession whose theory should be developed by the 'practitioner–research–theorist'.

The type of theory generated has certain similarities to 'grand theory'. No author acknowledges this but an examination of the frameworks shows that they are postulated as if they are relevant to social work practice *as a whole* without reference to different settings or contexts of practice. The component parts of each framework refer to timeless, contextless, universal truths about social work reality. In none of the eleven frameworks is acknowledgement made that they might only be theorizing about one particular aspect of social work reality, that is, the peculiar socio-economic/social welfare context of the country in which it was formulated, and its influence on theory development.

In this regard, a comment by Mills on the grand theories of sociologists is apt. These attempts

> represent a partially organized attempt to withdraw from the effort
> plainly to describe, explain, and understand human conduct and
> society . . . [the difficulties are] in their initial choice of so general
> a level of thinking that one cannot logically get down to
> observation; and secondly, in the seemingly arbitrary elaboration
> of distinctions which do not enlarge one's understanding of
> recognizably human problems or experience.
>
> (Mills 1967 : 62)

All of the frameworks *attempt* to construct 'formal' theory; however, it is suggested that because of the naïve view of formal theory construction, this appears as an attempt at informal theory construction because assumptions are not made explicit and concepts ill-formed and linked to one another. In terms of formal theory construction, these frameworks can be viewed as embryonic because they contain very little explanation of the concepts (or elements) which help to link the different parts of the social work reality. Most of the frameworks are unable to explain either the nature of the component parts or the relationships of these component parts. An example of this, already discussed, is the 'common base' of practice where there is agreement neither about which elements constitute this nor the substantive content of these elements.

The lack of explanatory power can also be related to the frameworks' inability to invoke and to apply substantive theories from other disciplines. Where this is attempted it is restricted almost totally to theories related to the psychology of the individual. In none of the frameworks is sociological theory invoked to help explain the nature of society and social problems. Neither is organizational theory nor theory on the sociology of professions invoked in order to attempt to explain professional concerns of social work practice.

The failure of the frameworks to *explain* adequately the nature of their elements or concepts, and the relationships between them, results in theory being 'contentless' and 'empty'. Similar terms have been used in relation to a critique of social systems analysis. A certain similarity between these two theories exists: they both outline 'process' guidelines rather than formulating 'substantive theory'. Even these process guidelines have poor prescriptive qualities, because of the lack of explanation and their dislocation from reality.

Chapter Eight

NOMENCLATURE

INTRODUCTION

Any undertaking which depends upon the effective communication of ideas and concepts relies upon a set of nomenclature the meaning of which is clear and which is used consistently. It is one of the profound difficulties of the present study that terminology which is fundamental to effective communication of ideas and concepts is used differentially and inconsistently. This is the major reason why it is impossible to use one term to accurately describe this genre of writing and the related literature.

The differential use of terminology and the variable attribution of meaning to terms has resulted in a number of important difficulties in relation to the present study.

- Difficulties in determining whether particular frameworks or writings could be included in the study. A reliance on key terms alone is insufficient.
- Difficulties in knowing exactly what different authors mean by the use of particular terminology particularly when the terms are used as if their meaning was self-evident.
- Difficulties in trying to group writings for the purposes of critique.
- Difficulties in deciding meaning where similar terms have been used to describe different purposes or intentions, e.g. the use of terms related to educational issues in contrast to terms related to practice.
- Difficulties related to the meaning of terms when used in writings about theoretical constructs of practice on the one hand,

and the operationalization of those constructs within specific settings and organizational arrangements on the other.

● Difficulties in determining meaning when the same terms are used by authors from different contexts with apparent disregard for historical influences on their work.

● Difficulties arising from the use of terms to refer to frameworks whose authors themselves do not use those particular terms. This problem is exacerbated by the lack of cross-reference to frameworks developed earlier.

The purpose of this chapter, then, is to demonstrate the confusion which results from a differential and inconsistent usage of terms.

Nine years prior to her *Common Base of Social Work Practice*, in 1970, Bartlett recognized the different usages of the terms 'generic' and 'specific'.

> At various times 'generic' has been taken to mean elementary, nonspecialized, common, basic, core, fundamental, essential, comprehensive, and whole. Some of the meanings attached to 'specific' have been specialized, different, particular, and unique. Thinking and doing, education and practice, have not been kept distinct.
>
> (Bartlett 1961 : 175)

The inconsistent usage and different attribution of meanings has resulted in confusion over the reality the terms are supposed to describe. In this state of affairs, she claims the term itself has become the reality.

> Terms are thus bandied around until the term itself becomes the reality in the social worker's mind. Effort is expended in defining the term rather than in examining its relation to actual phenomena of social work and its usefulness in explaining them.
>
> (Bartlett 1961 : 176)

In reviewing the work at the Milford Conference (1929) and also the work of Grace Marcus (1938), Bartlett notes that the generic-specific concept

> referred to: (1) a body of common concepts and methods – the *generic* aspects of social casework; and (2) their application in practice, in a wide range of different settings – the *specific* aspects of social casework.
>
> (Bartlett 1961 : 162)

It should be noted that Bartlett (1961 : 159) herself believes it is helpful, for the purposes of analysis, to think of 'generic-specific' as an 'inclusive concept, composed of two subconcepts which are interdependent and complementary in meaning.'

A further important observation Bartlett makes (1961 : 162-3) is the confusion which results when the intention behind the use of a term is not made clear. This is particularly the case when the terms 'generic' and 'specific' are used for both practice and educational purposes. In its early development schools emphasized the 'generic' in formulating curricula, while practitioners in different fields emphasized the specific. Bartlett (1961 : 168-9) traces the strong influence which 'generic' thinking had upon the development of curricula but notes the 'fallacy of translating to practice, concepts originally intended for education'.

> Education and practice are both concerned with the same subject matter – knowledge, skills, and values – but from different orientations. Education is concerned with formulating suitable teaching objectives in terms of the changes to be brought about in the students. Learning experiences appropriate for attainment of these objectives must be planned and organized into a curriculum. . . .A general curriculum has been established and appropriately placed within the total framework of social work education. . . .
>
> (Bartlett 1961 : 185)

Had this distinction between education and practice objectives been heeded and made explicit, then a similar confusion may have been avoided in the frameworks being studied here.

Bartlett further draws attention to the Milford Conference recommendation that a research programme be established to test the manner in which generic principles are applied in practice in various settings. Such research could have clarified the relationship between the generic and the specific. However, the pressures in the post-war period for the establishment of a unified profession tended to reinforce the generic concept and gave the false impression that a common practice really existed and was understood (Bartlett 1961 : 166).

This reflects Bartlett's recognition of the influence of historical factors upon the formulation of practice as well as asserting the need to ensure that terms reflected reality. A call to have a closer scrutiny of practice is still relevant. Indeed terms can only be used consistently, if they are used to refer to consistent sets of behaviour and practice.

It should be noted, however, that Bartlett herself is inconsistent regarding this point and one could postulate that it is this ambivalence towards asserting the existence of something but then not testing it out which has caused the confusion to remain. Her commendation to research is demonstrated thus:

> The concepts and the criteria are to be derived from examination of what one social worker after another is doing in his work, using all forms of analysis from informal examination to disciplined research.
>
> (Bartlett 1961 : 181, see also 1961 : 173)

Yet on the other hand, Bartlett makes certain claims as if they had been established by the processes just mentioned, e.g. 'Social work has now arrived at a point as a unified profession where the relation between the whole and its parts can be understood clearly' (Bartlett 1961 : 159).

Connaway's (1975) observations indicate that little improvement has taken place since Bartlett's outlining of the problems associated with differential and inconsistent usage of terms. Connaway concludes, *inter alia*:

(1) The profession has a history which suggests that our use of terms and concepts to describe and explain what we are all about has been somewhat imprecise.

(a) We have not always been able to clearly and precisely say all that we know.
(b) We have used nonsimilar terms interchangeably which suggests the basic idea may not be clear to us.
(c) We have been concerned from the beginning with something like a 'core' and something like 'particulars'.

(2) Our emphasis on either the generic or core and on the specific or the particular has served various functions related to our historical development. . . .

(Connaway 1975 : 8–9)

A review of key terms will demonstrate the differences in meaning attributed to them. This will serve to highlight the difficulty in using any one of these terms to refer to this group of practice frameworks.

It also alerts future writers to the need to clearly define key terms, to explicitly relate new work to previous similar work, and to clarify in what ways key terms are used in a similar or different way to terms used previously.

'GENERIC'

The Milford Conference used this word in relation to social casework. It did not define substantively what was common but said that there are 'sufficient commonalities among the various specialities to preserve the idea that all social workers are part of one profession', and affirmed that a 'fundamental conception . . . of "generic social case work" was much more substantial in content and much more significant in its implications for all forms of social case work than were any of the specific emphases of the different case work fields' (Brieland 1977 : 31). The Conference claimed that aspects of generic casework included (i) knowledge; (ii) method; (iii) philosophy. Specific casework was described as the application of this generic content to the requirements of a particular setting or field (see Connaway 1975 : 3).

Bartlett (1970 : 129) uses the term 'generic' to describe the underlying principles of practice, but not practice itself. Her term 'generic' refers to the body of common concepts, values, and principles of practice, and 'specific' is the application of this in specific settings. 'The common base of social work practice consists of . . . abstract ideas. Practitioners learn these "common elements" in school and apply them in their professional practice. The base is not the doing but what *underlies* the doing' (Bartlett 1970 : 123).

However, the term 'generic' is not used synonymously with the 'common base', either. 'The idea of the common base, the elements of which are applied together in practice but with variations according to the particular characteristics of the practice, brings together the concepts of generic and specific, of basic and specialized' (Bartlett 1970 : 195).

This highlights the inconsistency of use of 'generic', 'common base', 'basic', and 'specialized' by one author within the one book.

Middleman (1977) uses the analogy of 'distilling' in an attempt to convey what the 'generic' means. She says generic refers to 'what is left over after adding together diverse processes, skills, and the like, when you take *away* all the differences. It is a subtractive process. Perhaps it should be termed distilling' (Middleman 1977 : 143). She

163

says that it is through this process we hope to get to what is basic or core, but in the process we will have lost some of the 'special flavour' of the components.

This is certainly a different usage from Bartlett, given that the latter restricts 'generic' to the *contemplation* of the common body of concepts, values, and principles and does not include the actual application in specific settings. Middleman's definition would appear to include both thinking *and* action.

A further variation in usage is noted in Haines's (1975) framework. He refers to 'generic elements', that is, those which are common to the practice of all social workers. He distinguishes between 'generic' methods and skills, and 'specialized' knowledge. This usage appears to be different from both Bartlett's and Middleman's.

Timms (1968), in noting the problems of defining the 'generic' and the 'specific', argues that these terms have been used to promote particular causes, namely 'generic' courses of training and a 'common' profession. He says that while these may or may not be 'worthy causes', 'the terms employed in their promotion have not been used to deepen any sense of curiosity about the nature of social work' (Timms 1968 : 26).

Referring to the experience in the USA he observes:

It was some time before it was appreciated that arguments in favour of generic social work education did not support any idea of generic social work practice, and that to consider methods divorced from specific application was like looking for the family but ignoring all the members.

(Timms 1968 : 31)

Likewise Connaway notes the confusion with educational goals at an earlier point in history. She notes the use of 'generic' to describe both general knowledge and skills, but then notes:

Shortly, however, the concept was picked up by education and used to denote both curriculum policy or goals and curriculum content. In fact, educators used the generic half of the concept nearly to the exclusion of the specific half while the concept had originated with two interdependent parts. As a result of the use of the concept by educators, 'specific' became confused with specialization.

(Connaway 1975 : 3)

Thus the problem relates not only to meaning *per se*, but also to the association with *causes* and with particular goals related to both practice and educational contexts.

One of the ways out of such confusion would be to follow Vickery's advice. She prefers not to use 'generic' at all because of its original use within social casework to refer to the common base of knowledge used in the various functional areas in which casework was practised (Vickery 1977 : 15–16).

However, the term is still being used and indeed its meaning further embroidered, e.g. Anderson (1983) uses 'generic' to refer to the universal elements of social work practice and maintains it is the core, base, common, or unitary aspects and is synonymous with those terms.

'SPECIFIC'; 'SPECIALIZATION'

The terms 'specific' and 'specialization' have likewise been confused. Bartlett (1961 : 162) notes that 'specific' and 'specialization' have been used interchangeably without recognizing different connotations. 'Specific' is the application of generic principles in practice (Bartlett 1961 : 186). It is the 'doing' component within a particular context, but she also recognizes there is concept thinking involved at the specific level.

'As applied originally in casework, the word "specific" meant the application of generic knowledge and principles in specific settings. Gradually, however, it came to mean specific practice itself' (Bartlett 1961 : 172–3). 'Specialization', on the other hand, 'means continuous and disciplined effort in relation to some particular problem over many years. The specialist is the expert, who must often pass severe technical tests' (Bartlett 1961 : 184). She also notes the meaning as applied in education, where 'specialization' means a concentration of courses. 'Specialization' of practice means expertise in performance (1961 : 163).

A similar meaning is attributed to 'specialist' by Anderson (1983). Specialization is continuous and disciplined effort in relation to some particular problem over many years. It refers to technical expertise of intervention.

'GENERALIST'

This term can mean one who moves from direct service to community organization and back. It can mean one who can provide a direct service utilizing a systems-oriented perspective and emphasizing environmental manipulation, or it can mean a practitioner with a baccalaureate degree.

> One becomes a generalist by learning and doing practice one plus practice two plus practice three, and so forth. Through such an additive learning process it seems possible, at least theoretically, to perform various types of practice to the extent one knows and can faithfully enact their differential requirements *if* one can also accept and live out the unique ideological, value differences (and be allowed to do so by the service providers). In the additive process of learning to be a generalist the *differences* as well as the likenesses are blanketed in.
>
> (Middleman 1977 : 143)

A similar meaning is given by Anderson (1983). The generalist, he claims, in contrast to the specialist, has a wide range of knowledge, skills, and methods to bring to bear on a social work situation. This can be compared to the general practitioner in medicine.

Minahan and Pincus (1977 : 352), however, do not equate 'generalist' and 'specialist' with beginning and advanced practice. They note that some social workers equate the generalist with the expert who has a bachelor's degree, and the specialist with the expert who has a master's degree. They do not agree with these definitions. They cite the Council on Social Work Education (CSWE) of March, 1976 which stated that base-level education could be achieved either at undergraduate or graduate level.

Their position is explicated by an example of a social worker in an institution for mentally retarded adults. They say that this person is viewed by a lay person as a 'specialist' – that is, a specialist in social work. From within the profession,

> if a generalist is defined as a person with a broad view who can look at an entire social situation, analyse the interactions between people in all the resource systems connected to that situation, intervene in those interactions, determine which specialists are needed from a variety of disciplines, and co-ordinate and mobilize the knowledge and skill of many disciplines – this worker is a generalist.
>
> (Minahan and Pincus 1977 : 352)

Is this person also a specialist? 'If she continued working there she would become more of a specialist in mental retardation than people who were not in that field.' She could acquire education in different treatment modalities and in supervision, consultation, or administration, and become a specialist in one or more of these functions. These authors also recognize that further advanced education could also lead to 'a more expert generalist': 'that is, acquire increased competence in assessment, knowledge, and skills related to interactions between resource systems' (Minahan and Pincus 1977 : 352).

In contrast to this position, Compton and Galaway (1979) use the term 'generalist' in a way which seems similar to Bartlett's use of the term 'generic'. They use the term 'generalist' for someone who is skilful in 'deciding what to do'. The 'doing the decided' can be by either a general social worker or a specialist.

The effects of content on the use of terms is a further factor which some writers take into account. Vickery notes that 'generalist' refers to a particular type of social worker rather than to social work practice. She cites the Younghusband Report which makes reference to the 'general purpose social worker' who carries out a wide range of functions (Vickery 1977 : 38 and 15–16).

However, Vickery states that she

has come to prefer 'generalist social work practice', on the understanding that most problem situations should be examined first from a 'generalist' perspective. Any decision to apply 'specialist' knowledge and skills should be in consequence of, and subsequent to, a 'general' assessment. [However,] . . . Unfortunately, in the UK the term 'generalist' is often confused with 'generic', and wrongly attached to a worker in a local authority social services or social work department dealing with the full range of people whose difficulties make them legally eligible to receive specific social service and/or the attention of a social worker. While local authority social workers *may* practise as 'generalists' in the sense outlined in this chapter, the social philosophy underlying their statutory obligations and the organization of their departments do not make it easy for them to avoid what is in effect a quite 'specialist', almost pre-determined, approach to each of their clients. Nevertheless, they deal with a very wide range of problems, and cannot be an expert in all of them. So in that sense they are general practitioners or general purpose social workers rather than specialists. Already, we can see the difficulty in knowing what is meant by the word 'generalist'.

(Vickery 1979 : 1)

Indeed!

A further example of this kind of confusion is provided by Teigiser (1983) who claims that the notion of 'generalist' social work has been widely adopted by Bartlett, among other writers. However, as we have seen, Bartlett wrote about the 'generic'. This was operationalized in specific settings by invoking methods and skills.

Anderson (1983) likewise compounds this confusion by taking the terms 'generic' and 'generalist' out of any historical context and developing their meanings further. He defines a 'generic framework' (for the direct practice generalist) as one which specifies the common elements of social work practice and depicts their relationship to each other, e.g. in the work of Bartlett. These common elements flow from social work's unique and central purpose – that is, matching the needs and resources of individuals with the needs and resources of their environmental systems for the self-actualizing growth of both (Anderson 1983 : 5).

The 'generalist framework', Anderson asserts, is for the use of the Bachelor of Social Work (BSW) 'direct service general practitioner'. As he uses this term it refers to delivering direct services to individuals, families, and groups.

> . . . it connotes a worker who selects and uses methods for practice
> based upon the assessed needs of individual service consumers in
> their particularized situations. These methods include an
> interventive repertoire for working with individuals, families,
> groups, organizations, and communities in behalf of individual
> service consumers and other groups of consumers.

(Anderson 1983 : 7–8)

This framework is 'organized very generally' around the works of Pincus and Minahan (1973), and Middleman and Goldberg (1974).

'UNITARY'

This term has been used by Baker (1980), Goldstein (1973) and Olsen (1978) among others. However, this term has failed to make any clearer what the authors intend by it, and has brought further problems by its own connotations. Among other meanings, the *OED* says of 'unitary': 'marked by unity or uniformity'. The term implies oneness, unity, lack of diversity, all-embracing, and to some even hegemony.

Whether the consequences of the use of this term were recognized ahead of time will never be known. Whether this attribute of 'unity' was seen only in the utilization of a 'common base' or a 'common constellation of components' to underpin all social work activities, has never been clarified.

The recognition of the historical context of this term is important, because the term has been more widely used in relation to UK writings than those from the USA. Goldstein is the only American writer in this current study to use 'unitary', however he makes no attempt to explicate its meaning although it forms part of the title of his work. He does refer to a 'common base' so one might question whether he associates 'unitary' with 'common base'.

Apart from Goldstein's (1973) use of this term in the title of his book, the only other author to use the term (from the frameworks being studied) is Baker, and he uses it synonymously with 'generic' and 'integrated'.

In their introduction, Specht and Vickery say:

> A unitary method of social work practice . . . would provide a
> common set of principles and concepts which *all* social workers
> could use in dealing with social problems as they are manifest in
> a single individual, a group or a community.
>
> (Specht and Vickery 1977 : 15)

Yet their book is entitled *Integrating Social Work Methods*. Further, in response to the question of how the use of the 'unitary method' changes current practice, Specht notes:

> social workers will do the same things as they do now; they will
> counsel, guide, advocate for and treat their clients; they will work
> with groups and organizations. Thus the integration of social work
> methods will not change many of the features of current social
> work practice. Nor does it provide any methodology or technique
> which is not, at present, available.
>
> (Specht and Vickery 1977 : 28)

This appears to be in contradiction to the findings of Stevenson and Parsloe (1978) which claim that there is little evidence of this kind of practice in the UK at the present time. Such contradictions raise the question of just what conceptualizations of practice these authors had in mind.

Further differences emerge when Gilbert and Specht's position (1977 : Ch. 13) is presented. They acknowledge that the 'generic model' represents extreme unification through mixing (Gilbert and Specht, 1977 : 226) – mixing implies creating a new whole by fusing separate entities of constituent elements. This is in contrast to 'linking' which implies creating a new whole by connecting separate identities of constituent elements (Gilbert and Specht 1977 : 224). Such a model, they say, trains professionals to know a little about a lot, but then they 'are not well enough versed in the practice requirements of any specific area to offer a substantial contribution to either service or welfare' (Gilbert and Specht 1977 : 226).

Vickery differentiates 'integrating methods' and 'unitary method'. The former she says seems to describe what we are in the process of doing as we attempt to find the means by which to join the different bodies of knowledge and the different methods of practice. 'Unitary method' is the term to describe what it is hoped to produce from these efforts (Specht and Vickery 1977 : 16).

However, Bywaters equates 'unitary approach' with 'multi-methods approach'. He says, 'Our practice in no way implies a rejection of individual casework but only that, like other methods, it should be used as and when appropriate' (Bywaters 1978 : 19).

This equation of 'unitary' with 'multi-methods' is rejected by Baker (1980) who differentiates 'method', 'multi-method', and 'unitary':

> The unitary (generic) approach reinterprets social work practice
> into new holistic models which attempt to capture the core
> variables of the discipline and present them within an integrative
> comprehensive frame of reference applicable to all social work
> intervention, with any target group and in any setting.
>
> (Baker 1980 : 29)

This seems to be the meaning attributed to 'unitary' by Armstrong and Gill: 'the unitary approach is claimed to be a major reformulation of social work theory incorporating community work, groupwork, and casework within one theoretical framework' (Armstrong and Gill 1978 : 18).

Given that some authors claim the unitary approach is about re-conceptualization of social work practice one might have assumed that this could be linked to the 'generic', that is, the search for something common or core underlying the whole of social work practice. However, some authors still wish to invoke the orthodox methods and to 'integrate them', other authors wish to not only conceptualize the practice in a particular way but also operationalize it in a particular way (e.g. Pincus and Minahan 1973, Minahan and Pincus 1977, Baker 1976, 1976a, 1980b). This clearly contradicts at least Bartlett's view of the 'generic'.

Jones asserts that the unitary framework is not itself a method, and nor should it be identified with

> the futile search for the grand theory. . . . It is a conceptual organization of the activity of social work into an integrated meaningful whole. [Its aim is to delineate the nature of social work itself] . . . and from this to give the practitioner a sense of identity without the constraining influence of pre-determined client or problem.
>
> (Jones 1978 : 7)

However, in two major works, Specht and Vickery (1977) and Olsen (1978), the integration of disparate conceptions of practice into a 'new holistic model' is not convincingly demonstrated. Rather than demonstrating how 'integration' can occur, they present a collection of writings based on particular methods or practice settings, loosely linked to an overall, yet ill-defined, framework of social work.

Far from demonstrating how integration can occur, one of the Olsen authors, Wilkes (1978), actively warns against embarking on a unitary approach. 'The idea that "all is one" is dangerous because when some concept of unity "makes sense" of everything our minds are consoled and the danger of reductionism is great' (Wilkes 1978 : 3). In trying to solve the problem of 'facile eclecticism', 'it provides a justification for almost every approach and it might be said that a set of ideas that tells us so much finishes by telling us nothing'.

This picture is further confused by the use of the term 'unification' (Vickery 1977 : 37), because, again, it is not clear how this term is being used. She does note how the 'search for a unifying framework' has taken a different form in the USA in comparison with the UK.

> Whereas in the last two decades we have sought to unify specialized caseworkers in one professional body, to provide a common social work education and to unify administratively most

of our statutory social services, the Americans in varying degrees have been concerned with conceptualizing the whole of social work practice in a unitary method. The purpose of this [unification] is not only to bring [different methods] . . . under the one roof, but . . . more importantly, to avoid fragmentation and distortion in the reality of people's lives. . . .In the same way that the British social worker is concerned to avoid defining client problems solely in terms of his or her agency's function, the American social worker is concerned to avoid defining problems exclusively in terms of his or her particular method of practice.

(Vickery 1977a : 40–1)

Having acknowledged the effects of different historical influences on the development of this type of framework, it is surprising that Vickery (1976 : 113) can then invoke all American authors in the application of such a framework in the UK.

'INTERACTIONIST'

The term 'interactionist' recognizes the relationship between the person and environment and the relationship therefore between private trouble and public issues (Schwartz 1969). Thus there is the need to bridge the practice concerns of dealing with clinical and individual approaches with wider community, social, and political issues more generally. Thus Vickery sees the need:

to conceptualize practice in such a way as to encourage practitioners to devote as much, and sometimes more, attention and skill to intervention in the social and material environments of individual people and groups of people as to intervention with the people themselves.

(Vickery 1976 : 113)

This need to recognize the interdependence between person and environment and public and private is recognized by Evans (1976 : 192) but such an integrated model, he claims, requires an integrated theory to underpin it.

Similarly Bywaters (1982 : 303–17) sees one of the key benefits of an interactionist perspective as the ability to handle the relationship between public issues and private troubles. However, the difficulty with the term 'interaction' is one of defining *who* are the people who

172

interact, and more specifically when to stop the chain of interactions in order to place a boundary around the interacting components for the purpose of analysis, assessment, and intervention. A further difficulty is making a 'choice' between 'trouble' and 'issue' for the purposes of social work action. For while Schwartz (1969) declares 'there can be no choice . . .', in regard to a practitioner with competing claims on his/her time and resources, and with a defined range of expertise, it appears that from this point of view, a choice for action *has* to be made.

The interactionist approach claims to offer a conceptual framework which bridges the gap between the 'individual' and 'society'. It views the world 'as an interdependent network of individuals, groups, institutions and structures . . .' (Bywaters 1982 : 305). But Bywaters questions how this works in practice.

Bywaters (1982 : 305ff.) demonstrates that an approach which *always* builds from the particular to the general 'is inadequate and will founder on a series of obstacles':

1. As a matter of priority a social worker or team could never afford to take action on the structural level in order to help one family. Each case has to be seen not in isolation, but in relation to the total workload and aims of the team.
2. As a matter of priority, a social worker or team could never afford the time and other resources needed to analyse all the systems involved in every case every time.
3. Working at and from the general level of problems creates new perspectives which inform the individual case by removing agency and method-based blinkers.
4. The value of a general as well as an individual analysis is further indicated by the fact that some problem areas identified fall far outside the boundaries of 'normal' case discussion and action, that clients are unlikely to raise them, and the social worker unlikely to be conscious of them as problems, e.g. media reporting of crimes and its effects on people in such areas; study of fuel debt problems at a general level.
5. Office systems tend to reinforce problems as private troubles.
6. The interactionist approach requires a shift in team organization, workloads, tasks, etc.

Thus Bywaters (1982 : 308) concludes that it is necessary to work from private troubles to public issues, and vice versa.

'DIRECT' AND 'INDIRECT' PRACTICE

These terms are attributed a range of meaning. They are used as two important complementary aspects within some frameworks (e.g. Baker 1976a) but in others the framework is limited to 'direct service practice' (e.g. Middleman and Goldberg 1974).

Vickery (1977 : 43) points out some of the different meanings of 'direct' and 'indirect' practice. She refers to Richmond's use where 'direct' refers to the practitioner who relates to the client or client group, and 'indirect' to intervention in which the practitioner, on the client's behalf, relates to individuals, groups, and agencies in the client's environment. This latter intervention is designed to influence the client's behaviour and/or circumstances in an indirect way.

Vinter (1967a) uses the terms in relation to groups, where 'direct' refers to the influence upon an individual in the group by relating to him personally. 'Indirect' is used to refer to influence upon an individual through intervention in the structural relations of the rest of the group.

In other usages, 'direct' refers to where the worker is directly involved with the problem situation, and 'indirect' refers to discussions with individuals or groups about problematic situations. Sometimes 'direct' refers to encounters with clients and includes all work on their behalf with other agencies and professionals and other members of the community. 'Indirect' refers to activities concerned with the development and allocation of social service resources, inter-organizational work, policy formation and change, and social planning (Vickery 1977 : 44).

It seems to be in this latter sense that Gilbert and Specht (1977 : 219) develop their two-track system for social work education. For them, 'direct service' refers to therapy, counselling, education, advocacy, information gathering, and referral. These activities belong to casework, group work, and to that part of community work which provides services to community groups and organizations. 'Indirect service' refers to professional activities that focus on both change in and maintenance of the institution of social welfare. This does not deal directly with those in need, but focuses on the institution structures through which those in need are served (Gilbert and Specht 1977 : 220).

Frameworks such as Baker's utilize both 'direct' and 'indirect' as integral parts of the framework and emphasize this as a crucial feature of the 'unitary' approach. For Baker 'direct service' refers to the work done directly with the client (be that individual, group, family, community), and 'indirect service' refers to those activities done on behalf of the client such as advocacy. Baker stresses the importance for both these types of activity. This usage means that an adequate definition of 'client' has to be used. It also implies that a 'client' is present to activate social work intervention. This stresses the 'individual nature' of problem definition, that is, the presence of a designated 'client' to start the social work process. This further poses difficulties referred to by Bywaters (1982), who from his experience stresses the need for reciprocal movement between private troubles–public issues.

Although Middleman and Goldberg (1974) do not use the terms in any particular way, if one accepts the Baker definition, then 'direct' service could be used to designate those activities of the social worker in Quadrants A and B of their model (1974 : 19–23) and 'indirect service' used to refer to activities in Quadrants C and D. Middleman and Goldberg employ the terms 'sufferers' and 'non-sufferers' which, despite their emotive connotations, do serve to differentiate those *with* the problem and those *without*. Work with the latter is invariably necessary in order to find some resolution to the problem, particularly if one takes the view that problems and the means of their resolution do not reside solely within the individual with the problem.

Whittaker (1974 : 111) includes both 'direct' and 'indirect' helping in his framework. 'Direct helping' is 'what the worker does directly with the client in their face-to-face encounter'. 'Indirect helping' 'refers to all activities that the worker undertakes on behalf of the client to further the mutually agreed-upon goals of the helping relationship' (Whittaker 1974 : 166). But for pragmatic reasons, this author restricts the number of variables considered. He restricts his focus to 'interpersonal helping' rather than dealing with the 'big questions' of society. Hence in discussing 'indirect helping' roles, these are limited to 'advocate–ombudsman', 'broker of services and resources' (Whittaker 1974 : 166ff.).

The focus is further restricted when one considers this author's definition of 'client'. The 'client' is limited to those who freely engage in a helping relationship with the worker in order to reach contractual arrangements. The 'involuntary client' is incompatible with this author's view of 'social treatment'. This would seem an unnecessarily restricted view in the face of the wide range of persons social workers appear obliged to deal with.

CONCLUSIONS

This review of nomenclature demonstrates the confusion which results when different meanings are attributed to the same words, when terms are used interchangeably and inconsistently and when terms and their meanings are divorced from particular contexts. The problems result, first, when the terms inaccurately represent what a conceptual framework actually does, and second, the inconsistent use of terms means that some of the attributes (and problems) of one framework can be carried over to other frameworks by the use of ill-defined terminology.

In other words, the ontology of this nomenclature has not been established. For example, what is the concept of 'generic', 'common base', and so on, and does this concept have a demonstrable reality which can be observed? Or is it something which is desired or hoped for, but not yet present? As noted above, there are differences of opinion as to whether a particular type of practice exists, where it exists, and whether it is desirable in order to achieve a particular goal or purpose.

At least some of those questions could be addressed if the recommendations made initially after the Milford Conference (1929), advocating empirical studies related to the actualities of practice, had been executed. Such systematic studies describing the realities of practice of social workers are still required. However, it will not be helpful if old terminology is used without clarifying its meaning, and unless key terms accurately reflect the interventions of the author. To continue using conventional terminology on the assumption that its meaning is unproblematic (such as Anderson 1983; Teigiser 1983), and further, to go on changing usage is to confound the problem which exists.

Social work theory development will progress no further until and unless key terms are defined in a way that the reader is clear about the meanings and concepts these terms represent. Terms can never be divorced from their historical contexts. Thus it is imperative that when terms are used, the meaning intended by their user is made absolutely clear. One can never assume effective communication will result when words such as 'generic' and 'unitary' are used without qualification.

Chapter Nine

HISTORICAL INFLUENCES

INTRODUCTION

The eleven frameworks span the period 1970 to 1981. With the exception of the Baker framework, they originate either in the UK or the USA. However, even the Baker framework can be linked to a British context rather than an Australian one given the writer's education and practice experience in the UK and the references he makes to the British context (Baker 1975 : 196).

It is not the purpose of this chapter to make a detailed analysis of the historical events which gave rise to or influenced the development of these frameworks. However, it is important to note some of the historical developments in social work practice which in all probability exerted influence on the development of the eleven frameworks being studied, and writings of a similar kind. And furthermore it is important to observe the extent to which the frameworks locate themselves within an historical context.

THE UNITED STATES OF AMERICA

The search for unifying concepts of a common base and common professional identity can be traced to writings of a much earlier period. The search for the linkage between the activities of the social worker relating to the 'personal' and to the 'social' can be traced back at least to the writings of Mary Richmond with her concern for both 'wholesale' and 'retail' methods of social reform (Richmond 1930 : 215–16). While Richmond stressed the need to move from the individual case to the general issue (Richmond 1930 : 221), 'she also stressed the significance of the client's relationship with others and to the social institutions of his community' (Goldstein 1973 : 28).

177

Goldstein argues that Richmond's work contained two major ideas:

> The first and most explicit presented an organized way of understanding the individual through a systematic collection of information which, if sufficient, would reveal a problem's ultimate cause and therefore an obvious cure. . . . But on a more implicit level, a somewhat visionary quality was evident. . . . [S]he encouraged an expanded view of the individual as a social being.
>
> (Goldstein 1973 : 29)

The writings of Porter Lee (1937), Jane Addams (1910), and Bertha Reynolds (1951) also highlight early attempts to focus upon the dual aspects of social work's commitment. Clark Chambers makes the following comment relating to the 'wholesale-retail' dimensions of social work:

> And so the two overlapping phases of social work continue to exist, not always harmoniously, but certainly in inter-dependence – the one focused on the individual and his welfare, strongly influenced by the psychological disciplines, introspective, dealing in personalized, retail services; the other concerned with reform, with reconstruction, informed primarily by the social sciences, extroverted, dealing in group or community or wholesale services.
>
> (Chambers 1962 : 52)

The development of the concept 'wholesale-retail' has resulted in its translation into the concept of the interaction of the private troubles of individuals and the public issues of collectivities. This is developed by Schwartz, who concludes:

> There can be no 'choice' – or even division of labor – between serving individual needs and dealing with social problems, if we understand that a private trouble is simply a specific example of a public issue, and that a public issue is made up of many private troubles.
>
> (Schwartz 1969 : 38)

A significant influence on the development of 'integrated' frameworks has been the search for the 'generic'. This has been, among other things, a search to find what is common to social work: that which helps differentiate social work from other occupations and professions. This has resulted in the search for a 'common base' of social work in order to provide a central frame of reference to which all forms of practice can be related. It has been seen as necessary in order to provide the necessary links between disparate parts of the profession in the hope that a greater degree of cohesiveness and solidarity would develop. This search significantly predated Bartlett's writing.

A landmark in the search for this 'commonness' can be found in the Milford Conference of 1929. This Conference, the culmination of five years' work, affirmed that there were 'sufficient commonalities among the various specialities to preserve the idea that all social workers are part of one profession'. It also affirmed that 'a fundamental conception . . . of "generic social case work" was much more substantial in content and much more significant in its implications for all forms of social case work than were any of the specific emphases of the different case work fields' (Brieland 1977 : 341).

However, having asserted this, the Conference did not attempt a definition of social casework because it believed that at that time no definition could sufficiently distinguish social casework from other professional fields (Brieland 1977 : 342). The Report did list twenty-five 'methods' used by the social caseworker and these included a range of activities associated with what later became known as fields of practice (e.g. adoption, relief allowance, institutional care), as well as social work processes and techniques (e.g. analysis, diagnosis, interviewing, participation, referral, treatment, and so on).

Leighninger (1980 : 4–5) points out that the Milford Conference had strong symbolic meaning for the profession. Its aim was to counter fragmentation by emphasizing common or generic principles uniting social workers into a single occupational group. She believes, however, that it is best seen as an ideological statement rather than a definitive list of basic casework skills.

Given its long period of deliberation and its difficulty in finding an adequate definition of social work, it might also be concluded that the sentiments expressed at Milford represented an aspiration rather than an accurate reflection of reality.

This search for a common identity continued, although it must be remembered that it was to find what was common (generic) within the method of social casework. While this is so, it is an historical influence on the current set of writings. It should be noted again that in the light of this early search being confined to social casework, Vickery (1977) prefers not to use the term 'generic' because of its historical association with one method.

Other significant milestones in the US included the Hollis-Taylor Report (1951), the Working Definition (1958), and the Curriculum Study (1959). The Hollis-Taylor Report (Hollis and Taylor 1951), sponsored by the National Council on Social Work Education, again attempted to address definitional problems. Difficulties and differences resulted in the acceptance of a United Nations 1950 Statement as a 'fair summary' of the profession:

1. It is a helping activity, designed to give assistance in respect to problems that prevent individuals, families, and groups from achieving a minimum desirable standard of social and economic well-being.

2. It is a 'social' activity, carried on not for personal profit by private practitioners but under the auspices of organizations, governmental or non-governmental or both, established for the benefit of members of the community regarded as requiring assistance.

3. It is a 'liaison' activity, through which disadvantaged individuals, families and groups may tap all the resources in the community available to meet their unsatisfied needs . . . .

(See Brieland 1977 : 343)

The objectives for social work were likewise selected from the United Nations (1950; see Brieland 1977 : 343):

1. Social Work seeks . . . to see – and assist – individuals, families, and groups in relation to the many social and economic forces by which they are affected . . . . The well-trained social worker makes the nearest possible approach to full and constant awareness of the interplay of social, economic and psychological forces in the lives of troubled people who come to him for assistance.

2. Thus the well-trained social worker seeks to perform an integrating function for which no other provision is made in contemporary society.

3. Social work fixes attention on specific social ills, pinpointing the need for appropriate remedial and preventive services and thus seeks to maximize the resources available in the community for promoting social well-being.

These statements reflect an optimism and a challenge for social work. The optimism almost verges on megalomania if one is to consider this in any other than the best possible circumstances of skills, resources, and power of the social worker. It is interesting to note the focus on 'disadvantage'. However, the terms are global and therefore open to many interpretations. It is of interest to note that this was formulated for the purposes of education, and again one can ask whether the optimism and isolation of the educator resulted in a prescriptive statement rather than one which was fully informed by the realities of practice.

The Working Definition of 1958 was the result of the NASW Commission on Practice chaired by Harriett Bartlett. It put forward the notion that practice consisted of five elements: *value, purpose, sanction, knowledge,* and *method.*

Later, Gordon proposed the following definition of social work practice:

Social work practice is interventive action directed to purposes and guided by values, knowledge, and techniques which are collectively unique, acknowledged by and identified with the social work profession.

(Gordon 1962 : 5)

Once again the statement is general, it is consensus-oriented, and it seeks to minimize differences which at the time were evident in the field. In this sense it could be said that it was a statement of aspiration rather than one which accurately reflected the realities of both practice and education.

It was the Curriculum Study of 1959 which resulted in Boehm bringing together in a unique way several concepts in order to formalize a definition of social work:

Social work seeks to enhance the social functioning of individuals, singly and in groups, by activities focused upon their social relationships which constitute the interaction between man and his environment. These activities can be grouped into three main functions: restoration of impaired capacity, provision of individual and social resources and prevention of social dysfunction.

(See Brieland 1977 : 346)

Boehm emphasized three factors. First, social work requires

technical skills. It is more than this, however, because 'the people it serves are the product of a multiplicity of circumstances.' Second, practitioners need to be aware of the factors which cause problems in relationships because this use of self-awareness is a tool to be used in a disciplined way in working with others. Third, it is important to understanding the humanity and uniqueness of man.

Because such statements are global, it is not possible to know how wide the context of social interaction was meant to be. The predominance of the casework method, and the strong hold within this method of psychodynamic theory (Field 1980), were factors in concentrating most of the practitioner's efforts on the individual and his or her internal dynamics rather than the wider social context. Further it is evident from these statements that techniques focused on the individual, and his or her roles in society. The concept of social functioning related to the performance of different roles, which individuals, by virtue of their membership of social groups, were required to carry out. This certainly linked the analysis to a structural-functional perspective, and gave no attention to conflict within society or within the profession itself.

The search for conceptual frameworks to accommodate 'centre-moving ideas' (Billups 1984) continued through the 1970s and 1980s. Two significant groups of writings summarize the major thrusts and their associated problems.

The first significant meeting was the Madison Conference reported in the Special Issue of *Social Work*, 1977 : 22(5).

This Conference arose because of concern and uncertainty over what social work's purposes were and what they should be, what social workers were and should be doing, and to see whether a consensus existed about these questions over and above the various specialities and interests. Both the NASW and the CSWE took the position that the methods of social work intervention can be clarified only if common social work objectives are clarified.

Authors were commissioned to address the following six questions (Minahan and Briar 1977 : 339):

1. What is the mission of social work?
2. What are the objectives of social work?
3. What do social workers currently do? What should they do, or not do, to achieve their objectives?
4. What sanctions should social workers have?

5. What knowledge and skills are available to social workers that would enable them to achieve their objectives?
6. What are the practical and educational implications of the mission in terms of the profession's objectives, interventions, sanctions, and knowledge of skills?

While the responses to these questions varied, a review of the papers reveals that not *one* satisfactorily addressed all the questions posed. One would have to agree with Briar's conclusions (1977 : 415) that the objectives set for Madison were too ambitious. He notes that, first, the Madison Conference provided only one opportunity in contrast to Milford which met over a period of years. Second, Milford restricted itself to social casework whereas Madison attempted to cover the whole of social work.

Briar concludes:

> A more modest and more accurate description of this special issue is that it is an attempt to assess the current state of thinking about the common base of social work as perceived by a group of thoughtful social workers representing a range of perspectives in the profession.
>
> (Briar 1977 : 415)

In attempting to address the mission of social work, Briar states, 'Based on this admitted limited experience, the seemingly inescapable conclusion is that at this time in the history of social work there is not a widespread consensus about the profession's mission and purpose.'

A reasonable conclusion to be drawn from this is that at that time, the profession was highly diversified and specialized. In the context of this diversity, the only way agreement could be reached was by highly-generalized statements. Fundamental issues were not adequately addressed, such as the diversity of social work values (particularly the emphasis to be placed on social change versus individual change), the differential use of specialists and generalists, and the way the use of different theories about persons and society affect the emphases on direct and indirect services.

The problem remains, notes Briar:

> Although it is good that many practitioners feel comfortable with a conception of social work that works for them, it is not good – in the long run at least – that the profession cannot clearly and

simply articulate to others what is common to the activities of all social workers. To be both a diverse and an undefined profession is not the best formula for professional survival. . . .

(Briar 1977 : 444)

Similar to the recommendation of the Milford Conference, Madison called for a major study to be undertaken in order to observe some realities of practice. This would at least help to clarify what social workers actually do. The continued resistance to these suggestions of the systematic analysis of practice has been one of the reasons why social work theory development has been impeded.

Simon makes a similar comment in reviewing descriptive-prescriptive aspects of practice realities of the contributors:

Clearly, both ways must be followed (descriptive-prescriptive), and it is hoped that the first will provide a basis for the development of the second. It is startling, therefore, to realize that the emphasis in the papers and the discussion was on what social workers should do.

(Simon 1977 : 396)

To ignore what the 'current picture' is, she claims, leads to the course of 'reinforcing the compulsion of the profession to reinvent the wheel every ten years!'

Likewise, Morales (1977) notes the gulf which exists between the stated mission of social work and what it is actually doing. If the focus remains on clinical services alone, then social work can easily lose sight of its mission to the poor. However, Alexander (1977 : 408) notes that a focus on social problems presents a serious dilemma: it directs the profession's responsibility to *solving* a social problem, rather than taking responsibility for a *process* that moves people toward solving a problem. He believes the profession's experience for declaring responsibility for the elimination of poverty and making social work claims in relation to public welfare systems should have taught an unforgettable lesson: one cannot be accountable for what one does not control.

These problems arising from the Madison Conference highlight a basic dilemma for social work: is it responsible for certain end states, e.g. elimination of poverty, better standards of living, etc., or only responsible for devising and refining processes which can achieve particular ends set by others?

These problems in teleology are further clouded by what *should* be the focus for social work related to person-environment. Simon (1977) notes the important differences in argument even within one selected component of this dialectic. For example, she takes the papers of Cooper (1977) and Morris (1977), both of whom could be grouped at the 'people-as-individuals' end of the continuum. She notes, however, that their similarities are only 'skin deep'. Cooper emphasizes that social work should pay equal attention to the individual's internal life and to the external forces that shape and affect internal processes. Morris, however, emphasizes the creation and management of social environments as they affect ('caring for') individuals. He suggests that primary professional attention to individual internal forces should be minimal and that the necessity for this is also minimal (Simon 1977 : 395).

A further area on which no agreement was reached related to the generalist-specialist debate. While Minahan and Pincus (1977) develop arguments for types of 'generalist' practice, Siporin (1978) replying the following year argues that the generic base or purpose, values, knowledge, method, and skill constitutes a foundation for specific practice and not for some still undefined ideal of a 'basic generalist.' He further argues that the schools provide a generic base of knowledge and skill, but they do not actually prepare students to be generalists of any kind in the sense of competent, multifunctional practitioners. 'This fantasy ought to be laid to rest!' he asserts.

Thus while the Madison Conference set out to define things which are common to social work, it can be argued that it demonstrated just the opposite. It also highlighted once again some confusion between authors as to where they were looking for that commonness. One can differentiate one or a mixture of:

- the need to define an end in terms of a 'social movement', e.g. improved health, housing, the elimination of poverty, etc.;
- the need to find better means for achieving some end, e.g. 'generalist practice' vs. specialist practice, etc.;
- the need to give equal attention to the person-environment concept.

The Conference referred only to one fully-developed framework, Pincus and Minahan (1973), and not to others which, as Siporin (1978) notes, led to an insularity of discussion and a lack of historical perspective.

185

The unresolved nature of this debate is further illustrated in the writings which resulted from the Chicago meeting (Minahan 1981), which again set as its goal the defining of the purpose of social work. The deliberations of the Chicago meeting were reported in 1981 and hence have no effect on the eleven conceptual frameworks under consideration here. Nevertheless, some discussion of this meeting is important because it serves to highlight the *continuing* debate and confusion around the central component of 'purpose' in social work.

The central difficulties and problems remain. While a statement of purpose was formulated (Minahan 1981 : 6) it can be criticized on a number of grounds. First, it is too global and general, reified, and locked into the problems of conceptualizing the *interaction* between persons and environments. Second, it makes the assumption that it is possible to have 'mutually beneficial interaction' between individuals and society. Third, it appears to assume a monolithic view of 'society'. Fourth, there is no recognition of the existence of conflict of interests either within social work or between client groups.

Further, there appears to be the assumption that the needs and potentials of everyone can be met. There also appears to be the assumption that people are altruistic rather than self-interested, and that social work has an interest in *everyone*, without consideration of the various sanctions, available techniques for helping, or the power social work and individual social workers hold.

There is a focus on processes rather than outcomes. There is no direction stated for social work's particular concern (e.g. with the poor or disadvantaged; or the type of social arrangements social workers ought to support). Whatever the desired outcome in defining a common purpose, the individual papers demonstrate a focus on specific fields of practice or with service populations, e.g. health care, the family, community mental health, school social work, industrial social work, work with the aged, etc.

Briar (1981 : 83) notes that at least dissensus appears to be neither greater nor deeper than at the Madison Conference, and remarks that in the context of a more varied and complex profession than ten or twenty years ago, that is remarkable. He notes too that social workers appear to *want* to perceive and analyse problems within the context of person-environment, although admitting that thus far, 'that desired ideal has eluded social workers, just as it has eluded social scientists for whom it has also been a goal' (Briar 1981 : 84). Part of the problem, Alexander notes, is that 'environment' is too abstract and idealistic. Environment cannot provide opportunities and resources, only *people* can make those available from the environment (Alexander 1981 : 87).

Likewise, Meyer notes that the 'person-environment transaction' is too 'missionary-like and insufficiently realistic for practice purposes. It is also too isolated from an institutional context to serve for *social work* purposes' (Meyer 1981 : 91).

The monolithic view of 'society' inherent in the definition of purpose can also be related to Alexander's (1981 : 87) criticism that no attention is given to the variation of resources of each society. Indeed both Gilbert (1981 : 88) and Meyer (1981 : 91) refer to the lack of an institutional base within the definition. For Meyer 'it is too global and benign'. To 'improve the quality of life for everyone' is 'unreal, impossible, out of sight' (Meyer 1981 : 91). To state that the environment *should* is naïve, according to Meyer. 'Of course, the environment *should*, but it does not!'

Meyer further notes that the profession remains 'hopelessly' bound up with its idealism. A *commitment* to certain values cannot easily be translated into social change. A further problem is social work's trying to be all things to all people. In spite of the difficulties, Meyer is still committed to finding consensus not just more ideas. 'Social workers cannot afford to wait too long to tell the public, the government, and themselves what it is they do well and what it is they will assume responsibility for managing' (Meyer 1981 : 74).

The search for unifying concepts has been a feature of North American social work since the 1930s. The search for a common knowledge base to clearly unite and differentiate social workers from other occupational groups has also been a part of the rhetoric of North American social workers for a long time. Under such influences, the development of practice frameworks to mirror this rhetoric is not surprising. This in part might account for the burgeoning of this type of conceptual framework in that country.

However, what this brief historical account has shown, is that whatever the ideals of some social work writers might be, fundamental problems remain around the following tasks: (i) to explicitly define the purposes for social work; (ii) to make a clear differentiation of ends and means of social work and an explication of social work ends; (iii) to commit the *concept* of 'person-in-environment' to a reality which can be operationalized in practice; (iv) to relate social work purposes and concepts (like person-in-environment) to an institutional context which takes into account access to power and resources; (v) to clearly differentiate prescriptions and descriptions; and (vi) to study the aspirations for social work in the context of current practices which have been accurately and systematically described.

THE UNITED KINGDOM

Vickery (1977 : 40) notes that writers in the USA have attempted to find a consensus around a common conceptual base for the *whole* of social work. As the above discussion has indicated, this has not been achieved. In contrast to these attempts, writers in the UK have been less universal in their aims, and they have made more explicit links to their particular social welfare system and the needs created by the Seebohm (1968) and Kilbrandon (1964) reorganizations. Furthermore, a more coherent 'radical critique' of establishment social work has been developed. The UK writings along these lines have a more recent history than their American counterparts.

The reorganization of the social services and social work departments meant that individual social workers or teams would be responsible for a far wider range of social work activities. Until then these activities had been performed by specialists who were identified with one particular field of practice. In addition 'social work' was mainly described in terms of 'casework method', and 'community work' was often seen as an undertaking in its own right and not linked to social work (see e.g. Armstrong and Gill 1978a). The need for an integrating framework was seen as necessary by some people in order to provide some cohesion to the vast array of otherwise disparate activities of social workers.

In addition it was not until 1970 that the 'separate interests' formed themselves into a common professional association, the British Association of Social Workers.

While the North American literature provides a record of attempts to describe the 'generic', the predominant emphasis in the British literature has been an attempt to link and integrate the orthodox methods of practice in a cohesive way. Two major collections of writing, *Integrating Social Work Methods* (Specht and Vickery 1977) and *The Unitary Model* (Olsen 1978), can be seen primarily as attempts to link orthodox methods into an overall integrating framework. Because the divisions remain between the methods, they can be seen in terms of what Baker describes as 'multi-methods' (Baker 1980 : 29). They do not attempt to devise a wholly integrated framework in their own right, but rather rely upon the frameworks developed by Pincus and Minahan (1973), and Goldstein (1973), in particular.

From a speculative point of view it is fortuitous that such American frameworks had been developed, because it appears that this type of framework was the type that was being searched for in the UK. Some British writers seem to have accepted these frameworks, not so much for what they implied in themselves, but because they appeared, at first sight, to fulfil some of the needs for an integrating framework to link the orthodox methods and specialist fields in such a way that they could be used within the reorganized social services structures, and possibly to help consolidate the newly created professional social work association.

The visits to the UK of Pincus, Minahan, and Goldstein in 1975 (see Parsloe 1975) can also be seen as having made a substantial impact on educators and practitioners, if the use of their particular frameworks, rather than others, is any indication. It is curious that given the copious writings about an integrated approach by British social workers, a framework similar to the Pincus and Minahan and Goldstein formulations was not developed by them, especially given the very different social welfare arrangements operating in each country (Parsloe 1975 : 1–16).

Evans (1976 : 177) notes, '*the recent introduction into this country, from the USA* [my italics], of an "integrated" or "unitary" model for social work practice has excited a good deal of discussion . . .'. Practitioners and educators appeared to take these frameworks and transplant them to their own situation. While there appear to have been very few questions raised about the viability of using a practice framework developed within one social welfare context and applying it in a different one, nevertheless the frameworks of Pincus and Minahan and Goldstein, in particular, appear to have acted as catalysts to the development of ideas of UK social work writers.

Parts of these two frameworks were extracted in order to develop ideas relevant to the UK. It is interesting to note the comment of Bywaters (1978) who, after discussing the 'four point method of analysis' of Pincus and Minahan, says, 'we would tend to argue that we managed OK before we knew about the model by working from the question, "What is the most effective way in which to tackle this problem?"' (Bywaters 1978 : 19). This comment, along with one of a similar nature by Specht referring to practice in the UK (Specht

1977 : 28), leads one to question whether this type of thinking may have emerged irrespective of what conceptual frameworks were developed elsewhere.

In some senses it is disappointing that both the American frameworks were so whole-heartedly accepted, because different frameworks may have emerged with a much closer linkage to the institutional and socio-political base, hence reflecting the specific context for practice more accurately. Nevertheless, these frameworks were seen to provide a foundation to develop a conceptual framework of practice which would meet the needs of multi-service social services departments.

Vickery notes a recurring theme of the Seebohm Report of the need to make available 'a more varied response to client problems' (Vickery 1977 : 41). The Report emphasized the need for forms of intervention in the social worker's repertoire to supplement casework approaches, as well as to extend generic training to equip students to work with individuals, groups, and communities.

The Report states:

> The justification for this approach is the belief that the different divisions between methods of social work are as artificial as the difference between various forms of casework and that in his daily work the social worker needs all these methods to enable him to respond appropriately to social problems which involve individual, family, group and community aspects. This newer concept of generic training has obvious attractions as a preparation for work in the social service departments.
>
> (See Vickery 1977 : 42)

Parsloe (1975 : 12) links the unitary approach to social services departments with the hope that 'a unified approach to methods can help' in relation to making choices. She notes that the 'unified social work departments confront social workers with inevitable choices about the allocation of scarce resources, including their own time, in a way which is not so apparent when social workers operate in separate agencies' (Parsloe 1975 : 11). She recognizes that 'people very low down in the system' have to make choices about the allocation of resources between groups in need (Parsloe 1975 : 12). Further,

> we should recognize that when we ask social workers in such an exposed position to consider a wide possible range of ways of

working, we are asking them to select without any proper criteria from a mass of clients, and then choose ways of working from an equally wide range again with ill-defined criteria for the choice.

(Parsloe 1975 : 12)

Optimistically she goes on,

I hope this Conference may help to develop some guide-lines for choice of system, otherwise our unified social work departments may prove less fruitful ground for a unified methods approach than their specialized American equivalents.

(Parsloe 1975 : 12)

Evans (1978 : 19–38) further links these approaches to organization of social services departments in his proposals for the use of joint teams. He argues that social work is 'case based' not only in terms of a 'method' but also the form of social work organization the method gives rise to. This represents

the tradition of the single social worker working with individual clients or occasionally client groups such as the family. Given this as the axis of the helping relationship this form of social work gives rise to a set of administrative practices and daily routines within social work agencies that belie an underlying ideology of need and a perspective on practice which is essentially individualistic. This is reflected in accepted forms of case allocation; in the keeping of individual case files; in the almost exclusive deployment of single social workers working largely independently of other members of the social work team; in the fact that individuals rather than social groups or institutions are most usually the target for intervention; and so on. . . .What I am suggesting then is that the form of social work organization associated with case based practice is not compatible either with the ideology of need, the practice perspective, or the style of intervention associated with a unitary approach.

(Evans 1978 : 20)

In his critique, Jordan (1977 : 448) links the 'unitary approach' directly to its use within local authority social services departments. He asserts that it is the unitary approach which has been adopted in order to provide an overall rationale 'for the many disparate tasks' social workers have to perform in these departments. 'Its appeal lies in the integration not only of the social worker's role, but also of the social services department as an organization.'

While the potential usefulness of this approach has been highlighted by UK writers, they have given much more attention to a critical evaluation of both specific conceptual frameworks as well as this group of writings in general, than have their North American counterparts. If conceptual frameworks and practice theory are going to develop, then critical evaluation is a necessary part of refinement and redevelopment. There is very little critical evaluation of this type of writing in the North American literature. It should also be noted that this critical context provides a significant historical context for 'integrated' theory to develop.

The criticisms can be grouped in the following ways:

- Criticisms of an ideological nature. These come mainly from the 'radical'/'socialist' writers who claim that the development of these kinds of writings in social work practice removes the arena of debate from one of ideology to one of methodology. This they reject (Bailey and Brake 1975; Mowbray 1977; Statham 1978; Simpkin 1979; Corrigan and Leonard 1978; Galper 1980; Brake and Bailey 1980; Bailey and Lee 1982).

- Criticisms relating to the use of *interactionism*. This is linked to the consideration of an increased number of variables including the use of a larger number of socio-behavioural theories, *without* criteria to help select and limit the wider number of choices (Sheldon 1978; Evans 1976).

- Criticisms which directly link this writing with systems theory and thus bring the full weight of a critique of systems theory to bear on these conceptual frameworks regardless of the strength of the links between these writings and systems theory. Furthermore, criticism which claims the frameworks are merely about processes and are 'contentless' and therefore are unable to provide substantive guidelines for the practitioner to follow. The method of the frameworks' development has only tenuous links with practice reality (Watts 1978; Jordan 1977; Triseliotis 1978; Bywaters 1982 : 314–15).

- Criticisms which deal with the operational problems of this approach. This includes an individual practitioner's capacity and ability to have all the necessary skills and resources for such a multi-faceted approach (Evans 1978).

192

● Criticisms related to the fact that there has only been limited use made of these frameworks in the field (Baker 1980c; Stevenson and Parsloe 1978).

● Criticisms of a moral nature. The focus is upon what is workable or normal rather than what is good, and thus there is the assumption (which is questioned) that man is 'social' rather than 'individual' (Wilkes 1978).

● Criticisms which highlight the critic's own ideology and end up demanding quite different qualities from these frameworks. For example, Van Krieken (1980), in making a critique of Baker's (1976) work, argues that while Baker's work masquerades as a broad, all-encompassing approach, it is no more than 'casework recycled'. From the opposite point of view, Wilkes (1978 : 7–10) criticizes the 'unitary' approach for not questioning 'social morality'. She questions why a profession which claims to value the individual now wants to put so much emphasis on the 'social' and on the 'interaction' of the individual with his social environment. The idea that salvation is social, rather than spiritual, is central to the unitary approach and indeed there seems to be an ontological mistrust of the solitary individual (Wilkes 1978 : 8).

Undoubtedly, the writings of the so-called 'radical' school have formed an influential part of this critique. In using the term school, this is not meant to imply that all these writings are similar, and indeed there are problems with the meaning of a term such as 'radical' (Mowbray 1981 : 2). While it is not my intention to review these 'radical' writings systematically, nevertheless they have important implications for the theory under consideration in this book.

While having different emphases, these critiques focus on a number of central issues. They question the role of social work in relation to the state, and more specifically to being used by the holders of power to help uphold the status quo by adjusting people to the norms of the existing social arrangements. Some arguments, more specifically, see social work as a central part of capitalist arrangements whereby certain disadvantaged groups are further deprived of their power by having some of their immediate needs met through residual welfare and personal services. The use of social casework in particular to help 'adjust' people to present social conditions, no matter how unjust or inequitable, is a powerful force in maintaining the status quo. Further, a concentration on technique and process has diverted attention away from a consideration of underlying ideological issues.

Whatever their specific prescriptions, the 'radical' writers make very different assumptions about the nature of social science knowledge, as well as about the nature of society, than do most writers of the 'integrated' approaches (see Leonard 1975 and 1975a; Longres 1981). They challenge the basic structure of capitalist society and the social welfare arrangements made under it. Their position is not one of looking for adjustments and accommodations for particular needs, but rather a change in the power and decision-making structures. This position is related to the development of particular social science concepts and hence development of theory (Leonard 1975).

These matters are highlighted by Armstrong and Gill (1978, 1978a), in their discussion on the importance of ideology to practice. They dispute that their kind of community work can be integrated with other forms of social work because to them their practice is influenced by what they see to be the fundamental causes of problems, that is, the social structures. They assert that (based on Batley and Edwards 1975) it is not possible to combine approaches based on an analysis of power and social structure with one based upon social pathology. To them the ideology and theory is part of the framework for practice. This they contrast with Pincus and Minahan (1973), who clearly differentiate their framework for practice from a number of theoretical orientations they maintain can be used with the framework. Thus there is the implication that the framework can be 'neutral' rather than aligned with one particular ideology.

In contrast to the seven major objectives listed by Pincus and Minahan (1973 : 15), Armstrong and Gill outline the purpose for social work accepted by the University of Concepción, Chile, namely:

> Social work as social praxis tries to promote in man a critical consciousness that will permit him to realize his own ontological vocation to transform the world through his own betterment.

> Social work must work in activating and consolidating the class consciousness of the urban and rural proletariat and in those

194

efforts which call for the organization and rescue of an authentic national culture.

(Armstrong and Gill 1978 : 20)

The authors note that the assumption made by Pincus and Minahan (1975) is that resource systems are benevolent in aiding everyone's life chances, and that these systems can be adjusted to increase the benefits of the majority. The assumption within the Chile statement, however, is that there are substantial conflicts of interest between classes and that social work must state its position on that clash.

Armstrong and Gill conclude:

We can therefore see that the unitary approach is not a neutral framework in which the worker can insert his own theories. It is located in a particular culture and ideology which promotes values such as consensus and integration and demotes values such as class and conflict.

(Armstrong and Gill 1978 : 20)

Another point of crucial difference is the role social workers play in bringing about fundamental changes through political processes. For most 'radical' writers, people's behaviour *is* political in terms of their support for or opposition to social arrangements and in terms of their interference in power relationships. In contrast, Pincus and Minahan (1973) proscribe 'political' behaviour and confine 'political' to the narrow 'party political'.

Referring to such assertions as these, McLeod and Dominelli reply:

Besides begging questions about the monolithic, reified and all powerful nature of 'society' this approach does little to help the social worker who feels that in order to secure justice for his/her client the status quo, with its acceptance of endemic poverty, should be challenged. We would maintain that concern over the necessity for social workers to make their contribution towards the process of promoting social change is neither limited to a small number of social workers, and, therefore, simply a matter to be conveniently set aside; nor is it simply a matter of current controversy. . . .

(McLeod and Dominelli 1982 : 113)

A recurrent theme in the writings of the 'radical school' is criticism of a 'monolithic and reified' view of society portrayed in 'integrated' or 'generic' theory. In a 'radical' view it is of fundamental importance to recognize the conflicting elements in society. The integrated approaches to social work paint a scenario based upon the assumption that there is agreement as to what the ends and means of social work ought to be. Clients can then be helped to adjust to those norms. The 'radical' school highlights the tensions created by conflict and dissensus. This brings attention to the inequalities and differential power relationships. For these theorists the role of social work is not seen as 'neutral' but rather upholding the interests of the powerful. Their view of 'politics' is not confined only to 'party politics' but rather to an analysis of power in relationships of all people.

The 'radical' writers see themselves as opposed to the consensus type arguments they claim are inherent in the integrated approaches. Rojek (1986), however, convincingly argues against a 'gladiatorial' paradigm in which the 'radicals' and 'traditionalists' are adversaries. In his use of post-structuralism, he argues that 'the continuities *between* theories of social work are at least as significant as the oppositions which divide them'.

HISTORICAL LOCATION OF THE FRAMEWORKS

Given the historical influences outlined, it might be expected that the frameworks would make some attempt to acknowledge their location within a particular social and welfare context. However, none of the eleven frameworks studied effectively puts itself in an historical context, although Goldstein (1973) and Haines (1975) include historical material. This material unfortunately is only indirectly related to the development of their frameworks. Furthermore, none of the eleven frameworks attempt to build upon the work of preceding authors, and the recognition or even acknowledgement of other contributions of this genre is very limited.

The importance of the need to acknowledge the influences of historical contexts is recognized by some authors, for example, Vickery (1977 : 40–1) and Evans (1976 : 180–2). While passing reference is made by some authors to the seminal work of Bartlett (1970), and to the early writings of Richmond (1930) and others supporting an interactionist position between person and environment, the failure to make links to other similar works gives the

196

impression that each framework stands in its own right isolated from its recent history. This failure means that it is difficult, if not impossible, to know in what ways each author sees his or her framework being similar to and different from other formulations within the genre. This has a serious implication for theory development because it deprives it of a sense of development.

As none of the frameworks locates itself within an historical or social context this gives rise to the question of what reality the frameworks refer to, and how important is a particular social welfare context to the reality of that framework. The consequence of not linking a framework to a particular social welfare context is to raise the question of how 'universal' a framework is – that is, can it be transferred and applied in a different context and still remain valid and effective?

It is Baker (1980c : 13) who argues that his framework is not connected with a particular social, political, and economic context which has given rise to social welfare arrangements. Indeed Baker makes no attempt to recognize the differential effects of historical context when formulating his framework whether this is taking place in the UK or Australia. However, without the necessity of a detailed analysis, there are striking differences in the form social work practice takes in different socio-political contexts, which one could assume result at least partly from a different mission for social work. The above analysis has demonstrated that the search for 'integration' and an 'integrated' theory has taken place against a backdrop of different historical concomitants in the US and the UK.

This raises the question of whether there is a social work practice over and above the context of agency, state, and country, or whether the type of practice is determined and influenced by a specific socio-cultural and political context. The issue of sanction is relevant here. It is interesting to note that Bartlett (1970) discards 'sanction' from her constellation of elements in the common base, yet this was a major consideration in the Working Definition (1958). The traditional forms of sanction for social work are the client, the agency, the professional organization, and the state. It is an interesting question and open to empirical analysis just how much these sanctions influence the practice of social work and hence its theory. To ignore this would seem to imply that a social work theory could stand unaffected by its context and hence suggest its construction either implicitly or explicitly within a positivist paradigm.

What becomes clear is the need to guard against the automatic transfer of a framework of practice from one socio-cultural setting to another without studying the implicit and explicit ideology contained within that framework. To make the transfer without such a study is to impose the values and beliefs of one context upon another without knowing it.

While none of the eleven frameworks puts itself in an explicit historical and cultural context, some authors (in passing) do make reference to their social welfare context. Haines (1975), for example, refers to the Seebohm reorganization and asserts that his approach is in response to the changing nature of social work under this legislation. He notes it reflects a shift away from predominantly social casework to a 'more effective assessment' of problems generally; and it links the social worker's role with its legislative context.

Likewise Baker (1975) makes reference to the British context when he says the approach will have popularity because of the limitations of the social worker who is trained only in one method; because of the creation of multi-service social services departments; and because of the advent of an integrated social work professional association. However, as noted earlier, Baker appears to make no accommodation to the fact that he is developing his model for a UK or Australian context, where social welfare arrangements are substantially different.

Referring to the reasons for developing his approach, Siporin (1975) notes: first it is in response to the pressures on the profession (e.g. the conflict between those who maintain that social work should be aligned to the poor and disadvantaged in society, in contrast to those who maintain that social work should maintain its contractual societal purposes within traditional social arrangements); he cites the inadequacy of the methods approach ('methodolatry'); and the need to have a single vision of social work's mission, knowledge, and methodology.

Compton and Galaway (1979), while asserting there is a need to link this material to the past, do not carry this out. They maintain their work is consistent with the ecological models of Baer and Federico, Germain, Meyer, and Pincus and Minahan. It is not clear just how the term 'ecological' is being used, and if indeed all the authors referred to would subscribe to an 'ecological metaphor', which Germain does.

Germain and Gitterman (1980) note the problems caused in the past by the creation of artificial boundaries of method and setting, and the failure to take into account the reciprocal relationships of individuals and social groups. They maintain their perspective covers the dialectics of cause–function (social action–client treatment); and generalist–specialist debates.

Apart from these alleged relationships with a past and contemporary history, the frameworks have little to say.

CONCLUSIONS

The historical context is an important consideration in studying the development of conceptual frameworks of social work practice. While this chapter does not systematically trace the events which have been influential on the development of these types of frameworks, nevertheless some significant contextual variables have been cited in order to demonstrate the differential effects these can have on theory development.

None of the frameworks explicitly locates itself within an historical context, although some authors refer, in passing, to effects from their social context. This failure to locate the framework in an historical context can imply that the framework is universally applicable, regardless of the social welfare context in which it has been developed.

If this is the case, then the universal applicability needs to be demonstrated. However, the failure to take into account the historical context, or to demonstrate the framework's universality, can be further linked to the authors' views regarding the nature of knowledge and theory development. To imply that an historical context is unimportant to theory development further reinforces the authors' commitment to positivism.

Furthermore, the authors' failure to make explicit links between frameworks and hence place their own work in context, proves a serious impediment to theory-building. The reader has to make his or her own evaluation. However, in the context of a confused nomenclature, this evaluation proves even more difficult.

In reviewing the frameworks and related writings, it is clear that the North American frameworks have not been subjected to the same degree of critical scrutiny as have their British counterparts. While UK writers cite US authors, particularly Pincus and Minahan, and Goldstein, the US frameworks appear to have been developed within a context totally insulated from the writings of social workers abroad.

This situation is a serious impediment to the development of social work theory, particularly to a study of the differential effects social welfare contexts have upon that theory development.

Chapter Ten

RELATIONSHIP TO SOCIAL SYSTEMS ANALYSIS

INTRODUCTION

This chapter will explore the use of 'social systems analysis' or 'systems theory'[1] not because its use can be linked explicitly to the frameworks under consideration, but because of the implicit parallels between the development of systems theory and the development of social work theory through the 'integrated' frameworks. These parallels can be observed in that systems analysis and the 'integrated' approaches both:

- attempt to deal with a very broad canvas of social reality;
- stress the importance of interdependence and interrelatedness at all levels;
- are couched in terms and concepts at a high level of abstraction;
- provide little in the way of explanation of social realities and hence have limited prescriptive qualities;
- emphasize technical, process, and procedural variables over substantive, historical, and ideological ones.

The use of systems theory in social work has a history covering the last twenty years, however, rarely has this theory been critically evaluated by social workers, as a theory in its own right, or for its potential use within social work. The dangers of such an uncritical acceptance of a 'theory' developed by another discipline have been outlined (Watts 1978; Roberts 1981).

Within this chapter, it is proposed to outline the basic tenets of systems theory, its definitions and attributes; problems with these definitions and attributes including its theoretical 'status'; its use within social work and particularly its relationship to the 'integrated' frameworks under consideration in this book.

CONFLICT OF VIEWS

Different attitudes to systems theory are reflected in the following quotations:

> [The words of James G. Miller in 1955 on systems theory] . . . seemed literally to jump from the page, capturing my attention and fancy in a vice-like grip that has persisted to the present time. From that day forward it is fair to say that I have been addicted to general systems theory and the general systems approach to theory building.
>
> (Hearn 1974)

> my objection to systems thinking is that it adds nothing new, interesting or significant to our understanding of social phenomena, and that it achieves this negative result per medium of confusion, ambiguity, fallacious logic, and old fashioned silliness. . . . The incorporation of this perspective into social work theory can only be regarded as an intellectual disaster of the first order.
>
> (Watts 1978)

> Systems analysis is one example of what the social sciences can contribute to the enrichment of our profession. It can give us the tools for moving towards an integrated micro–macro single model of social work practice, and partializing the knowledge or skills which are to be taught to the next generation of social workers. Systemic thinking offers a rich alternative to current ways of deciding on the type of intervention to undertake, especially since it makes possible a diagnostic perspective which links assessment with planning and intervention for the entire problem field.
>
> (Yanoov-Chetkow 1980)

> The systems thinker does not attempt to prove that systems 'principles', whatever they may be, fit the social world; he merely takes it for granted. The literature is totally one of abstract definitions, conceptualizations, formal structures, and commentaries on other abstract definitions, conceptualizations, and formal structures; nowhere can one find concrete, specific

empirical problems that have been defined, studied, worked with, and learned from. The few empirical materials to be found in the literature add up to a pastiche of minor illustrations which prove nothing.

(Lilienfeld 1975)

In view of the inadequacies of theoretical approaches that are limited to the micro level (as symbolic interactionism and exchange theory tend to be), to processes of harmonious co-operation based on consensus (as in functionalism), or to processes of coercion and conflict (as in conflict theory), it would seem that general systems theory could hold considerable promise for the future of sociological theory. An adequate theory must be able to deal with the complex linkages between the micro level of interpersonal interaction and the macro level of complex institutional patterns . . . an adequate theory must recognize that social systems may exhibit high or low levels of stability or rapid change, extensive or minimal degrees of interdependence, high or low levels of individual autonomy, and so on. Systems theory seems to offer an image of social reality that is sufficiently comprehensive and flexible to meet this requirement and to provide a framework within which these variations can be investigated empirically. As such, systems theory helps us to recognize the variability and complexity of the socio-cultural world.

(Johnson 1981)

EARLY USE

As these quotations illustrate, writers reach very different conclusions about systems analysis despite its relatively long period of influence throughout the physical and social sciences. One of its founders, von Bertalanffy (1901–72), developed open systems analysis for use within biology, but saw its potentiality for developing a theoretical approach which could span across disciplines. This approach may have been seen as the 'grand theory' to explain the nature of man, society, language, and human history. It was argued that such disciplines as operations research, communications theory, cybernetics, information theory, and modern linguistics were all subdisciplines of general systems theory. As Lilienfeld (1975 : 640) notes, 'The

203

purpose of general systems theory was to develop broad overarching concepts applicable to all fields, and to show that conceptual models fruitful in one field were transferable to other fields.'

The relevance of this kind of 'theory' was soon heralded by social work. Here was an approach having the backing of 'respectable scientists', an approach which was searching for commonalities across discipline boundaries:

> is it possible that a universal theory of human behaviour might be developed which would serve us at all levels when we are attempting to understand individuals, groups, organizations or communities? . . . if we could develop a universal theory of human systems behaviour, might this also serve as a base for the development of a general theory of social work intervention?
>
> (Hearn 1974 : 333)

Its popularity in social work education is demonstrated by Hearn (1974 : 339) who notes its use in 75 per cent of social work courses in the US.

BASIC PREMISE

The basic premise of open systems analysis is that each system except the largest system can be seen as a subsystem of another system; and that each system except the smallest has subsystems of its own. That is what is described as a *holon*, an entity which is simultaneously both a part and a whole.

While by definition any system is both a whole and at the same time a part, one has to designate which is the *focal* system, at any point in time. The concept of the holon requires one to attend to the component parts or the subsystems of that focal system and to simultaneously attend to the significant environment or the suprasystems of which the focal system is a part, or to which it is related.

If a family, for example, is viewed as the focal system within the holon concept, then attention must be given both to its members (subsystems) and to its significant environments such as schools, community, work organizations, other families, and the neighbourhood (suprasystems). The choice of the focal system is quite arbitrary. In the above example, the focal system might have been one person of the family, in which case the family would form part of the suprasystems of that individual.

Of fundamental importance to this theory or form of analysis, are the interrelationships of the component parts, for these create a whole that is greater than the sum of the parts. The interaction among the elements of a system give it characteristics that are not only different from, but often are not found in the components alone. As Compton and Galaway remark:

> Thus the 'sum of the parts' does not refer to the particular parts of the units added together or summed but to the aggregate of the units and the transaction and relationships between them that creates a 'whole' with some degree of continuity and boundary.
>
> (Compton and Galaway 1979 : 73)

DEFINITIONS

The following definitions of 'system' have been put forward: 'A set of units with relationships among them' (von Bertalanffy 1968 : 11); 'a totality of elements in interaction', 'the dynamic interrelatedness of components', 'a whole which functions as a whole by virtue of the inter-dependence of its parts' (Buckley 1968 : *xvii* and *xxiii–xxv*); 'a set of objects together with relationships between the objects and between their attributes' (Hearn 1974 : 335).

> [T]hat complex of activities which is required to complete the process of transforming an intake into an output . . . a system has a boundary which separates it from its environment. Intakes cross this boundary and are subjected to conversion processes within it. The work done by the system is therefore at least potentially measurable by the difference between its intakes and its outputs.
>
> (Miller and Rice 1967 : 6–7)

CHARACTERISTICS OF SYSTEMS

Openness and closedness

When applied to living organisms within an environment which allows for the exchange of information and energy (*input, throughput, output*) the analysis is in terms of the system being *open*. This is in contrast to a *closed* system (a black box), where an environmental boundary of one kind prevents the exchange of information and energy. Within open systems analysis, there are degrees of relative openness and closedness. For example, a closed or semi-closed institution like a prison or closed convent is less open to interaction with the rest of the world than a university. The former would be characterized as a 'semi-closed' system, whereas the latter is an 'open' system.

Entropy

This concept comes from Newton's Second Law of Thermodynamics, which holds that a certain quantity, called *entropy*, or degree of disorganization in the system, tends to increase to a maximum until eventually the process ends in a state of equilibrium. Open systems, because they are able to exchange energy and information with other systems, that is, receive input from and produce output to the environment, are able to grow and evolve towards increasing complexity. This condition is called *negative entropy*.

'Steady state' and homeostasis

While closed systems attain equilibrium or rest, in open systems, because of the dynamic interplay between systems and suprasystems, while they appear at rest, in reality they are in a 'dynamic steady state'. Open systems tend to maintain themselves in a steady state and after any disturbance, a system tends to re-establish a steady state, that is, it is *self-regulating*.

Equifinality

This means that the same end state may result from different initial conditions. Multifinality is the opposite of this, viz. similar conditions may lead to dissimilar end states.

Tension

Tension is seen as a necessary part of each complex adaptive system. This tension may manifest itself in either constructive or destructive ways. However, systems analysis does not put a value, either positive or negative, on the tension *per se*. Systems analysis is more concerned with the identification and analysis of how and to what purpose tensions operate within a system and between systems.

Feedback

Relying on information and communication theories, feedback is the mechanism by which open systems may be maintained in or near a steady state. Hall and Fagan (1956) note that a certain portion of the system output or behaviour is fed back to the input to affect succeeding outputs, e.g. thermoregulation in warm-blooded animals.

SOME PROBLEMS WITH THESE DEFINITIONS AND CHARACTERISTICS

Because general systems theory seeks to focus on the similarities of *organization* that may be found in otherwise dissimilar things (e.g. person, school, neighbourhood, etc.), definitions of a *system* are simple and general. However, if one is to isolate two key words in Hearn's definition (above), viz. 'object' and 'relationship', it is difficult to know what these words actually mean without relating them to some reality. The theory itself does not do this and as Kelk (1978 : 430–1) points out, the theory is not ontologically committed. What the theory does do 'is.to supply a relatively physicalistic language to describe systems . . . none of these terms supply any ontological commitments' (Kelk 1978 : 430).

A further problem, raised by Buck, is that in defining everything as a system (either sub- or suprasystem), it is open to question what then is not a system: 'with limitless vistas of systems . . . one is unable to think of anything, or any combination of things, which could not be regarded as a system. . . . [A] concept that applies to everything is logically empty' (Buck 1956 : 226). Because systems theory does not have the criteria for recognizing something which is not a system, Buck (1956) maintains it is a 'naïve and speculative philosophy.' Such statements as 'I am a system', 'the membership committee is a system', 'the species salmon is a system' cannot be shown to be false in systems terms.

In order to challenge any theory, one needs to gather anomalies which the original theory does not account for (Kelk 1978 : 434). However, because everything can be considered a system, this is not possible with general systems theory, and so its language is generally considered tautologous (see Kelk 1978 and Watts 1978).

A third major problem is that 'general systems theory' is used as a rubric to include 'systems models', 'systems analysis', and 'systems theory'. In defining one's terms it is essential that each of these concepts is differentiated. It is too easy for social workers in essentially *applying* systems formulations to assume that the numerous systems formulations are without significant differentiation.

This is related to the use of the word 'theory' and the subsequent expectations which this conjures. As pointed out in Chapter 2 'theory' can be used in different ways. When we observe the way systems 'theory' has been used in the social sciences we see that there is no group of concepts or propositions linked together in a coherent or explanatory way. The 'reality' which is used is a mixture of 'raw' empirical data, hypothesis, utilization of substantive content from other theories, and assumption.

There is no explanation to help understand the phenomenon, but a mere claim that *one group* of systematic phenomena is interdependent upon other systems. Indeed, the relationship between the systems is often an assumed one, rather than one which has been demonstrated empirically (Lilienfeld 1975 : 648; Buck 1956 : 231). Sallach (1972 : 56) raises the issue of whether systems theory has 'substance'; theory implies a more or less coherent framework that can be translated into testable propositions. While the systems perspective is not devoid of deducible propositions, it relies, however, on substantive literature and previous theories in order to provide the guidelines and specific content in which the systems propositions can emerge (Buck 1956 :231).

Likewise, Drover and Schragge (1977 : 32) note that it provides a useful typology of social organization, but this depends upon other substantive theories. The approach provides no criteria for ordering the relations between systems. 'The ordering is done by individual system analysts' (Drover and Schragge 1977 : 32).

Other writers have viewed 'systems theory' as a 'meta-theory' (Forder 1976 : 29), an 'exercise in modelling' (Evans 1976 : 180), a *Weltanschauung* (Watts 1978 : 19), and an 'ideology' (Lilienfeld 1975 : 656ff.)

Evans (1976 : 193) maintains it does not have the status of a theory, because it is 'without any historical or cultural content'. While at first sight it provides an account of the action structure relationship, on examination this is seen to be not an account but simply a description. At the same time it is described at such a high level of abstraction it is of little use for practice. The problem of definition applies not only to the terms 'system' and 'theory', but also to the language of the attributes of systems whose terms come mainly from the physical sciences.

For example, critiques of the use of systems theory in the social sciences go to great lengths to point out the difference between *homeostasis, equilibrium,* and *steady state* (Evans 1976 : 190). Yet in their framework, Compton and Galaway (1979 : 81) confuse them, treating the concepts as one and the same thing. This is a significant error and it highlights one of the problems associated with using analogies from the physical sciences and uncritically importing them for use within social work.

It is important to differentiate these concepts particularly because of their relationships to the concept of *entropy* and open-system and closed-system analysis. The terms *equilibrium* and *homeostasis* refer to aspects of closed system analysis. Homeostasis connotes the tendency for an organism to return to a state of rest that is relatively free of tension (Goldstein 1973 : 115). *Equilibrium* 'is similar to . . . homeostasis in that it refers to the processes in closed systems whereby they achieve a state of balance between the forces that bear upon them' (Evans 1976 : 191).

Now this is in contrast to an open system which receives continual inputs from other interdependent systems. Thus strain and tension are 'endemic to them because they are concerned with growth and elaboration' (Evans 1976 : 190). It was Buckley who argued that the term 'steady state' more accurately captured the way in which open systems not only maintain their structure but elaborate and change it in response to internal and external stimuli. As Forder remarks, 'The steady state is not a condition of equilibrium, but a condition short of equilibrium, in which some degree of tension is a permanent feature' (Forder 1976 : 25).

If this distinction is not kept clearly in mind, it is very easy to confuse 'social integration' with 'system integration' (Evans 1976 : 189). In fact, as Leighninger (1977 : 47) asks, 'Is every part related to every other part? How much integration is necessary to establish the existence of a whole? This should be a matter for investigation, not assumption.' He goes on to suggest that the danger of not asking these questions is to make the assumption that there is total integration. If this happens, the systems analyst is

liable to be locked into a defense of all aspects of the status quo because they may be necessary to the operation of the system.

Because of the stress on equilibrium and integration that is part of the biological heritage of systems theory, the approach lends itself easily to conservative, status-quo, political positions.

(Leighninger 1977 : 47)

On differentiating 'social integration' and 'system integration' Evans (1976 : 189) notes that the former of these is concerned with the degree of co-operation or conflict in society while the latter is concerned with the causal links of interdependence between groups and institutions. Causal interdependence need not imply social harmony. In fact in an open systems analysis there is nothing in the *method* of analysis itself which prevents the introduction of elements of power, conflict, and tension (see Forder 1976 : 28–31; Leighninger 1977 : 46). Leonard (1975a : 48), for example, claims that it is not the use of systems theory itself by which Pincus and Minahan have a 'reified and consensus view of society', but rather that this results because of their use of particular values. Furthermore, Leighninger (1977 : 48) suggests that open systems analysis may provide a framework for understanding the place of power in social work practice. Indeed, through continual feedback, information input can be seen as a form of power.

The failure to recognize the logic and potential use of systems analysis, over and above the way certain authors *choose* to apply it in particular instances, is a limiting and confusing aspect.

THE UTILITY OF SYSTEMS THEORY FOR SOCIAL WORK

The broad canvas

The first aspect most theorists mention is the potential afforded by systems analysis for considering a wide range of relevant systems which impinge on the focal system. This in turn, says Forder (1976 : 29), makes possible a review of a wider range of possible targets for intervention. By viewing systems in dynamic interaction with each other, it is claimed one becomes more aware of all the potential effects systems are having upon each other and this prevents a narrow unicausal, or simplistic approach to complex individual and social needs.

In this sense Vickery (1974 : 390) does not see general systems theory as an alternative theory to the many others from which social workers draw, but rather,

> we perceive it to be a theory that can help social workers to organize and integrate a multitude of perspectives and methodological approaches that may be used in attempts to achieve change of various kinds. . . . [It] serves to map out the variables in professional practice in such a way as to highlight the connections among variables within personality systems and within social systems. . . . [Its use] tends to encourage social workers to take into account a far wider range of variables than they otherwise might, and to see personal well-being not in terms of a static equilibrium, but in terms of openness to exchange with the environment.
>
> (Vickery 1974 : 390)

Indeed, Evans and Webb assert that:

> the systems approach, whatever its faults, has at least driven social work methods teachers (and some practitioners) to consider the wider structures within which clients live their lives and raises the possibility that it is an aspect of the system with which the client is interlinked which may be the problem rather than the individual *per se*.
>
> (Evans and Webb 1977 : 20)

However, it is alerting the social worker to the complex labyrinth of interdependent systems and the linkage of micro- and macro-systems which causes problems for those seeking to operationalize this theory in practice.

First, there is the tortuous business of deciding which is the 'focal' system. This relates to the concept of hierarchy of systems. While the presentation of a wider range of potential target systems may prevent the social worker from drawing a premature conclusion, little guidance on this point has been provided by social work application of 'systems analysis'. This is echoed by Drover and Schragge:

> it is . . . difficult to accept the idea that systems theory will provide a clear range of predictive alternatives for handling problems. The one thing systems cannot provide is a simple solution to a complex problem. If anything, it seems to compound the complexity. This

complexity results not only from the larger number of variables to be considered by a systems analysis, but also by the lack of explicit criteria upon which a hierarchy is organized.

(Drover and Schragge 1977 : 29–30)

Drover and Schragge argue that unless other substantive theory is invoked to guide the social worker's judgement, then the selection of some variables over others is merely arbitrary.

Leighninger (1977 : 46), in analysing the 'holistic promise' of systems theory, questions its contribution beyond the initial sensitization to the 'big picture'. 'If one stops to think, one realizes that *everything* cannot be equally relevant to everything else. . . . Can systems theory help to show us what is relevant? Can it rank variables according to relative importance?' (Leighninger 1977 : 46–47).

So while a systems analysis alerts the social worker to the range of possibilities which need to be taken into account both for assessment and for potential targets of intervention, systems theory *per se* provides no guidance or prescription on how the systems are to be placed in a hierarchy or which one(s) will become the focus for the social worker's attention.

Interaction

The second major claim of usefulness is the attention it gives to *interaction* between various systems, and within systems. This encourages an analysis of the interface between person and environment, between the individual and the structure in which that individual lives. As Leighninger points out:

systems theory represents a renewed interest in social, and particularly macrosocial, explanations of problems. . . . It provides a redress of the balance between sociological and psychological emphases which was swung in the latter direction by the psychotherapeutic preoccupations of the 1940s and 1950s.

(Leighninger 1977 : 45)

While not agreeing that systems theory *per se* has been responsible for this swing, it is fair to conclude that the form of analysis provided by systems theory has at least attempted to provide a conceptual tool for this to happen.

PROBLEMS ASSOCIATED WITH THE ANALOGISTIC METHOD AND ITS RELATIONSHIP TO REDUCTIONISM

Social systems analysis relies on observing a system at one level – its properties and how they relate to each other – and then moving to a system at some other level, where one can test to determine whether the properties and relationships are the same. 'Thus, a fact or phenomenon that is observed at one level suggests a hypothesis to be tested at all other levels' (Hearn 1974 : 343). The danger of this approach, however, is to assume there are similarities between different levels of system rather than treating this as hypothetical. Leighninger (1977 : 46) accuses systems theorists of making analogizing 'a major indoor sport'.

Buck argues that the kinds of analogies used in general systems theory are of the 'so what?' variety. 'Granting that you have shown that there is some analogy, what follows?. . . . [S]o they're structurally analogous, so what? My answer is "so nothing!"' (Buck 1956 : 225).

The use of analogy is condemned by Hoos, especially when it involves using aerospace systems analysis to tackle social problems:

> In the real world, there appears to be about as much justification for committing society's sundry malfunctioning systems to the care of a systems analyst whose sole claim to expertise is technical as to call a hydraulic engineer to cure an ailing heart because of his speciality in pumping systems. Although the term 'system' can be applied to both the space hardware and social problems, the inputs are vastly different, as are the controls and objectives.
> (Hoos 1969 : 23–24)

In social work, however, the problem relates to the use of structural analogies as well as to that of reductionism. This occurs by forcing one system of ideas into a mould that would fit another system that is, in fact, unlike it. The danger in this is that neither set of systems maintains its own integrity, especially when one is a theory of apples and the other a theory of oranges. While originating his ideas in biology, von Bertalanffy reaffirmed the fact that 'the organismic analogy does not imply "biologism", that is, reduction of social to biological concepts, but indicates system principles applying to both fields' (Stein 1974 : 52).

However, Drover and Schragge say the danger for social work is not reductionism to an organic analogy, but simplification. On the one hand systems analysis increases the scope of the range of interdependent variables to be considered, yet on the other, it is claimed there is likely to be a simplification of cause–effect relationships by the use of analogies. This is the kind of danger which Hoos has referred to in social policy, and that is the creation of artificial construction of reality (Drover and Schragge 1977 : 31).

While recognizing that systems theory has made some 'insightful contributions' to social work, particularly family practice, Drover and Schragge question the uncritical extension of the theory to other areas of practice, such as community organization, administration, planning, or policy: 'its extension is virtually impractical unless accompanied by alternative behavioural and historic theories' (Drover and Schragge 1977 : 29). It is difficult to disagree with their conclusion.

RELATIONSHIP OF 'SYSTEMS ANALYSIS' TO SOCIAL WORK

Uncritical acceptance of 'systems theory'

Where systems theory has been used in social work, it is the exception, rather than the rule, for this theory to be treated in a critical manner. Most writers appear to accept the basic tenets of systems theory as valid. Perhaps without exception they choose to select only parts of systems analysis which suit their own ends giving no explanation of how the selected parts relate to the theory as a whole. Maybe this reflects an 'eclectic' tradition in social work. However, if this is the case, then it is always open to enquire to what ends is systems theory being used? What goals does the worker have for his or her piece of intervention? What if there is no agreement on the meanings of the goals and no boundaries are discernible? Does this mean that the concept of a social welfare system is no more than private geometry, as Robert Albritton suggests (see Drover and Schragge 1977 : 31)? The apparent uncritical acceptance by social workers of this theory highlights the dangers of accepting any theory developed outside this discipline without first examining the validity of the construct, and second relating it to social work's own principal *modus operandi*.

214

Crude and simplistic applications of systems analysis

Second, it is important for any social work writer to make explicit in what ways he or she is using a particular theory derived from the social sciences. Some writers (e.g. Yanoov-Chetkow 1980; Watts 1978), mistakenly in my view, claim that the 'integrated' approaches to practice rely heavily on systems theory. Thus, in the case of Watts (1978), he has attributed many of the flaws of systems analysis to the integrated approaches in general and Pincus and Minahan (1973) in particular. Elsewhere (Roberts 1981), I have argued that the integrated approaches use only a crude and elementary form of systems analysis.

In the case of Pincus and Minahan the development of their 'client', 'action', 'target', and 'change agent' systems (Pincus and Minahan 1973 : 53–68) could be achieved without reference to systems analysis. These authors use 'systems' to denote 'collectivities' thus emphasizing the multi-faceted nature of assessment and intervention in social work situations. These authors do not discuss the use of systems analysis in their work; they do not study the structure and function of these systems, nor do they examine specific processes occurring within and between these systems, nor do they invoke social systems analysis for case analysis and assessment.

Goldstein claims he makes use of open systems analysis, however, his systems analysis is not integrated with the rest of his framework (Forder 1976 : 24).

It is enlightening to see how Goldstein proposes to use systems analysis. First 'the worker constructs his notion of the system in his own mind. This depends on the *range of circumstances* and things that he needs to encompass *relative to the task*. He then enlarges or narrows his field and the targets within it as the relevant strategies and goals become apparent' (Goldstein 1974 : 186). Like Watts (1978 : 35–6), I would question what these stressed phrases actually mean. Likewise what criteria does the worker use in order to 'enlarge or narrow his field and targets'? Goldstein does not demonstrate how systems theory informs these decisions.

It is interesting to study Goldstein's example (1973 : 106ff.). While asserting that 'its use for the analysis of the problem–client configuration may prescribe interventions or modalities of service . . .' (Goldstein 1973 : 117), Goldstein does not demonstrate how systems theory is used prescriptively with the case material presented. He says that as the social worker

> extends his study of the initially presented persons and problems to take into account *all of the relevant systems* in relation which affect and are affected by the conditions described, many avenues of attack are open to him. Which he selects depends upon the assumptions he makes about the nature and dynamics of the problem, his purposes and objectives, and the most effective point of entry.
>
> (Goldstein 1973 : 118; author's emphasis)

Presumably the social worker at this point needs to refer to substantive theories to make these judgements because it is not demonstrated that they are made on the basis of systems theory.

'All of the relevant systems' (my emphasis above) presupposes the social worker has used criteria external to systems analysis for deciding what is relevant. While systems theory tells us that systems may be interdependent, it does not tell us where to place the boundaries, and in as much as this has to be done to make some sense of the world, it is done using other criteria.

But having considered all of the relevant systems (somehow), Goldstein then proceeds with a set of 'coulds' for the social worker (1973 : 118). This is hardly prescription, or if it is, there is no apparent logic to it. In fact a choice has to be made and if that choice is going to rise above 'private geometry', a justifiable rationale for that choice must be made.

Goldstein concludes his chapter on the client 'in and as a system' as follows:

> a systems orientation, even with its exigencies and limitations of the practicalities of practice, would enable the social worker to determine and predict which sequence or combination of these functions would be most efficacious and where, within either his or other systems, they can best be implemented.
>
> (Goldstein 1973 : 119)

Unfortunately this is completely without substantiation or demonstration.

Goldstein (1974 : 186) maintains in using systems theory, 'determinations do not occur by chance, instead, they are the product of the careful study of order, relations and effect in a given system.' However, one does not come to a determination by mere 'study' alone, however careful, one has to resort to other strategies to determine priorities, relationships, interdependence, and so on.

So beyond announcing that a systems orientation 'gently nudges the profession' (Goldstein 1974 : 187) to recognize that all problems can no longer be viewed in uni-directional terms, and explicating its potential for broadening the scope of problems through inter-dependence, Goldstein gives no clue to how this analysis can actually be used.

In reviewing the case of Mr A., presented by Vickery (1974), one can ask what is the purpose of using *systems language* to describe the situation? Indeed Forder (Forder 1976 : 30–1) appropriately takes her to task for (i) failing to deal with goals and objectives in the systems analysis and diagram; (ii) failing to be clear about the central concept of 'transformation' in her analysis; and more seriously (iii) not taking' into account issues of power pertinent to Mr A.'s situation.

Vickery (1974 : 401) herself makes the astonishing comment after the case exposition:

> This outline of a practice model exemplified by the case of Mr A. *does not say anything new to social workers* but it does help to present a unified view of the social work processes and to identify what are likely to be the most effective and essential points of entry into the client and environment intersystem and the most appropriate inputs for the social worker to make.
>
> (Vickery 1974 : 401; my italics)

The latter part of this claim is totally suspect. While a systems analysis might assist in delineating relevant impinging systems on Mr A. and his environment (and that is a useful exercise in itself), the analysis *per se* gives no indication regarding likely effectiveness nor any indication apart from the worker's judgement regarding 'points of entry' and the 'most appropriate inputs'.

*Parallels between the 'integrated approaches' and
'social systems analysis'*

Interdependence and breadth of analysis

A central feature of social systems analysis is the assumption that the systems of a holon are interdependent. This parallels the assumption made by the 'integrated' frameworks of the interdependence between person and environment and their related systems. It is the identification of these various interdependent systems which will enable the practitioner to look for aetiology not necessarily confined to one system and as well to consider a variety of points for intervention.

Process vs. content

The debate from systems analysis concerning its 'substantive content' in contrast to its 'process of analysis' has a parallel in the integrated approaches. Both approaches have been criticized for their lack of explanatory power and hence their prescriptive capacity. The integrated frameworks, like systems analysis, provide process guidelines of one kind or another, but in order to make an assessment of a problem situation, and to choose techniques and skills for intervention, the user has to invoke other theory. The choice of this theory, in the absence of explicit criteria, has to be arbitrary. Whether in making a decision about a 'case' or providing guidelines for curriculum development, it has been shown (Roberts 1981) that other criteria have to be invoked.

In both instances, the problem which remains is the substitution of technical processes for a proper consideration of the substantive theories which might explain a problem in its historical and ideological context.

Use of analogy

Systems models employ the analogistic method whereby structures and functions observed to be present in one set of observations are *assumed* to be present in another context. As noted already, often this assumption is taken as fact rather than as something to be tested. The use of analogy in the ecological metaphor used by Germain and Gitterman (1980) presents such a problem. These authors do not acknowledge that unlike some biological and physical systems, social systems do not necessarily acquire an 'optimal' level of existence. If the biological metaphor is taken too literally in the principles which are applied to social systems, then it can be argued that social systems analysis should be used to help maintain a *particular* 'steady state', rather than another kind. This has led to the linkage of social systems analysis with structural functionalism, and hence its being labelled as a conservative form of analysis.

It should be noted however that both Evans (1976 : 189–90) and Leonard (1975a : 48) draw distinctions between the *logic and method* of systems theory, and the way it is *used*. Both these authors see a potential in the use of systems analysis for dealing with conflict, although they recognize it has been used by some writers to uphold the status quo (e.g. in Pincus and Minahan), because of the set of values they invoke (Leonard 1975a : 51). The same parallel can be drawn with the logic and design of the 'integrated' frameworks in contrast to the particular substantive content of the parts, e.g. the values underpinning the framework.

Reductionism

In attempting to deal with such a broad canvas, all integrated frameworks suffer from gross reductionism. Such a situation results in highly distorting the reality they claim to deal with.

Depoliticization

It is claimed (Drover and Schragge 1977 : 35) that systems theory, by introducing an 'aura of neutrality and scientific, technical know-how', has depoliticized practice. In a similar way, some frameworks provide technical solutions to ethical dilemmas. In both systems analysis and the use of 'integrated' frameworks, value positions, including political preferences, need to be invoked. Neither of the approaches will provide substantive content on these vital questions. The fault remains, that in attempting to provide a 'means', both approaches fail to provide explicit normative 'ends'. This can give the false impression that social work is an apolitical, technical activity. In fact, its very nature is about the power relationships between people and any 'technical' means will affect those power relationships, and hence take it into the arena of normative activity.

CONCLUSIONS

While systems analysis has a number of parallels with the development of the 'integrated' frameworks of practice, none of the frameworks are dependent upon this form of analysis, and each could be enunciated without it. Nevertheless, the parallels are striking: the attempt to cover a 'broad canvas' by looking for interdependent and interrelated systems at all levels; a form of 'analysis' with little or no explanatory or predictive capacity; and a substitution of technical processes for a proper examination of political and social theory.

Where systems analysis has been explicitly invoked, e.g. Goldstein (1973) and Vickery (1974), its uncritical use can be seen to compound the problems already faced by an 'integrated' framework. The lesson from this is the need for social work not to accept uncritically theories formulated within other disciplines. By so doing, social work stands in line to be targeted for criticism far beyond what it might have bargained for in the first place. The mere use of the word 'system' by Pincus and Minahan (1973) has resulted in the full weight of critique of systems theory falling on them as well. While this is not warranted, by the way such a term itself is used, the lesson is salutary in that social work needs to be critical about its use of words, especially those borrowed from other disciplines, and with a different history.

Part 4

CONTRIBUTION

Chapter Eleven

THE CONTRIBUTION OF 'INTEGRATED' THEORY TO SOCIAL WORK

The findings resulting from an analysis and evaluation of the conceptual frameworks representing 'integrated' theory in social work will be used as a basis for assessing the contribution that this type of theory makes to social work. In view of the problems outlined, the central contribution of this type of 'grand theory' is in the lessons it teaches us about undertaking theory construction on such a vast scale.

The listing of a 'catalogue of errors' should not be seen in a pejorative way. Nor does this question the motives of the authors. I have no doubt they were working hard to produce social work theory to assist practitioners to be more effective and efficient in their work, as well as for the advancement of the profession as a whole. While the demands are great for social workers to provide so many different types of services to assist in the resolution of personal and social problems, it is vitally important for there to be a clear point of reference to anchor social work activity and to ensure that practitioners understand why they undertake certain tasks and not others.

This central reference for social workers must be realistic. The mission for social work must be realizable in terms of the skills and techniques possessed by practitioners and in terms of the power and authority vested in social workers. Social work cannot be held responsible or accountable for things over which it has no control. For social workers to offer more to individual clients, or to society as a whole, than they know they can deliver, is both deceptive and foolish. While the frameworks studied here have attempted to provide a central point of reference, I believe they have been far too ambitious in what they say they offer.

Whatever the merits of this undertaking, at this point in social work's history, I believe it is not unfair to conclude that these attempts at 'integrated' theory on such a grand scale have so far failed. This points to the theoretical homework which social workers need to undertake in the future. If a long-term goal to construct theory of this kind becomes pressing in the future I believe the following needs will have to be met.

THE NEED FOR CONSISTENT USE OF NOMENCLATURE

The findings demonstrate the confusion which results from the differential and inconsistent usage of terms, even by the same author. This highlights the need to develop a meaningful terminology: one that accurately describes a reality and avoids reification and jargon. Hopefully, the closer a term is seen to reflect a reality, the more consistent its use will be. The effects of the differential and inconsistent use of terminology, as demonstrated here, have been serious.

First, unless writers define their own terms it is difficult and often impossible to attribute accurate meaning to them. Few writers do this, apparently making the assumption that the meaning of terms is self-evident, or that a range of terms is synonymous.

Second, when the meaning of basic terms is ambiguous it is difficult, if not impossible, to comprehend the component parts of formal theory construction, because these 'building blocks' or concepts comprising the theory are not properly explained. If these basic concepts are unclear, so too are the relationships between them, thus it is not easy to communicate with precision the theory being advocated.

Third, if the meaning of terms is unclear, then the reality which they are meant to represent is uncertain. This may account for Bartlett's comment that the term itself often becomes the reality. Time can then be spent in further definition of the 'term' or 'concept' without its ontology being clearly established. This time could be more fruitfully spent on making an accurate statement about reality in the first place.

Fourth, the meaning of terms is impeded by lack of clarity concerning the context of their use. Thus the writer's intention in his or her use of terms should be made explicit; for example, whether the terms can be used in an educational or practice context, or both.

Fifth, in addition to impeding the development of ideas and hence theory, the inconsistencies in terminology can be exploited by various critics who are able to attribute *any* meaning they like, whether because of real confusion or to suit their own purposes of criticism. Hence the problems associated with the terminology have resulted in critiques which take the debate nowhere, because each side has its own interpretation which remains 'private' because common ground in terms of meaning is never established.

The Milford Conference noted the confusion in terminology even then, and called for research in order to bring clarity to the terms and the reality they were meant to describe. Since that time, more terms have been developed, older terms used inconsistently, and still no proper research has been carried out to bring some order into this situation.

While the call for empirical research to accurately explicate practice realities remains current, it can be argued that the continued use of *these* terms, even with careful definition, will prove troublesome. Terms by their day-to-day usage take on a particular meaning for their users, regardless of the differential usage and confusion which results. The word 'generic', for example, is still being used *as if* it had an agreed-upon meaning within the profession (e.g. Bailis 1985).

The implications of this situation are clear, that until and unless writers are clear about the concept they are trying to communicate and choose a unique term for that concept, then further research and theory development will be impeded. I am not suggesting that terms become straitjackets and are used to stifle the recognition of diversity, confusion, and inconsistency. It is clear, however, that one cannot go on using terms which have a history of differential use and hope to effectively communicate ideas to others.

It does appear that a major difficulty rests in attempts to make one term represent an idea which is too complex, for example the term 'common base'. Terms are invented as shorthand devices for portraying ideas. Despite the inconvenience which can result from a long-hand description of an idea, this would appear to be the preferable course of action until there is a wider agreement on terminology and a more consistent use of that terminology.

THE NEED TO BE LESS AMBITIOUS
AND LESS IDEALISTIC

In order for both social work and its theoretical development to progress it is necessary for their domain to be less ambitious, less idealistic about what might be desirable in an ideal world. It is necessary to link any conceptual and theoretical activity to the 'real' world. It is necessary to link the ideals to the realities of social work's place in a particular society (or community), to the sanctions given to social work by different levels of government, to the techniques available to social work practitioners to achieve desired outcomes at a particular time and in a particular place, and to the powers and authorities which social workers have.

I agree with Howe (1980 : 321–3), that social work, at least in some countries of the world, is valued and has a legitimate place, but its mission is not furthered by either immodest purposes or the 'high baroque' in theory development. It is clear that 'integrated' theory has itself attempted to achieve too much without being explicit about what exactly this is.

What social work has been striving to achieve since its early beginnings is clear occupational identity. It was the explicit need to help define clear occupational boundaries which concerned Bartlett (1970). However, it has been the confusion of purpose for the development of subsequent 'integrated' frameworks which has clouded the issue: each framework is expected to fulfil too many functions – to help define occupational boundaries, provide guidelines for practice, provide underpinning theory for the skills of practice, and so on.

These claims became more ambitious as frameworks of this genre burgeoned: they were expected to do more and more, they took on a life of their own, which at least in some cases appeared to supersede all other conceptualizations. Bartlett (1970) clearly limited her work: she was writing *about* practice, she was providing ideas to help link a variety of different concerns of social work to a 'common base' in order to provide (among other things) a common occupational identity in order for social work to develop in its own unique path.

The components of Bartlett's 'common base' were described in a crude way, but at least this started writers thinking about how these components provided the foundations for a social work 'thinking' which might have the potential for linking quite disparate types of practice. What subsequent writers did was to *leave* these components of the 'base' in this crude form. Then they proceeded to build a more complex framework onto a base which had in no way been validated. Indeed more and more capabilities were assumed for the base of the framework on the assumption that it had been validated, just because it had been *described* in a particular manner.

At this stage, social work needs to properly document what it does, rather than formulating what it would like to do in an ideal world. Such a call echoes the call put out at Milford!

THE NEED TO LIMIT THE UNIVERSALITY OF THE CLAIMS

In making no effort to define their applicability within a particular social or geographic context, the frameworks make universal claims, implying that they can be applied in any setting, either within one country or in other cultures or geographic locations.

In the absence of evidence on the viability and utility of importing theories to foreign settings (see e.g. Midgley 1981), the author(s) ought to detail the setting from which the framework grew, and the setting in which its operationalization has applicability. In other words, it cannot be assumed that a framework has any universality until this can be tested.

In addition to failing to properly locate a framework in an historical context at a particular point in time, there has been a failure to consider the usefulness of frameworks within the one country but with different socio-economic-educational groups. The frameworks of Compton and Galaway (1979) and Loewenberg (1977), for example, rely on a high degree of rationality and decision making on the part of the 'client'. They assume a capacity and motivation on the part of the client to be articulate about his or her needs, to be self-determining, and able to put into practice a 'rational' plan of action. Even within the one geographic area, levels of motivation and capacity to be self-determining vary. Even more so when one crosses socio-cultural and sub-cultural boundaries with an increased differentiation in terms of education, access to resources, and life needs.

It has been shown that not only are historical variables important to the definition of social work within one country, but more so when those factors result in quite different conceptualizations and methods of practice between different countries (see e.g. Kendall 1973, 1977).

The clear implication is the need to consider how contextual factors have been influential in the development of particular approaches to practice at particular times. Furthermore, it cannot be assumed that a framework of practice will be viable in another context, particularly as the key elements of 'purpose', 'values', and 'knowledge' change. In addition, the role of social work within various social welfare systems cannot be assumed to be the same in all instances. Thus the usefulness of a particular framework of practice cannot be assumed, unless some relationship to a context can be demonstrated.

Such appraisals can only be undertaken by cross-cultural studies and the application of frameworks and techniques across these boundaries. The amount of published material in this regard is very scarce. What material does exist suggests that the particular socio-economic-cultural and geographic contexts vitally affect the application of frameworks and techniques (Midgley 1981 and Kendall 1977).

Thus in developing proper guidelines for practice it is clear that at least at this point in time, claims about the applicability should be more modest rather than universal. Such applications are to be tested and reported on in the future. Until this happens, it is desirable that frameworks and techniques be seen in particular and limited contexts.

Furthermore, the ambiguous use of the words 'society' and 'environment' requires clarification. Proper debate cannot occur until the domain over which the theory has applicability is defined. To remain unsure if 'society' or 'environment' refer to an immediate 'social milieu' or the whole of society, means that an assessment of 'integrated' theory and its relationship to the 'radical critiques' cannot proceed in any meaningful way.

THE NEED TO DEAL ADEQUATELY WITH BOTH 'BREADTH' AND 'DEPTH' ISSUES

This study demonstrates the difficulty of dealing with 'depth' and 'breadth' issues at the same time, and in the end shows these attempts prove unsuccessful because they fail to deal adequately with either. By 'breadth' issues I mean the attempt to set parameters for the profession of social work, to develop a conceptual framework on which all relevant practice activities can be mapped, and provide the justification for the multifarious activities of social work. By 'depth' I mean an examination of the minutiae of details required for the individual 'acts of practice'. Unless both these sets of activities can be linked there is the danger of individual acts of practice becoming ends in themselves rather than means to a particular end. At the other extreme there is the danger of drawing such grandiose and idealistic parameters for the occupation that there are few specific guidelines for the practitioner to follow in deciding upon acts of practice. In this latter case an effective technology is lacking and/or the required sanction is absent.

This is further evidenced by the failure in these frameworks to link theories of behaviour on the one hand, and theories of society on the other. It has been demonstrated that the frameworks fail to give a proper consideration of the nature of society and its effect upon the practice of social work in any given context. It has also been noted by some writers (e.g. Webb and Evans 1972) that many of the observations within sociology have failed to be taken up in social work. In all of the frameworks the emphasis is upon the psychological and individualistic components rather than the sociological and collective components. This is despite the claims that social work should deal with both. However, the ambiguity in presentation results in critics from either side being left dissatisfied, for example, Wilkes (1978) argues that the approach does not give sufficient attention to the individual, while Armstrong and Gill (1978) argue it does not concern itself enough with collectivities.

It is suggested that the undertaking as presently defined is too complex to deal adequately with both 'breadth' and 'depth' issues within the space of *one* framework. Parameters need to be explicitly set.

THE NEED TO RECOGNIZE THE PROCESSES OF THEORY CONSTRUCTION AND THEIR UNDERLYING ASSUMPTIONS

The authors under consideration have demonstrated a relatively simplistic understanding of theory construction and the different sets of underlying assumptions which affect that theory. Even in Siporin's text (1975) where a full glossary relating to the terminology of the nature of theory is included, there is not a corresponding treatment in the text itself which states clearly the theoretical status of the framework being developed. Furthermore, writers are prepared to use terms like 'theory', 'framework', 'model' in a haphazard manner.

There appears to be a lack of understanding about different types of theory construction. It is only by implication, or 'reading between the lines', that the theorist's approach to theory construction can be gleaned. In order for proper evaluation to take place, the assumptions of the author should be made as clearly as possible, including assumptions relating to theory construction.

Such defects in these social work writings are possibly related to a lack of understanding concerning the philosophy of 'knowledge' and 'theory'. An implication of this is the need for social workers to have both more input and better teaching of these matters to ensure they can be applied in their work.

THE NEED TO DEVELOP PRINCIPLES TO HELP GUIDE THEORY CHOICE

It is argued that in developing guidelines for practice it is necessary to develop criteria by which the practitioner can choose from a variety of sources of information, knowledge, or theory. One of the features of 'integrated' theory is it sets broad parameters for practice which increases the number of factors which have to be taken into account in making assessments and interventions. In addition to increasing the number of variables, it also increases the amount of knowledge and theory from within and outside social work required because of its attempt to deal with both personal problems as well as public issues, the individual client as well as the larger groups of clientele, and others.

It has been shown that while these approaches increase the number of variables to be taken into account, they provide no criteria to assess the relative importance of these variables. For example, they provide no criteria by which to develop a hierarchy of importance of factors to influence an assessment. Thus the practical implication of this is to widely increase the number of variables required to be considered by the practitioner but to provide no tools as to how this might be achieved systematically and within realistic constraints of time and personnel. While this approach has the advantage of delaying assessment until all 'relevant' factors are taken into consideration, it does not give any assistance in the determination of what is 'relevant'. Thus the assignment is complex, but in the end other factors have to be invoked, such as other theory, ideology of the practitioner, and so on.

There is no guidance for the choice of material 'borrowed' from other sources; there is no direction as to what is more likely to achieve particular ends. Thus the practitioner is mainly left with his or her 'practice wisdom' or 'professional judgement': both nebulous qualities which one assumes can only be acquired over time, and then based upon implicit rather than explicit theory.

The implication from this is the need to develop criteria by which the relative importance of data collection at the assessment stage can be evaluated. Second, the development of criteria by which the utility of material 'borrowed' from relevant disciplines can be assessed.

A further implication for practice is the necessity to determine priority of intervention on behalf of different people with different circumstances. It can no longer be assumed that people's interests and needs are compatible. It has already been demonstrated by way of example that there are groups of people, all with legitimate claims to client status, but whose needs are often opposed to each other's and in conflict. A failure to have explicit criteria for choice means that social work resources will be used haphazardly. For example, there is nothing within 'integrated' theory to direct its interests towards one group of people (e.g. the poor and disadvantaged) or to another. To assume, on the other hand, that social work has the power and resources to deal with *everyone* is naïve.

Thus the theoretician needs to be aware of the influence of ideology on theory construction, and most importantly the requirement to explicate the assumptions which underpin a particular theory.

THE NEED TO ESTABLISH PROPER RELATIONSHIPS BETWEEN DIFFERENT THEORIES

'Integrated' theory differentiates between 'practice theory' and 'theory for practice'. While this might serve a worthwhile purpose, it has not been demonstrated how the two types of theory can be linked or integrated. Thus this separation remains of little use as far as operationalization of the theory is concerned.

It has been shown that the use of theories and knowledge 'borrowed' from other disciplines can influence the practitioner and can distract the user from the central purposes and goals of social work to the purposes and goals of those other disciplines. However, social work remains dependent upon this 'borrowed' material for at least part of its operation. Thus to avoid the risks described above it is necessary to demonstrate concretely in what ways particular knowledge and theory from other sources can be used in the service of social work purposes.

This task will involve an analysis of the assumptions upon which social work is predicated and the assumptions of the borrowed materials. This analysis will involve the entities of 'social work' and 'borrowed materials' being broken down into small components, because different parts of each of these components are predicated upon different assumptions. Within discipline boundaries, knowledge and theory develop because of different assumptions which are made about the nature of man, the nature of knowledge, and so on. Such conflicts can be demonstrated in the differences between existential and phenomenological versus behaviourist approaches in psychology, and structural–functional and conflict–critical approaches in sociology.

This study of 'integrated' theory has shown that no such detailed study has been made of 'borrowed' knowledge. As indicated previously the principle of eclecticism has operated. Without an explication of the assumptions there can be no development of predictive theory.

A further serious consequence of 'borrowing' ideas, theory, and terminology, is the risk of having the social work framework branded with the faults of the materials being borrowed. A clear example of this is the link between 'integrated' theory and social systems analysis.

The implication in both the above instances is the need for an author to be quite explicit about how 'borrowed' material is being used and how the social work theory is similar to and different from the borrowed material. In the case of Pincus and Minahan (1973) one might conclude that given their framework does not depend on 'social systems analysis' the term 'system' should have been avoided altogether.

THE NEED TO RECOGNIZE THE EXISTENCE
OF OTHER PARADIGMS

The preponderance of sociological positivism has been demonstrated. However, if debate is to proceed in an informed manner, at least the existence of other sets of assumptions requires recognition. My argument is not that a particular paradigm should or should not be used, but the need to acknowledge the existence of other sets of assumptions which may result in the construction of different theory. In order for theory to be challenged, in order for events and relationships of events to be accounted for in different ways, conflicting accounts need to be weighed up against each other. Lecomte's (1975) study illustrates the use of a descriptive versus a dialectic approach in contrasting different sets of underpinning assumptions. Rojek (1986) argues for the need to study the 'continuities' between theories as well as their 'oppositions'. However, in order to undertake such a process, differences and conflicts need to be *recognized* before their effects can be taken into account. By and large the theory under consideration here does not even recognize conflict and difference. It is presented *as if* agreement exists. Such an assumption clouds reality and in as much as it does, inaccurate theory results.

THE NEED TO MAKE EXPLICIT THE PURPOSE OF FUTURE THEORY

There are similarities and differences of purposes in each of the frameworks examined in relation to the deployment of a 'common base', the treatment of the *interface* between 'person and environment', the universality of the claims, and the confusion in purpose in relation to providing an introductory text for educational purposes on the one hand, and developing a coherent frame of reference for the purpose of guidelines for practice on the other.

A significant implication arising from this is the need to clearly relate a framework to others already in use, and to explicitly identify the similarities and points of difference. To lump frameworks together in very crude categories (e.g. the move towards 'unifying concepts' (Billups 1984; Rosenfeld 1983)) masks important differences.

Furthermore, it is important to demonstrate a theory's historical context. The creation of conceptual tools grows from a writer's experience and this experience has been influenced by practice within a socio-cultural context. To present 'new' ideas as if they were generated in a vacuum does not reinforce a writer's innovation, but rather has the effect of masking the experiences and context which helped formulate that innovation. A fundamental part of this is the experience of the writer not only in terms of his or her personal background, beliefs, and values, but also the particular set of professional experiences.

The failure of the American authors in particular to make reference to similar work elsewhere reinforces the insularity and ethnocentrism of their theory.

THE NEED TO REDUCE THE GAP BETWEEN SOCIAL WORK AND OTHER DISCIPLINES

This study has revealed the lack of flow of information from other disciplines into social work, despite social work's dependence upon other related disciplines for 'knowledge' and 'theory'. This is most obvious in relation to the sociology of social problems and the nature of 'society'. Its breakdown has occurred at two levels: between other disciplines like sociology, political science, etc., and second, between social work and philosophical enquiry: both moral philosophy and the philosophy of knowledge.

The dependence of social work upon knowledge and theory from other sources has always been acknowledged. However, despite the recognition of the skew psychological-type knowledge has had upon social work, the predominance of psychology over other disciplines remains. That it remains with 'integrated' theory which claims to redress the balance between psychological and sociological concerns, is problematic.

Evans and Webb (1977) suggest reasons why the discipline of sociology has had comparatively little impact on the practice of social work. Likewise, one can open for investigation why major related concerns from economics, politics, religion, have played such an insignificant part in the writings of authors claiming to be interested in the 'person-in-society'. For an informed social work assessment, it is not adequate to consider only the variables that present themselves through a client's perception and description of particular needs or problems. These must be understood against a socio-political-cultural backdrop if the reasons for this state of affairs are to be understood and if any hope of remedy is contemplated. To perceive stated needs and problems only in psychological terms, or even broader social welfare terms, is inadequate.

Furthermore, because social work intervention is about choice, and choice involving human beings, then the ethical basis of that decision making is likewise important. Lawrence (1983, 1985, 1986) calls for a study of moral philosophy so that social work can develop its justification through detailed moral analysis. While the author agrees with this, unless there is a direct connection to social work 'reality' and practice, then an isolated study of moral philosophy will most likely end up in the same position as disciplines like sociology: there will be little explicit application.

THE NEED FOR A REALISTIC DESCRIPTION OF THE PURPOSES OF SOCIAL WORK

To develop social work theory, a clear understanding of the goals to be achieved is required. Thus it is necessary to consider the purposes or 'mission' of social work. This undertaking is not easy mainly because of the breadth and ambitiousness of social work purposes (Howe 1980). An approach which attempts to take into consideration this whole has a mammoth task ahead.

However, this is not assisted by 'artificially' limiting the breadth of purpose or deliberately ignoring a significant component of it. What is essential is to give recognition to the various and divergent aspects. A recognition of conflict of purpose is necessary, given that social work has different relationships to 'society' (Cowger 1977). The cause of many problems is the view that *one* version represents the *whole* of social work, without due recognition being given to conflicting view points. The theorists under discussion in this book have a propensity to create the impression of homogeneity and consensus, rather than heterogeneity and conflict, in the purposes of social work.

Having recognized this, then the purpose of *any* theory is to attempt to accurately account for this state of affairs, and to give some explanation as to why this is. What is imperative is the need to clearly differentiate between description and prescription.

An endemic problem in the analysis and evaluation of 'integrated' theory has been caused by the failure of authors to be clear on whether they are describing a reality *or* prescribing what ought to happen under certain circumstances. The problem with the frameworks under study is that the aims of the authors in relation to prescription and description remain unclear and therefore the reader is given no basis on which to justify the conclusions.

Both the descriptive and prescriptive elements need to be developed: an analysis of various practices as they occur, and a justification of

235

why they ought or ought not to occur. To take the former of these positions by itself can result in the continuation of practices to meet some (often undefined) end which has not been justified except in terms of perhaps meeting someone's current need. To pursue the latter path of writing from the prescriptive view point alone, while providing an argued justification, can result in the 'opinion' being seen in a vacuum and removed from the real contexts of day-to-day practice.

For a start it is suggested that writers make it clear what route they are following. A task at some future point in time will be the linking of both the descriptive and prescriptive aspects of practice and how they affect social work theory.

THE NEED TO GIVE DUE RECOGNITION TO SOCIAL WORK'S PROFESSIONAL RESPONSIBILITIES

'Integrated' theory, as characterized by the eleven conceptual frameworks studied here, appears to view social work as an 'applied science'. As such the frameworks neglect to give due weight to the sanctions, both prescriptive and proscriptive, under which social work operates; its power and authority base; its rights and obligations; and the available techniques to fulfil its defined purposes.

The behaviour of social workers is not directed *solely* by social science theory. Social work behaviour is deployed within a context, and that context is affected by the way social work is viewed by key institutions of that context. Thus social work theory needs to take these influences into consideration.

CONCLUSIONS

This chapter has looked at the implications which arise from study and evaluation of the eleven conceptual frameworks which represent 'integrated' theory in social work. These implications for the future development of social work theory are a legacy left to us by writers attempting to develop 'integrated' theory. In terms of what can be learnt from this 'movement', especially in terms of what to avoid in the future, the contribution has been considerable. Santayana once remarked, 'Those who do not know their history are condemned to repeat it.' If this is a valid observation, then it is very important that the lessons from attempts to develop 'integrated' theory are recorded and known, so the same mistakes will not be replicated.

This chapter has listed a series of needs which will require addressing if such large-scale attempts at social work theory continue to be undertaken in the future. I believe, however, that at this point in social work's history we are not ready to undertake theory construction on such a scale. The requirements are too complex and such a task should be undertaken by a 'practitioner–research–theorist'.

In the meantime, the interests of social work and its clients will be better served if the goals for theory construction are more modest, and its approach to theory more rigorous. I am not optimistic that such grand theory construction will cease. However, if the subject matter is narrowed, that is, if social work's purposes are more realistically delineated, and if the aims of its theory are better explicated, then there will be a greater chance of achieving something which is not only a more accurate account and explanation of social work thinking and action, but will be better able to direct social workers' actions for more effective practice.

Part 5

CONCLUSION

Chapter Twelve

THE NEED FOR A MORE MODEST AND RIGOROUS SOCIAL WORK THEORY

This study commenced with the assumption that the development of 'integrated' theory in social work was a useful way of bringing divergent elements of the profession into a coherent whole. These divergent elements were apparent at the professional organizational level, where different approaches to practice based on 'methods', fields, settings, social problems, or practice techniques, encouraged disparate interest groups to form and to specialize. This had adverse effects for social work theory development because many of these separate undertakings made little or no attempt to relate to a defined 'social work' frame of reference. It also resulted in some problems being initially assessed by specialists which meant that suggested solutions were skewed toward the specialists' own interests and skills rather than considering the range of aetiology of a problem before embarking on any form of intervention. Furthermore, failure to relate 'borrowed' theory from other professions and the socio-behavioural sciences to a social work frame of reference posed the risk that social workers would merely try to emulate these often more prestigious occupational groups.

While 'integrated' theory attempted to consolidate these disparate approaches, it has been concluded on the basis of a study and evaluation of a number of conceptual frameworks representing this genre that their most significant contribution to social work has been the 'lessons' which can be learnt from this 'catalogue of mistakes'. If theory construction on such a broad scale is going to continue, then there are many concerns and needs which will have to be addressed. These form the basis of Chapter 11. The identification of these needs really calls for a period now in which social workers do some 'stocktaking'. This stocktaking needs to be undertaken by the combined efforts of both practitioners and academics. Indeed, while recognizing some historical circumstances which have kept these two sub-cultures relatively separate, a major implication of this study is the need for these two sides to make greater efforts to establish cordial relations. Had cordial relations existed between the practice and theoretical sub-cultures in the past, then perhaps some of the mistakes identified in this study may never have occurred.

The concerns which Bartlett raised are still very relevant. Social work stands to lose its *raison d'être* unless it can state quite clearly what it is about, what it can realistically achieve, and what skills it has at its disposal. With increasingly limited resources social workers cannot afford to be the idealists they were in the 1960s. No funding agency will believe that social work by itself can cure such a wide range of ills from individual problems of coping through to structural changes to rectify political and social inequities. The rhetoric of accepting special responsibility for problem solving at the interface of 'person and environment' sounds impressive, even if a little unconvincing. So far, the exact meaning of this 'interface' has escaped practical explanation.

As a start, I believe social workers need to recognize their diversity instead of trying to *create* similarities. While international collectivities of social workers exist, thus signalling that a wide cross-section of practitioners is ready to identify with the term 'social work', it only takes a short time while attending an international conference, for example, to observe the very real differences which exist between social workers from different countries: how they conceptualize their assignment and the actions they propose to meet it. I was struck by this incongruity at one international conference where a North American social worker was elaborating on her latest dream analysis which she claimed benefited her clients. At the same time a social worker from the depressed countryside of Thailand was talking about the problems of obtaining suitable manure fertilizer to assist crop growth in a poor rural area. Their assessment of problems, their mandate as they perceived it, their education and skills, appeared at face value to be vastly different. Instead of masking these by looking for commonality, it may be better to start by recognizing the differences.

The same incongruities can often be observed in the very different types of intervention of social workers within one country and working with different social classes, different ethnic groups, urban or rural populations, disadvantaged or privileged groups, and so on. To assume there is one social work mission, let alone uniformity in intervention, is problematic. What enables social workers to identify with one occupational category when one practitioner is quite content to help clients adjust to the demands of the status quo, and another is outraged by certain social and economic arrangements and does all he or she can to change them? These two types of social workers can be observed in practice. Again, I believe it will be more productive in the long run to recognize these differences rather than imposing a false 'commonality', and to describe their various frames of reference rather than attempt an all-inclusive generalization. The latter is usually fairly meaningless.

The Milford Conference called for a more accurate description of the social work task. I believe this assignment has yet to be successfully undertaken in such a way that differences of mission for social work as well as practice are fully recorded, and where the researcher is able to maintain a clear separation between description and prescription. I believe that the need for a close liaison if not total integration between the theorist and practitioner has been well argued. An accurate description and analysis of practice, and an understanding of this, will only occur through studies by the 'practitioner–research–theorist'. To be realistic these studies need to be small-scale, they need to be culture and sub-culture specific. They need to focus on the 'peculiarities' of practice taking into account the client population, particularly race, class, gender, and its social location. The effects of context affect both the types of problems and how they are identified as well as the efficacy of preferred intervention methods and skills. A recognition of this will at least make practitioners cautious of importing concepts, ideas, skills, and techniques which have been developed under one set of circumstances for use in an entirely different set of circumstances.

The concepts of 'disadvantage' and 'need', as well as the differential effects of social welfare systems, need to be taken into account. Thus practitioners need to be wary of social work theory developed in another country. Even importation of theory between western countries can pose problems and this can only be magnified when ideas are imported from highly-developed and industrialized countries to the Third World. The power and authority given to social workers varies enormously from setting to setting. However much social workers would like to believe their practice was not constrained in some way by a variety of sanctions, the reality is that all occupational groups and professions operate under various types of approval. This factor then forms an important part of how a practitioner will work. Thus the influence of this should be clearly acknowledged in theory.

I do not wish to endorse the idea that social workers should never attempt to find commonalities in the various endeavours, nor seek to make generalizations across practice contexts. However, after a critical examination of 'integrated' theory it would appear that the making of generalizations and the seeking of commonalities will have a much better chance of being accurate, and thus useful for theory development, after accurate scrutiny of small-scale practice tied to various contexts. To start from the general and move to the specific runs a high risk of imposing prescriptions in the absence of properly understood descriptions.

I am not saying either that social work theory will only be enhanced by perpetuating what 'is'. What I am trying to emphasize is that the differences between accurate description and justified prescription need to be made quite clear. Masking differences in the pursuit of integration or generalizing in order to deal with timeless, contextless problems of interest to social workers, will inhibit proper understanding and therefore useful theory.

Social workers who write about their experiences, their problems, and attempted solutions, need to be particularly cautious that they make explicit the assumptions they are making about their work. The influences from positivism have already been noted. I believe many social workers in the past have not written about their experiences and their practice because they have been of the opinion that it would not be of interest to others, or that it was not rigorously developed in terms of a methodology. I am not wanting to encourage 'sloppy' thinking or writing, but often this failure to recognize something as a viable practice intervention has been because the practitioner has thought it would not stand the 'test of methods'. Yet the 'method' often has been perceived only in terms of the dictates of positivism, without the realization that this belongs only to one paradigm of meta-theory which can be used in developing and testing theory.

The mere realization that there is nothing axiomatic about theory formed on the basis of positivist assumptions may be sufficient to encourage social workers to value the theory resulting from other sets of assumptions. In this way it would seem that the processes involved in the development of informal theory should be given recognition.

Few writers are willing to share any part of themselves, their beliefs, hopes, and aspirations. Perhaps this also has resulted from the dictates of positivism whereby knowledge creation is seen as something external to the theorist. However, the influence of personal ideology may have a considerable bearing on the choice of subject for investigation as well as the method of investigation. The 'theorist in the theory' needs much greater attention than heretofore. The motives of the researcher form part of this influence and may have a decisive effect on the research effort. The researcher who grew up in a culture of poverty or discrimination (if he or she has survived) is quite likely to have different motives and purposes than the researcher who has been brought up in privileged circumstances and who now wants to 'look through the window' and then withdraw.

Likewise, at least some people enter social work because they believe they have a responsibility to facilitate change. This might be to help an individual or a neighbourhood or a group change some of their ways of behaving merely to survive or with a slightly improved quality of life. This responsibility might be to help some people cope better with separation, or grief, or find a better home, or hospice. It might be to help a person gain a little more information about themselves or about their immediate social world. On the other hand, this responsibility might be seen by others as raising some people's conscience about their circumstances in life whether that relates to their housing, their place in the workforce, their powerlessness in relation to social systems, or the repercussions resulting from their gender, skin colour, ethnicity, or sexual orientation. By a reconsideration of their place in society, their power or lack of it, and their motivation to change, some structural changes may be brought about.

Whatever its focus, such a responsibility and its concomitant duties should not be diminished by its relegation to formulae for practice. Often the motivation of practitioners comes from a personal recognition of these responsibilities. What is important for social work is that its practitioners are able to articulate a public justification for their intervention into these concerns, and further, can describe, no matter how crudely, a reasonable *modus operandi*. It would be unreasonable at this point in time to say that any means will justify a particular end, particularly in financial terms. Nevertheless, social workers must take even more care now that both their ends and their means are properly accounted for.

The 'integrated' theory studied in this book has shown quite clearly that a failure to state ends in reasonably concrete terms makes it impossible to justify any particular means simply because it is not quite clear what they are going to be used to achieve.

Underlying much of what I am saying is the need to encourage in future social workers an attitude which will value the need for properly designed theory. This will not be achieved if students leave the universities and colleges with some kind of 'distaste' or even fear of theory, and believe they can safely leave that to the academics at the places of learning they have left. The hopes and aspirations of the 'integrated' theorists have not resulted in a greater appreciation of the complexity and variety of theory construction, nor of the range of differing assumptions which can be made. Such requires greater understanding of the enterprise of theory construction and its influence from the gathering of data itself through to how this is eventually interpreted and used for practice.

As the social work assignment is becoming increasingly diversified, so the social work curriculum is becoming increasingly overloaded. Internationally there are marked differences in length of courses. Especially in two-year social work programmes, the amount of specialist knowledge which has to be 'crammed in' is massive. Yet, the mere adding of content without a sound appreciation of theory construction will provide no tools for the social worker to evaluate others' efforts or to feel a part of the responsibility to foster and develop useful social work theory for the future.

The proponents of 'integrated' theory have been far too ambitious in their aims, too naïve and simplistic in their attitude towards theory construction, and too impractical in their aspirations for social work. Their intentions and motives to further the causes of social work are not questioned. The difficulty of the assignment they undertook is recognized. However, their attempts have failed.

It is my hope that social work has moved *beyond* the era of the 'high baroque', to a conception of itself which is more manageable: a conception which is more confined to specific responsibilities within specific contexts. Social work cannot be 'all things to all people'. It needs to be more modest in its domain and this will enable a more rigorous approach to its theory.

NOTES

GENERAL EDITOR'S FOREWORD

1 Gladstone, I. (1955) 'How social is social work?', quoted by L. Rapoport in 'In defence of social work', *FWA, Social Work*, April 1962, p.12.
2 Quoted in *The Principle of Normalisation of Human Services*, by W. Wolfenberger, p.59.

CHAPTER THREE: 'THEORY' AND 'ACTION ', 'PRACTICE THEORY', AND 'THEORY FOR PRACTICE'

1 For a history of the concepts of 'theory' and 'practice', see Lobkowicz (1967).
2 Studies observing practitioner behaviour have a significant contribution to make to the development of social work theory. See, for example, Wallace (1980); Raynes *et al.* (1982); O'Connor and Dalgleish (1986); Sheldon (1986); Hallett (1983); Mispelblom (1985); Reay (1986); Vreugdenhil (unpublished).

CHAPTER FOUR: META-THEORY: 'ENDS' AND 'MEANS', AND THE CONTEXT OF PRACTICE

1 Goldberg and Warburton (1979) provide an interesting empirical description of practice as it relates to 'ends' and 'means'. Their study, however, is in no way justificatory.
2 Although writing in a different context there are some similarities between this argument and that of Fay (1975 : 74ff.) in his explication of an 'interpretive social science'.

CHAPTER FIVE: EXPLICATION AND CRITIQUE OF FOUR CONCEPTUAL FRAMEWORKS

1 Reference is made to Goldstein (1973, 1974, 1975, 1975a, 1977, 1981, 1982, 1982a, 1983, and 1983a). Reviews of his work have been made by

Specht (1974), Meyer (1974), Nelson (1975), and Seed (1975).

2 Further aspects of this critique are elaborated in Roberts and Zulfacar (1986).

3 Statham (1978 : 5) notes: 'There is a gentle, almost imperceptible slide from principles and theories designed to operate in private psychoanalytic practice to social work whose locus of activity is mainly in large, bureaucratically organized agencies with boundaries set by statute.'

CHAPTER TEN: RELATIONSHIP TO SOCIAL SYSTEMS ANALYSIS

1 The terms 'systems theory', 'systems analysis', 'systems models' are variously used (Roberts 1981 : 223). In view of the disputed theoretical status (is it a 'theory', a 'meta-theory', an exercise in modelling, an ideology, or a *Weltanschauung?*) (Roberts 1981 : 223), I prefer to use the term 'systems analysis' because as used in social work, it primarily provides procedures for analysing complex situations. It does not provide explanations of situations, and thus has little prescriptive capacity.

REFERENCES

Addams, J. (1960) *Jane Addams: A Centennial Reader*, New York: Macmillan.

Akhurst, C. (1977) Book review of Specht and Vickery *Integrating Social Work Methods, British Journal of Social Work* 7(4) : 487–8.

Albritton, R. (1976) *The Systems Approach: A Marxist Critique*, Toronto: York University.

Alexander, C.A. (1977) 'Social work practice: a unitary conception', *Social Work* 22(5) : 407–14.

Alexander, C.A. (1981) 'Reactions to the working statement on purpose', *Social Work* 26(1) : 87–8.

Allport, F.H. (1955) *Theories of Perception and the Concept of Structure*, London: John Wiley.

Anders, J.R. (1975) 'Internationalism in social work education', *Journal of Education for Social Work* 11(1) : 16–21.

Anderson, C.H. (1974) *Toward a New Sociology*, Homewood, Illinois: Dorsey Press.

Anderson, J.D. (1982) 'Generic and generalist practice and the BSW curriculum', *Journal of Education for Social Work* 18(3) : 37–45.

Anderson, J.D. (1983) 'Generic and generalist practice and the BSW curriculum', paper presented at the National Association of Social Workers' Symposium, Washington, D.C., November.

Anderson, J.D. (1983a) 'Conceptual models of direct service generalist practice – current issues and curricular implications', paper presented at the National Association of Social Workers' Symposium, Washington, D.C., November.

Anderson, R.E. and Carter, I.E. (1974) *Human Behaviour in the Social Environment*, Chicago: Aldine.

Andrew, G. (1974) 'Forecasting social work practice as a base for curriculum development', *Journal of Education for Social Work* 10(3) : 3–8.

Argyris, C. and Schon, D. (1974) *Theory in Practice: Increasing Professional Effectiveness*, San Francisco: Jossey-Bass.

Armstrong, J. and Gill, K. (1978) 'The unitary approach – what relevance for community work?', *Social Work Today* 10(11) : 18–21.

249

REFERENCES

Armstrong, J. and Gill, K. (1978a) 'The unitary approach – lessons from community work practice', *Social Work Today* 10(11) : 22–5.

Austin, D.M. (1978) 'Consolidation and integration', *Public Welfare* 36(3) : 20–8,

Baer, B. and Federico, R.C. (1978) *Educating the Baccalaureate Social Worker*, Cambridge, Mass.: Ballinger.

Bailey, R. (1982) 'Theory and practice in social work – a kaleidoscope', in Bailey, R. and Lee, P. (eds) *Theory and Practice in Social Work*, Oxford: Basil Blackwell.

Bailey, R. and Brake, M. (eds) (1975) *Radical Social Work*, London: Arnold.

Bailey, R. and Lee, P. (eds) (1982) *Theory and Practice in Social Work*, Oxford: Basil Blackwell.

Bailis, S.S. (1985) 'A case for generic social work in health settings', *Social Work* 30(3) : 209–12.

Baird, P. (1977) 'Confessions of a reactionary', *Social Work Today* 8(23) : 16.

Bakalinsky, R. (1982) 'Generic practice in graduate school work curricula: A study of educators' experiences and attitudes', *Journal of Education for Social Work* 18(3) : 46–54.

Bakan, D. (1966) 'Behaviourism and American urbanization', *Journal of the History of Behavioural Sciences* 2(1) : 5–28.

Baker, R. (1975) 'Towards generic social work: a review and some innovations', *British Journal of Social Work* 5(2) : 193–215.

Baker, R. (1976) *The Interpersonal Process in Generic Social Work: An Introduction*, Bundoora, Victoria: Preston Institute of Technology Press.

Baker, R. (1976a) 'The multirole practitioner in the generic orientation to social work practice', *British Journal of Social Work* 6(3) : 327–52.

Baker, R. (1978) *A Career in Social Work: Seven Personal Accounts*, edited by Lawrence, R.J., University of New South Wales: School of Social Work, 47–57.

Baker, R. (1980) 'Building and implementing unitary social work practice – a personal account', *Contemporary Social Work Education* 3(1) : 23–9.

Baker, R. (1980a) 'Responding to a critique of "The interpersonal process in generic social work"', *Australia Social Work* 33(4) : 34–8.

Baker, R. (1980b) 'Exploring the use of the bio-psychosocial model in one unitary framework for social work practice', unpublished paper, University of New South Wales.

Baker, R. (1980c) 'Notes on a conceptual framework for unitary social work practice', *International Social Work* XXIII(4) : 10–25.

Baker, R. (1982) 'Is there a future for integrated practice? Obstacles to its development in practice and education', paper presented at the Twenty First International Congress of Schools of Social Work, University of Sussex, 26 August.

Baker, R. and Campbell, M.D. (1976) 'A model for the planning and promotion of change in generic social work', *International Social Work* XIX(2) : 23–8.

Baker, R., Campbell, M.D., and Picton, C. (1976) 'Curriculum planning for education of the generic practitioner', in Boas, P. and Crawley, J. (eds)

REFERENCES

Social Work in Australia - Responses to a Changing Context, Melbourne: International Press.

Barbour, R.S. (1984) 'Social work education: tackling the theory–practice dilemma', *British Journal of Social Work* 14(6) : 557–77.

Bartlett, H.M. (1961) 'The generic–specific concept in social work education and practice', in Kahn, A.J. (ed.) *Issues in American Social Work*, New York: Columbia University Press.

Bartlett, H.M. (1964) 'The place and use of knowledge in social work practice', *Social Work* 9(3) : 36–46.

Bartlett, H.M. (1970) *The Common Base of Social Work Practice*, New York: National Association of Social Workers.

Batley, R. and Edwards, J. (1975) *CDP and the Urban Programme in Action – Research in Community Development*, London: Routledge & Kegan Paul.

Berger, P.L. and Luckmann, T. (1966) *The Social Construction of Reality*, Garden City, N.Y.: Doubleday.

Bernabo, L. (n.d.) 'Toward a theory of knowledge change in social work', unpublished paper available from author: Long Island Jewish-Hillside Medical Centre, Jamaica, New York.

Berreen, R. and Browne, E. (1986) 'Maiden aunt or earth mother: social welfare within the social work curriculum', *Advances in Social Work Education 1986*, University of New South Wales, School of Social Work.

Biestek, F. (1957) *The Casework Relationship*, Chicago: Loyola University Press.

Billups, H.O. (1984) 'Unifying social work: importance of centre-moving ideas', *Social Work* 29(2) : 173–80.

Bisno, H. (1969) 'A theoretical framework for teaching social work methods and skills with particular reference to undergraduate social welfare education', *Journal of Education for Social Work* 5(9) : 5–17.

Bisno, H. (1982) 'The conceptualization of social work practice in social work education: a perspective and interpretation', based on a paper presented at the 2nd National Conference of the Australian Association for Social Work Education, Adelaide, 1981. Available from the author, La Trobe University, Melbourne.

Bisno, H. (1984) 'Conceptualizing social work practice in social work education', in Dinerman, M. and Geisman, L.L. (eds) *A Quarter-Century of Social Work Education*, New York: National Association of Social Workers, CSWE and CLIO Press.

Bitensky, R. (1973) 'The influence of political power in determining the theoretical development of social work', *Journal of Social Policy* 2(2) : 119–30.

Blalock, H.M. (1969) *Theory Construction*, Englewood Cliffs, N.J.: Prentice Hall.

Block, A.M. (1972) 'The dilemma of social work education: restructuring the curriculum', *Journal of Education for Social Work* 8(1) : 19–23.

Blocksberg, L.M. and Lowy, L. (1977) 'Toward integrative learning and teaching in social work: an analytic framework', *Journal of Education for Social Work* 13(2) : 3–10.

Bloom, M. (1969) 'The selection of knowledge from the behavioural sciences and its integration into social work curricula', *Journal of Education for Social Work* 5(1) : 15–27.

Blyth, M.J. and Hugman, B. (1982) 'Social work education and probation', in Bailey, R. and Lee, P. (eds) *Theory and Practice in Social Work*, Oxford: Basil Blackwell, pp. 61–77.

Boas, P. and Crawley, J. (1975) *Explorations in Teaching Generic Social Work Theory*, Bundoora, Victoria: Preston Institute of Technology Press.

Boehm, W.W. (1958) 'The nature of social work', *Social Work* 3(2) : 10–18.

Boehm, W.W. (1976) 'Social work education: issues and problems in light of recent developments', *Journal of Education for Social Work* 12(1) : 20–7.

Bowker, L.H. and Cox, F.M. (1982) 'Sociologists in schools of social work: marginality or integration', *Journal of Sociology and Social Welfare* IX(2) : 220–32.

Bradshaw, J. (1972) 'The concept of social need', *New Society* 19–20(496) : 640–3.

Brake, M. and Bailey, R. (1980) *Radical Social Work and Practice*, London: Edward Arnold.

Brawley, E.A. (1974) *The New Human Service Worker*, New York: Praeger Publishing Co.

Brennan, W.C. (1973) 'The practitioner as theoretician', *Journal of Education for Social Work* 9(2) : 5–12.

Breshers, J.M. (1957) 'Models and theory construction', *American Sociological Review*, 22(1) : 32–8.

Briar, S. (1977) 'In summary', *Social Work* 22(5) : 415–16 and 444.

Briar, S. (1978) 'Toward the integration of practice and research', paper presented to the National Conference on the Future of Social Work Research, San Antonio, Texas, October.

Briar, S. (1981) 'Needed: a simple definition of social work', *Social Work* 26(1) : 83–4.

Briar, S. and Miller, H. (1971) *Problems and Issues in Social Casework*, New York: Columbia University Press.

Brieland, D. (1977) 'Historical overview', *Social Work* 22(5) : 341–6.

Brieland, D. (1981) 'Definitions, specialization and domain in social work', *Social Work* 26(1) : 79–84.

Brill, N. (1973) *Working with People, The Helping Process*, New York: Lippincott.

Briscoe, C. and Thomas, D.N. (1977) *Community Work: Learning and Supervision*, London: Allen & Unwin.

British Association of Social Workers Working Party (1975) 'The social work task: a preliminary report', *Social Work Today* 5(24) : 747–51.

Bromberger, S. (1963) 'A theory about the theory of theory and about the theory of theories', in Baumrin, B. (ed.) *Philosophy of Sciences*, New York: Interscience, Delaware Seminar 2 : 79–105.

Brooks, E.E. (1980) 'The rationale for generic social work in an undergraduate course in a developing country: the Zambian case', *International Social Work* XXIII(1) : 37–46.

252

REFERENCES

Buck, R.C. (1956) 'On the logic of general behaviour systems theory', in Feigl, H. and Scriven, M. (eds) *Minnesota Studies in the Philosophy of Science* vol. 1 : 223–38.

Buckley, W. (1967) *Sociology and Modern Systems Theory*, Englewood Cliffs, N.J.: Prentice Hall.

Buckley, W. (ed.) (1968) *Modern Systems Research for the Behavioural Scientist*, Chicago: Aldine.

Bullock, A. and Stallybrass, O. (1977) *The Fontana Dictionary of Modern Thought*, London: Fontana Books.

Burrell, G. and Morgan, G. (1979) *Sociological Paradigms and Organizational Analysis*, London: Heinemann.

Butrym, Z. (1976) *The Nature of Social Work*, London: Macmillan.

Bywaters, P. (1978) 'The unitary approach in practice', *Social Work Today* 9(35) : 17–19.

Bywaters, P. (1982) 'An international model: an answer or just a better question?', *British Journal of Social Work* 12(3) : 303–17.

Cannon, M.A. (1939) 'Where the changes in social case work have brought us', in Lowry, F. (ed.) *Readings in Social Case Work: 1920–1938*, New York: Columbia University Press.

Carew, R. (1979) 'The place of knowledge in social work activity', *British Journal of Social Work* 9(3) : 349–64.

Carroll, N.K. (1975) 'Areas of concentration in the graduate curriculum: a three-dimensional model', *Journal of Education for Social Work* 11(2) : 3–10.

Carroll, N.K. (1975a) 'Ideology and rationality in social work education', *Journal of Education for Social Work* 11(3) : 30–7.

Carroll, N.K. (1977) 'Three-dimensional model of social work practice', *Social Work* 22(5) : 428–32.

Chamberlain, E.R. (1976) *Cases, Courses and Competence*, St. Lucia, Queensland: University of Queensland Press.

Chamberlain, E.R. (1977) 'Social work: practice models and theory development', unpublished paper dated 13 April available from author: Faculty of Social Work, University of Queensland.

Chambers, C.A. (1962) 'An historical perspective on political action vs. individualized treatment', in *Current Issues in Social Work Seen in Historical Perspective*, New York: Council of Social Work Education.

Chescheir, M.W. (1979) 'Social role discrepancies as clues to practice', *Social Work* 24(2) : 89–95.

Clarke, M.J. (1975) 'The impact of social science on conceptions of responsibility', *British Journal of Law and Society* 2(1) : 32–44.

Clarke, M.J. (1976) 'The limits of radical social work', *British Journal of Social Work* 6(4) : 501–6.

Cocozzelli, C. and Constable, R.C. (1985) 'An empirical analysis of the relation between theory and practice in clinical social work', *Journal of Social Service Research* 9(1) : 47–64.

Cohen, S. (1975) 'It's all right for you to talk: political and sociological manifestos for action', in Bailey R. and Brake, M. (eds) *Radical Social Work*, London: Arnold, pp. 76–95.

253

REFERENCES

Collins, S. (1977) 'Casework – more than good intentions?', *Social Work Today* 8(31) : 11–12.

Compton, B.R. and Galaway, R.R. (1979) *Social Work Processes*, Homewood, Ill.: Dorsey Press.

Connaway, R. (1975) 'Comments on the generalist–specialist debate', paper delivered at the Agency Educational Consultants–Faculty Workshop, College of Social Professions, University of Kentucky, 2 April.

Considine, R. (1978) 'The death and resurrection of conservative ideology: Australian social work in the seventies', *Social Alternatives* 1(2) : 50–5.

Cooper, S. (1977) 'Social work: a dissenting profession', *Social Work* 22(5) : 360–7.

Corrigan, P. and Leonard, P. (1978) *Social Work Practice Under Capitalism*, London: Macmillan.

Coulshed, V. (1977) 'A unitary approach to the care of the hospitalized elderly mentally ill', *British Journal of Social Work* 7(41) : 19–31.

Cowger, C.D. (1977) 'Alternative stances on the relationships of social work to society', *Journal of Education for Social Work* 13(3) : 25–9.

Coyle, G.L. (1958) *Social Science in the Professional Education of Social Workers*, New York: Council on Social Work Education.

Crouch, R.C. (1979) 'Social work defined', *Social Work* 24(1) : 46–8.

Curnock, K. and Hardiker, P. (1979) *Towards Practice Theory: Skills and Methods in Social Assessments*, London: Routledge & Kegan Paul.

Curriculum Study (1959) – see under Boehm, W.W. (1959) *Objectives of the Social Work Curriculum of the Future*, New York: Council on Social Work Education.

Currie, R. and Parrott, B. (1981) *A Unitary Approach to Social Work – Application in Practice – An Analysis of a Patch System and Team Approach within a Unitary Framework in a Social Services Department*, Birmingham: British Association of Social Workers.

Curtis, J.E. and Petras, J.W. (1970) *The Sociology of Knowledge*, New York: Praeger.

Davey, I. (1977) 'Radical social work: what does it mean to practice?', *Social Work Today* 8(23) : 8–10.

Davies, M. (1974) 'Reassessment of environment in social work research', *Social Casework* 55(1) : 3–12.

Day, P.R. (1981) *Social Work and Social Control*, London: Tavistock.

De Maria, W. (1982) 'The dreaming and the doing: Utopian foundations of social action', *Journal of Sociology and Social Welfare* IX(2) : 186–202.

Deutscher, I. (1966) 'Words and deeds: social science and social policy', *Social Problems* 13:233–54.

Deutscher, I. (1973) *What We Say/What We Do*, Glencoe, Ill.: Scott, Foresman & Co.

Dewey, J. (1933) *How We Think*, New York: Heath.

Drover, F. and Schragge, E. (1977) 'General systems theory and social work education: a critique', *Canadian Journal of Social Work Education* 3(2) : 28–39.

Dubin, R. (1969) *Theory Building*, New York: Free Press.

REFERENCES

Dubin, R. (1971) 'Theory and research', in O'Toole, R. (ed.) *The Organization, Management and Tactics of Social Research*, Cambridge, Mass.: Schenkman.

Duncan, H.D. (1962) *Communication and Social Order*, New York: Bedminster.

Duncan, H.D. (1968) *Symbols in Society*, New York: Oxford.

Duncan, H.D. (1969) *Symbols and Social Theory*, New York: Oxford.

Durkheim, E., quoted in Pinker, R. (1971) *Social Theory and Social Policy*, London: Heinemann, pp. 97–8.

England, H. (1986) *Social Work as Art*, London: Allen & Unwin.

Ephross, P.H. and Reisch, M. (1982) 'The ideology of some social work texts', *Social Service Review* 56(2) : 273–91.

Epstein, W.M. (1986) 'Science and social work', *Social Service Review* 60(1) : 145–60.

Evans, R. (1976) 'Some implications of an integrated model for social work theory and practice', *British Journal of Social Work* 6(2) : 177–200.

Evans, R. (1978) 'Unitary models of practice and the social work team', in Olsen, M.R. (ed.) *The Unitary Model: Its Implications for Social Work Theory and Practice*, Birmingham: British Association of Social Workers.

Evans, R. (1978a) 'Worth defending', letter, 12 December, *Social Work Today* 10(16) : 16.

Evans, R. and Webb, D. (1977) 'Sociology and social work practice: explanation or method? *Contemporary Social Work Education* 1(2) : 15–26.

Falck, H.S. (1970) 'Twentieth century philosophy of science and social work education', *Journal of Education for Social Work* 6(1) : 21–7.

Fay, B. (1975) *Social Theory and Political Practice*, London: Allen & Unwin.

Feyerabend, P.K. (1975) *Against Method*, London: Humanities Press.

Field, M.H. (1980) 'Social casework practice during the "psychiatric deluge",' *Social Service Review* 54(4) : 482–507.

Findlay, P.C. (1978) 'Critical theory and social work practice', *Catalyst* No. 3.

Fischer, J. (1973) 'Is casework effective? A review', *Social Work* 18(1) : 5–20.

Fischer, J. (ed.) (1973a) *Interpersonal Helping: Emerging Approaches for Social Work Practice*, Springfield, Ill.: Thomas.

Fischer, J.(1976) *The Effectiveness of Social Casework*, Springfield, Ill.: Thomas.

Flexner, A. (1915) 'Is social work a profession?', *Studies in Social Work* 4 : 2–24.

Folkhard, M.S. (1976) *Intensive Matched Probation and After Care Treatment, Vol. 2, The Results of the Experiment*, London: HMSO.

Forder, A. (1976) 'Social work and systems theory', *British Journal of Social Work* 6(1) : 23–42.

Foster, Z.P. (1965) 'How social work can influence hospital management of fatal illness', *Social Work*, 10(4) : 30–45. Also cited in Pincus, A. and Minahan, A. (1973), *Social Work Practice: Model and Method*, Itasca, Ill.: Peacock.

Frankel, C. (1968) 'The relation of theory to practice: some standard views', in Stein, H.D. (ed.) *Social Theory and Social Intervention*, Cleveland: Case Western Reserve University Press.

REFERENCES

Friedlander, W. (ed.) (1976) *Concepts and Methods of Social Work,* Englewood Cliffs, N.J.: Prentice Hall.

Friedrichs, R.W. (1970) *A Sociology of Sociology,* New York: Free Press.

Galper, J. (1975) *The Politics of Social Services,* Englewood Cliffs, New Jersey: Prentice Hall.

Galper, J. (1976) 'Introduction to radical theory and practice in social work education: social policy', *Journal of Education for Social Work* 12(2) : 3–9.

Galper, J. (1980) *Social Work Practice – A Radical Perspective,* Englewood Cliffs, N.J.: Prentice Hall.

Gammack, G. (1982) 'Social work as uncommon sense', *British Journal of Social Work* 12(1) : 3–22.

Garvin, C. and Glasser, P. (1970) *The Bases of Social Treatment,* New York: Columbia University Press, pp. 149–77.

Garvin, C. and Glasser, P. (1977) 'The integration of individual and environmental change efforts: a conceptual framework', *Contemporary Social Work Education* 1(1) : 13–23.

Germain, C.B. (1970) 'Casework and science: a historical encounter', in Roberts, W. and Nee, H. (eds) *Theories of Social Casework,* Chicago: University of Chicago Press, pp. 3–32.

Germain, C.B. (1973) 'An ecological perspective in casework practice', *Social Casework* 54(6) : 323–30.

Germain, C.B. (1976) 'Time: an ecological variable in social work practice', *Social Casework* 57(7) : 419–26.

Germain, C.B. (1977) 'An ecological perspective on social work practice in health care', *Social Work in Health Care* 3(4) : 67–76.

Germain, C.B. (1978) 'Space, an ecological variable in social work practice', *Social Casework,* 59(9) : 515–22.

Germain, C.B. (ed.) (1979) *Social Work Practice: People and Environments,* New York: Columbia University Press.

Germain, C.B. and Gitterman, A. (1979) 'The life model of social work practice', in Turner, F.J. (ed.) *Social Work Treatment,* 2nd rev. edn, New York: Free Press.

Germain, C.B. and Gitterman, A. (1980) *The Life Model of Social Work Practice,* New York: Columbia University Press.

Gilbert, F. and Specht, H. (1977) 'The incomplete profession', in Specht, H. and Vickery, A. (eds) *Integrating Social Work Methods,* London: Allen & Unwin. Reprinted from *Social Work* 19(6) : 665–74, 1974.

Gilbert, N. (1977) 'The search for professional identity', *Social Work* 22(5) : 401–6.

Gilbert, N. (1981) 'Reactions to the working statement on purpose', *Social Work* 26(1) : 88–9.

Gitterman, A. and Germain, C.B. (1976) 'Social work practice: a life model', *Social Service Review* 50(4) : 601–10.

Glasser, B.G. and Strauss, A.L. (1967) *The Discovery of Grounded Theory,* Chicago: Aldine.

Goldberg, E.M. and Warburton, K.W. (1979) *Ends and Means in Social Work,* London: Allen & Unwin.

REFERENCES

Goldberg, G. (1974) 'Micro-level intervention: a frame of reference and a practice model', *Journal of Education for Social Work* 10(3) : 25–9.
Goldberg, G. (1974a) 'Structural approach to practice: a new model', *Social Work* 19(2) : 150–5.
Goldstein, H. (1973) *Social Work Practice: A Unitary Approach*, Columbia, South Carolina: University of South Carolina Press.
Goldstein, H. (1974) 'Theory development and the unitary approach to social work practice', *The Social Worker – Le Travailleur Social* XLII(3–4) : 181–8; also reprinted in Specht, H. and Vickery, A. (eds) (1977) *Integrating Social Work Methods*, London: Allen & Unwin.
Goldstein, H. (1975) 'Some critical observations on the relevance of social systems theory for social work practice', *Canadian Journal of Social Work Education* 1(3) : 13–23.
Goldstein, H. (1975a) 'A unitary approach. Its rationale and structure', and 'A unitary approach: implications for education and practice', in Parsloe, P. et al. (eds) *A Unitary Approach to Social Work Practice – Implications for Education and Organization*, University of Dundee: School of Social Administration, pp. 17–45.
Goldstein, H. (1977) 'Theory development and the unitary approach to social work practice', in Specht, H. and Vickery, A. (eds) *Integrating Social Work Methods*, London: Allen & Unwin, pp. 60–72.
Goldstein, H. (1981) *Social Learning and Change: A Cognitive Approach to Human Services*, Columbia, South Carolina: University of South Carolina Press.
Goldstein, H. (1982) 'Cognitive therapies: a comparison of phenomenological and mediational models and their origins', *Journal of Mind and Behaviour* 3(1):1–16.
Goldstein, H. (1982a) 'Cognitive approaches to direct practice', *Social Service Review* 56(4) : 539–55.
Goldstein, H. (1983) 'Starting where the client is', *Social Casework: The Journal of Contemporary Social Work* 64(5) : 267–75.
Goldstein, H. (1983a) 'Integration of theory and practice in social work education', mimeographed and available from the author, School of Applied Social Sciences, Case Western Reserve University, Cleveland.
Gordon, W.E. (1962) 'A critique of the working definition', *Social Work* 7(4) : 3–13.
Gordon, W.E. (1965) 'Knowledge and value: their distinction and relationship in clarifying social work practice', *Social Work* 10(3) : 32–9.
Gordon, W.E. (1965a) 'Toward a social work frame of reference', *Journal of Education for Social Work* 1(1) : 19–26.
Gordon, W.E. (1969) 'Basic constructs for an integrated and generative conception of social work', in Hearn, G.A. (ed.), *The General Systems Approach: Contribution Towards an Holistic Conception of Social Work*, New York: Council on Social Work Education, pp. 5–11.
Gordon, W.E. and Schutz, M.L. (1977) 'A natural basis for social work specializations', *Social Work* 22(5) : 422–6.
Gouldner, A. (1970) *The Coming Crisis of Western Sociology*, New York: Basic Books.

REFERENCES

Gouldner, A. (1973) *For Sociology*, London: Allen Lane.

Grace, C. and Wilkinson, P. (1978) *Negotiating the Law: Social Work and Legal Services*, London: Routledge & Kegan Paul.

Gray, A. (1976) 'A generic approach to providing residential care for mid-adolescents in Victoria', in Baker, R. *The Interpersonal Process in Generic Social Work: An Introduction*, Bundoora, Victoria: PIT Press.

Greenwood, E. (1957) 'The attributes of a profession', *Social Work* 2(3) : 45–55.

Grinnell, R.N. (1973) 'Environmental modification – casework's concern or casework's neglect?', *Social Service Review* 47(2) : 208–20.

Grinnell, R.N. and Kyte, N.S. (1974) 'Modifying the environment', *Social Work* 19(4) : 477–83.

Gurman, A.S. (1974) 'The efficacy of therapeutic interventions in social work. A critical re-evaluation', *Journal of Health and Social Behaviour* 15 : 136–41.

Gutierrez, F.R. (1978) 'Theory selection: some considerations for social work', *Journal of Applied Social Sciences* 2 : 82–97.

Gyarfas, M. (1969) 'Social science, technology and social work: a caseworker's view', *Social Service Review* 43(3) : 259–73.

Habermas, J. (1974) *Theory and Practice*, London: Heinemann.

Haines, J. (1975) *Skills and Methods in Social Work*, London: Constable.

Haines, J. (1978) Book review of Loewenberg, F.M. *Fundamentals of Social Intervention*, *British Journal of Social Work* 8(4) : 497–8.

Hall, A.D. and Fagan, R.E. (1956) 'Definitions of system', *General Systems* 1 : 18–29.

Hallett, C. (1983) 'Social workers: their role and tasks (1982)', *British Journal of Social Work* 13(4) : 395–404.

Halmos, P. (1978) *The Personal and the Political: Social Work and Political Action*, London: Hutchinson.

Hamilton, G. (1951) *Theory and Practice of Social Case Work*, New York: Columbia University Press.

Hamilton-Smith, E. (1975) 'Issues in the measurement of "community need",' *Australian Journal of Social Issues* 10(1) : 35–45.

Hanna, E.A. (1979) 'An integration of psychosocial concepts into the education of general practitioners', *Social Work in Health Care* 4(4) : 393–406.

Hanson, N.R. (1958) *Patterns of Discovery*, Boston: Cambridge University Press.

Hardiker, P. (1972) 'Problems: definition; an interactionist approach', in Jehu, D. *Behaviour Modification in Social Work*, London: Wiley, pp. 99–125.

Hardiker, P. (1977) 'Social work ideologies in the probation service', *British Journal of Social Work* 7(2) : 131–54.

Hardiker, P. and Barker, M. (1981) *Theories of Practice in Social Work*, London: Academic Press.

Hartford, M. (1976) 'Group methods and generic practice', in Roberts, R. and Northern, H. (eds) *Theories of Social Work With Groups*, New York: Columbia University Press.

REFERENCES

Hartman, A. (1974) 'The generic stance and the family agency', *Social Casework* 55(4) : 199–208.

Hartman, A. (1980) 'But all knowledge is one: a systems approach to the dilemmas in curriculum building', *Journal of Education for Social Work* 16(2) : 100–7.

Haworth, G.O. (1984) 'Social work research, practice, and paradigms', *Social Service Review* 58(3) : 343–57.

Hearn, G. (1958) *Theory Building in Social Work*, Toronto: University of Toronto Press.

Hearn, G. (ed.) (1969) *The General Systems Approach Contributions Towards an Holistic Conception of Social Work*, New York: Council of Social Work Education.

Hearn, G. (1974) 'General systems theory and social work', in Turner, F.J. (ed.) *Social Work Treatment: Interlocking Theoretical Approaches*, New York: Free Press, pp. 343–71.

Heaton, J.M. (1979) 'Theory in psychotherapy', in Bolton, N. (ed.) *Philosophical Problems in Psychotherapy*, New York: Methuen: 176–96.

Hellenbrand, S.C. (1978) 'Integration takes time', *Social Service Review* 52(3) : 456–67.

Heraud, B.J. (1970) *Sociology and Social Work*, Oxford: Pergamon Press.

Hernandez, S.H. (1985) 'Integrated practice: an advanced generalist curriculum to prepare social problem specialists', *Journal of Education for Social Work* 21(3) : 28–35.

Holder, D. and Wardle, M. (1981) *Framework and the Development of a Unitary Approach*, London: Routledge & Kegan Paul.

Hollis, F. (1966) *Casework: A Psychosocial Therapy*, New York: Random House.

Hollis, F. (1980) 'On revising social work', *Social Casework* 61(1) : 3–9.

Hollis–Taylor Report (1951): Hollis, E.V. and Taylor, A.L. *Social Work Education in the United States*, New York: Columbia University Press.

Hoos, I. (1969) *Systems Analysis in Social Policy: A Critical Review*, London: Institute of Economic Affairs.

Horn, D. and Clews, R. (1981) 'A unitary approach to teamwork: some payoffs and pitfalls', in Martel, S. (ed.) *Supervision and Team Support*, London: Bedford Press.

Horton, J. (1970) 'Order and conflict theories of social problems as competing ideologies', in Curtis, J.E. and Petras, J.W. (eds) *The Sociology of Knowledge*, New York, Praeger.

Howe, D. (1980) 'Inflated states and empty theories in social work', *British Journal of Social Work* 10(3) : 317–40.

Hudson, W.W. (1982) 'Scientific imperatives in social work research and practice', *Social Service Review* 56(2) : 246–58.

Imre, R.W. (1984) 'The nature of knowledge in social work', *Social Work* 29(1) : 41–5.

Irvine, E. (1964) 'The right to intervene', *Social Work* (UK) 21(2) : 13–16.

Jarvie, I.C (1972) *Concepts and Society*, London: Routledge & Kegan Paul.

Johnson, D.P. (1981) *Sociological Theory: Classical Founders and Contemporary Perspectives*, New York: Wiley.

REFERENCES

Johnson, H.C. (1978) 'Integrating the problem-oriented record with a systems theory approach to case assessment', *Journal of Education for Social Work* 14(3) : 71–7.

Jones, H. (1975) *Towards a New Social Work*, London: Routledge & Kegan Paul.

Jones, J.W. (1978) *Giving Shape to Social Work – Use of Unitary Concepts*, Preston: Preston Polytechnic, School of Social Sciences.

Jordan, B. (1978) 'A comment on "Theory and Practice in Social Work",' *British Journal of Social Work* 8(1) : 23–5.

Jordan, W. (1977) 'Against the unitary approach to social work', *New Society* 40(765) : 448–50.

Kahn, A.J. (1954) 'The notion of social work knowledge', in Kasins, C. (ed.) *New Directions in Social Work*, New York: Harper & Row.

Kahn, A.J. (1959) *Issues in American Social Work*, New York: Columbia University Press.

Kahn, A.J. (ed.) (1973) *Shaping the New Social Work*, New York: Columbia University Press.

Kamerman, S.B. (1973) 'Knowledge for practice: social science in social work', in Kahn, A.J. (ed.) (1973) *Shaping the New Social Work*, New York: Columbia University Press.

Kaplan, A. (1964) *The Conduct of Inquiry*, San Francisco: Chandler.

Kelk, N. (1978) *The Writings of Mary Ellen Richmond: A Study in the Logic and Structure of Social Work Theory*, Ph.D. Thesis, University of New South Wales, Sydney.

Kendall, K.A. (1973) 'Dream or nightmare? The future of social work education', *Journal of Education for Social Work* 9(2) : 13–23.

Kendall, K.A. (1977) 'Cross-national review of social work education', *Journal of Education for Social Work* 13(2) : 76–83.

Kendall, K.A. (1978) *Reflections on Social Work Education, 1950–1978*, New York: International Association of Schools of Social Work.

Kettner, P.M. (1975) 'A Framework for comparing practice models', *Social Service Review* 49(4) : 629–42.

Kiel, H. (1978) 'The radical approach: considerations for social work education', unpublished paper available from the author, University of Sydney, Department of Social Work.

Kiel, H. (1980) 'The multirole practitioner model: a critical examination', unpublished paper, available from the author, University of Sydney, Department of Social Work.

Kilbrandon Report (1964) *Children and Young Persons in Scotland*, Cmnd. 2306, Edinburgh: HMSO.

Klein, A.F. (1970) *Social Work Through Group Process*, Albany: School of Social Welfare, State University of New York.

Klenk, R.W. and Ryan, R.M. (1974) *The Practice of Social Work*, Belmont, Ca.: Wadsworth.

Kolevzon, M.S. and Maykranz, J. (1982) 'Theoretical orientation and clinical practice: uniformity versus eclecticism?', *Social Service Review* 56(1) : 120–9.

REFERENCES

Kuhn, T.S. (1970) *The Structure of Scientific Revolutions*, Chicago: University of Chicago Press.

Lawrence, J. (1983) 'The relevance of moral philosophy for professional education', paper presented at the Rutgers University School of Social Work and University Committee on the Professions Colloquium, 20 April, available from the author, University of New South Wales, School of Social Work.

Lawrence, J. (1985) 'Hunger survival and development: an urgent need for a reflective universal morality', *22nd International Congress IASSW Proceedings*, Montreal, pp. 3–24.

Lawrence, J. (1986) 'Future directions for social work education', *Australian Social Work* 39(4) : 19–26.

Lecomte, R. (1975) 'Basic issues in the analysis of theory for practice in social work, Ph.D. Thesis, Ann Arbor, Mi.: Bryn Mawr College, The Graduate School of Social Work and Social Research.

Lee, P.R. (1937) 'Social work as cause and function', in Lee, P.R. (ed.) *Social Work as Cause and Function and Other Papers*, New York: Columbia University Press.

Leighninger, L. (1980) 'The generalist–specialist debate in social work', *Social Service Review* 54(1) : 1–12.

Leighninger, R.D. (1977) 'Systems theory and social work: a re-examination', *Journal of Education for Service Work* 13(3) : 44–9.

Leonard, P. (1975) 'Explanation and education in social work', *British Journal of Social Work* 5(3) : 325–33.

Leonard, P. (1975a) 'Towards a paradigm for radical practice', in Bailey, R. and Brake, R. (eds) (1975) *Radical Social Work*, London: Edward Arnold, pp. 46–61.

Leonard, R.C. and Skipper, J.K. (1971) 'Integrating theory and practice', in O'Toole, R. (ed.) *The Organization, Management and Tactics of Social Research*, Cambridge, Mass.: Schenkman.

Levy, C.S. (1973) 'The value base of social work', *Journal of Education for Social Work* 9(1) : 34–42.

Levy, C.S. (1976) 'Personal versus professional values: the practitioner's dilemma', *Clinical Social Work Journal* 4(2) : 110–20.

Lewis, H. (1972) 'Morality and the politics of practice', *Social Casework* 53(7) : 404–17.

Lewis, H. (1973) 'Apology, animation, conscientization: implications for social work education in the United States of America', *Journal of Education for Social Work* 9(3) : 31–8.

Lilienfeld, R. (1975) 'Systems theory as an ideology', *Social Research* 42: 637–60.

Lippitt, R., Watson, J., and Westley, B. (1958) *The Dynamics of Planned Change*, New York: Harcourt, Brace & World.

Lobkowicz, N. (1967) *Theory and Practice: History of a Concept from Aristotle to Marx*, London: University of Notre Dame Press.

Loewenberg, F.M. (1977) *Fundamentals of Social Intervention – Core Concepts and Skills for Social Work Practice*, New York: Columbia University Press.

REFERENCES

Loewenberg, F.M. (1977a) 'The current crisis in social work education', *Contemporary Social Work Education* 1(1) : 16–68.

Loewenberg, F.M. (1984) 'Professional ideology, middle range theories and knowledge building for social work practice', *British Journal of Social Work* 14(4) : 309–22.

Longres, J.F. (1981) 'Reactions to the working statement on purpose', *Social Work* 26(1) : 85–7.

Lutz, W.A. (1969) 'Emerging models of social casework practice', West Hartford: University of Connecticut School of Social Work, cited in Siporin, M. (1975) *Introduction to Social Work Practice*, New York, Macmillan.

McDermott, F.E. (ed.) (1975) *Self-determination in Social Work*, London: Routledge & Kegan Paul.

McInerney, A. (1981) *The Application and Evaluation of the Pincus and Minahan Model of Unitary Social Work Practice, with Special Reference to Social Work Practice on a Neonatal Intensive Care Nursery*, MSW Project, School of Social Work, University of New South Wales.

Mackey, R.A. (1976) 'Generic aspects of clinical social work practice', *Social Casework* 57(10) : 619–24.

McLeod, D.L. and Meyer, H.J. (1967) 'A study of the values of social workers', in Thomas, E.J. (ed.) *Behavioural Science for Social Workers*, New York: Free Press.

McLeod, E. and Dominelli, L. (1982) 'The personal and the apolitical', in Bailey, R. and Lee, P. (eds) *Theory and Practice in Social Work*, Oxford: Basil Blackwell, pp. 112–27.

Maluccio, A.N. and Marlow, W.D. (1974) 'The case for the contract', *Social Work* 19(1) : 28–36.

Marcus, G. (1938) 'The generic and specific in social case work – recent developments in our thinking', *News Letter*, American Association of Psychiatric Social Workers, VIII 3–4, in Bartlett, H.M. (1961) 'The generic–specific concept in social work education and practice', in Kahn, A.J. (ed.) *Issues in American Social Work*, New York: Columbia University Press.

Martindale, D. (1960) *The Nature and Types of Sociological Theory*, Boston: Houghton Mifflin.

Maslow, A.H. (1954) *Motivation and Personality*, New York: Harper.

Mayer, J.E. and Timms, N. (1970) *The Client Speaks: Working Class Impressions of Casework*, London: Routledge & Kegan Paul.

Meadows, P. (1957) 'Models, systems, and science', *American Sociological Review* 22(1) : 3–9.

Meenaghan, J.M., Powers, G.T., and Feld, A. (1978) 'Developing curricular options in the pursuit of integration', *Journal of Education for Social Work* 14(1) : 94–101.

Meinert, R.G. (1976) 'What do social workers do?', *Social Work* 21(2) : 156–7.

Merton, R.K. (1968) *Social Theory and Social Structure*, New York: Free Press.

Meyer, C.H. (1970) *Social Work Practice: A Response to the Urban Crisis*, New York: Free Press.

REFERENCES

Meyer, C.H. (1973) 'Lydia Rapoport Memorial Lecture: practice models – the new ideology', *Smith College Studies in Social Work* XLIII(2) : 85–93.

Meyer, C.H. (1973a) 'Purposes and boundaries – casework fifty years later', *Social Casework* 54(5) : 268–75.

Meyer, C.H. (1973b) 'Direct services in old and new concepts', in Kahn, A.J. (ed.) *Shaping the New Social Work,* New York: Columbia University Press.

Meyer, C.H. (1974) Book review of Goldstein, H. *Social Work Practice: A Unitary Approach, Social Work* 19(2): 241–2.

Meyer, C.H. (1976) *Social Work Practice: The Changing Landscape,* New York: Free Press.

Meyer, C.H. (1981) 'Social work purpose: status by choice or coercion?', *Social Work* 26(1) : 69–75.

Meyer, C.H. (1981a) 'Reactions to the working statement on purpose', *Social Work* 26(1) : 91.

Middleman, R.R. (1977) 'Generalists and specialists', *Social Work* 22(2) : 143.

Middleman, R.R. and Goldberg, G. (1972) 'The interactional way of presenting generic social work concepts', *Journal of Education for Social Work* 8(2) : 48–57.

Middleman, R.R. and Goldberg, G. (1974) *Social Service Delivery: A Structural Approach to Social Work Practice,* New York: Columbia University Press.

Midgley, J. (1981) *Professional Imperialism: Social Work and the Third World,* London: Heinemann.

Milford Conference Report (1929) *Social Casework Generic and Specific,* New York: American Association of Social Workers.

Miller, E.J. and Rice, A.K. (1967) *Systems of Organization,* London: Tavistock.

Miller, J.G. (1955) 'Towards a general theory for the behavioural sciences', *American Psychologist* 10:513–31.

Mills, C.W. (1959) *The Sociological Imagination,* New York: Oxford University Press.

Mills, C.W. (1967) 'IBM plus reality plus humanism = sociology', in Mizruchi, E.H. *The Substance of Sociology,* New York: Appleton-Century-Crofts, pp. 60–6.

Minahan, A. (1980) 'Theories and perspectives for social work', *Social Work* 25(6) 1980: 435.

Minahan, A. (1981) 'Purpose and objectives of social work revisited', *Social Work* 26(1) : 5–6.

Minahan, A. and Briar, S. (1977) 'Introduction to Special Issue', *Social Work* 22(5) : 339.

Minahan, A. and Pincus, A. (1977) 'Conceptual framework for social work practice', *Social Work* 22(5) : 347–52.

Mispelblom, F. (1985) 'Low key practices in social work. Toward a socio-historic method', *British Journal of Social Work* 15(1) : 67–86; 2(5) : 339.

Mizruchi, E.H. (1967) *The Substance of Sociology,* New York: Appleton-Century-Crofts.

263

REFERENCES

Monger, M. (1976) Book review of Parsloe *et al.* (eds) *A Unitary Approach to Social Work Practice – Implications for Education and Organization*, *British Journal of Social Work* 6(2) : 286–7.

Morales, A. (1977) 'Beyond traditional conceptual frameworks', *Social Work* 22(5) : 287–93.

Morales, A. (1981) 'Social work with Third World people', *Social Work* 26(1) : 45–51.

Morris, R. (1977) 'Caring for versus caring about people', *Social Work* 22(5) : 353–9.

Mowbray, M. (1977) 'Conservative ideology in social work – the politics of Pincus and Minahan', *Action for Social Work Education and Training Newsletter* 3(2) : 4–6.

Mowbray, M. (1981) 'A new orthodoxy: all-purpose radicalism', *Australian Social Work* 34(2) : 2.

Mune, M. (1980) 'Exploring the utility of the general systems approach', in Pavlin, F. (ed.) *Perspectives in Australian Social Work*, Bundoora, Victoria: Preston Institute of Technology Press.

Murphy, G.C. (1978) 'Client perceptions of professional helpers', *Australian Journal of Social Issues* 13: 207–15.

Nagel, E. (1955) 'On the statement, "The Whole is More than the Sum of the Parts"', in Lazarsfield, F. and Rosenberg, M. (eds) *The Language of Social Research*, New York: Free Press, pp. 519–27.

National Association of Social Workers Committee on the Working Definition of Social Work Practice for the Commission on Social Work Practice (1958) 'Working definition of social work practice', 3(2) : 5–9. Reprinted in *Social Work* (1977) 22(5) : 344–5.

National Institute of Social Work (1977) *Unitary Approach to Social Work Practice*, Report of Follow-up Workshop, 12 May, London.

Nelson, J.C. (1972) 'Users of systems theory in casework I and II: a proposal', *Journal of Education for Social Work* 8(3) : 60–4.

Nelson, J.C. (1975) Book review of Goldstein *Social Work Practice: A Unitary Approach*, *Journal of Education for Social Work* 11(3) : 116–17.

Nelson, J.C. (1975a) 'Social work's fields of practice, methods and models: the choice to act', *Social Service Review* 49(2) : 264–70.

O'Connor, I. and Dalgleish, L. (1986) 'Cautionary tales from beginning practitioners: the fate of personal models of social work in beginning practice', *British Journal of Social Work* 16(4) : 431–47.

O'Hagan, K. (1986) 'There isn't an effective, tested crisis training course for generic social workers anywhere in Britain', *Social Work Today* 18(5) : 12–13.

Olsen, M.R. (ed.) (1978) *The Unitary Model: Its Implications for Social Work Theory and Practice*, Birmingham: British Association of Social Workers.

Olsen, M.R. (ed.) (1981) *Differential Approaches to Social Work With the Mentally Disordered*, Birmingham: British Association of Social Workers.

O'Toole, R. (ed.) (1971) *The Organization, Management and Tactics of Social Research*, Cambridge, Mass.: Schenkman.

Parsloe, P. (1976) 'Social work and the justice model', *British Journal of Social Work* 6(1) : 71–89.

REFERENCES

Parsloe, P. (ed.) (1975) *A Unitary Approach to Social Work Practice –*
Implications for Education and Organization, University of Dundee: School of
Social Administration.

Parsons, T. (1970) 'Some problems of general theory in sociology', in
McKinney, J.C. and Tiryakian, E.A. (eds) (1970) *Sociology: Perspectives*
and Developments, New York: Appleton-Century-Crofts.

Pavlin, F. (ed.) (1980) *Perspectives in Australian Social Work,* Bundoora,
Victoria: Preston Institute of Technology Press.

Pearson, G. (1975) *The Deviant Imagination,* London: Macmillan.

Pemberton, A. (1982) 'Theory, practice and "public knowledge" in the helping
professions', *Journal of Sociology and Social Welfare* IX(2) : 287–304.

Perlman, H.H. (1957) *Social Casework: A Problem-Solving Process,* Chicago:
University of Chicago Press.

Perlman, H.H. (1965) 'Social work method: a review of the past decade',
Social Work 10(4) : 166–78.

Perlman, H.H. (1970) 'Casework and the diminished man', *Social Casework*
51: 216–25.

Perlman, H.H. (1971) *Perspectives on Social Casework,* Philadelphia: Temple
University.

Perlmutter, F.D. (1977) *A Design for Social Work Practice,* New York:
Columbia University Press.

Philp, M. (1979) 'Notes on the form of knowledge in social work', *Sociological*
Review 27(1) : 83–111.

Pilalis, J. (1986) ' "The integration of theory and practice": a re-
examination of a paradoxical expectation', *British Journal of Social Work*
16(1) : 79–96.

Pilsecker, C. (1978) 'Values: a problem for everyone', *Social Work* 23(1) :
54–7.

Pincus, A. (1978) 'Implications of the unitary model', *Social Work Today*
10(11) : 29.

Pincus, A. and Minahan, A. (1969) 'Toward a model for teaching a basic
first year course in methods of social work practice', in Ripple, L. (ed.)
Innovations in Teaching Social Work Practice, New York: Council on Social
Work Education.

Pincus, A. and Minahan, A. (1973) *Social Work Practice: Model and Method,*
Itasca, Ill.: Peacock.

Pincus, A. and Minahan, A. (1975) 'An integrated framework for social
work: some implications for education and practice', in Parsloe, P. (ed.)
A Unitary Approach to Social Work Practice – Implications for Education
and Organization, University of Dundee: School of Social Administration.

Pincus, A. and Minahan, A. (1977) 'A model for social work practice', in
Specht, H. and Vickery, A. (eds) *Integrating Social Work Methods,* London:
Allen & Unwin.

Plamenatz, J. (1970) *Ideology,* New York: Praeger.

Plant, R. (1970) *Social and Moral Theory in Casework,* London: Routledge &
Kegan Paul.

Polansky, N.A. (ed.) (1975) *Social Work Research,* Chicago: University of
Chicago Press.

REFERENCES

Poloma, M.M. (1979) *Contemporary Sociological Theory*, New York: Macmillan.

Pray, K.L.M. (1949) *Social Work In a Revolutionary Age*, Philadelphia: University of Pennsylvania.

Pritchard, C. and Taylor, R. (1978) *Social Work: Reform or Revolution?*, London: Routledge & Kegan Paul.

Pumphrey, M.W. (1959) *The Teaching of Values and Ethics in Social Work Education*, New York: Council on Social Work Education.

Raynes, N.V., Whinney, J., and Mulgrew, K. (1982) 'What do social workers do? A method for classifying social workers' activities', *British Journal of Social Work* 12(4) : 353–62.

Reay, R. (1986) 'Bridging the gap: a model for integrating theory and practice', *British Journal of Social Work* 16(1) : 49–64.

Reid, W.J. (1977) 'Social work and social problems', *Social Work* 22(5) : 374–81.

Reid, W.J. and Epstein, L. (1972) *Task-Centred Casework*, New York: Columbia University Press.

Rein, M. and White, S.H. (1981) 'Knowledge of practice', *Social Service Review* 55(1) : 1–41.

Reynolds, B.C. (1951) *Social Work and Social Living*, New York: Citadel Press.

Richan, W.C. (1973) 'The social work educators' dilemma: the academic versus the social revolution', *Journal of Education for Social Work* 9(3) : 51–7.

Richmond, M.E. (1917) *Social Diagnosis*, New York: Russell Sage Foundation.

Richmond, M.E. (1930) 'The retail method of reform', in Colcord, J. (ed.) *The Long View*, New York: Russell Sage Foundation.

Ripple, L. (ed.) (1969) *Innovations in Teaching Social Work Practice*, New York: Council on Social Work Education.

Ritzer, G. (1975) *Sociology: A Multiple Paradigm Science*, Boston: Allyn & Bacon.

Roberts, R.J. (1980) Book review of Loewenberg F.M. *Fundamentals of Social Intervention*, *Contemporary Social Work Education* 3(1) : 110–13.

Roberts, R.J. (1981) 'Further notes on a "systems" analysis of social work practice', *Contemporary Social Work Education* 4(3) : 220–8.

Roberts, R.J. (1982) 'Some implications of unitary approaches to social work practice for curriculum design', *Contemporary Social Work Education* 5(3) : 237–59.

Roberts, R.J. (1987) 'The contribution of recent "integrated" social work theory to social work: an analysis and evaluation of eleven conceptual frameworks', Ph.D. Thesis, University of New South Wales, Sydney.

Roberts, R.J. and Zulfacar, D. (1986) 'Developing complementarity between generic and methods approaches to social work practice: an exploration of some problems in curriculum design', *Australian Social Work* 39(4) : 27–34.

Roberts, R.W. and Nee, R.H. (eds) (1970) *Theories of Social Casework*, Chicago: University of Chicago Press.

Roberts, R.W. and Northern, H. (eds) (1976) *Theories of Social Work with Groups*, New York: Columbia University Press.

REFERENCES

Robinson, J.N.G. (1972) 'The dual commitment of social work', *British Journal of Social Work* 2(4) : 471–80.

Rojek, C. (1986) 'The "subject" in social work', *British Journal of Social Work* 16(1) : 65–77.

Rosen, A. (1978) Book review of Rischer, J. *The Effectiveness of Social Casework*, *Social Casework* 59 : 121–2.

Rosen, J. (1983) *An Evaluation of the Pincus and Minahan Conceptual Framework of Unitary Social Work Practice, With Special Reference to its Implications for Social Work Education and Social Work Practice*, MSW Project, School of Social Work, University of New South Wales.

Rosenberg, G. (1978) Book review of Specht H. and Vickery A., (eds) *Integrating Social Work Methods, Journal of Education for Social Work* 14(2) : 119–20.

Rosenfeld, J. (1977) 'Professional education for social work: the universal and the particular', in International Association of Social Work *Social Realities and the Social Work Response*, pp. 14–42.

Rosenfeld, J.M. (1983) 'The domain and expertise of social work: a conceptualization', *Social Work* 28(3) : 186–91.

Ross, B. and Khinduka, S.L. (eds) (1976) *Social Work in Practice*, New York: National Association of Social Workers.

Rothman, J. (1964) 'An analysis of goals and roles in community organization practice', *Social Work* 9 : 24–31.

Rychlak, J.H. (1968) *A Philosophy of Science for Personality Theory*, Boston: Houghton Mifflin.

St George Henry, C. (1974) 'The application of generic principles and theory to the practice of generic social work in the field', *Journal of Education for Social Work* 10(1) : 27–34.

Sallach, D.L. (1972) 'Systems analysis and sociological theory', *Sociological Focus* 5(3) : 54–60.

Schrag, C. (1967) 'Elements in theoretical analysis in sociology', in Gross, L. (ed.) *Sociological Theory Inquiries and Paradigms*, New York: Harper & Row.

Schutz, A. (1963) 'Common sense and scientific interpretation of human action', in Natanson, M. *Philosophy of the Social Sciences*, New York: Random House, pp. 302–46.

Schutz, M.S. and Gordon, W.E. (1977) 'The social work generalist as specialization', paper presented at the 24th Annual Program Meeting on the Council of Social Work Education, Phoenix, Arizona, 27 February.

Schwartz, E.E. (1977) 'Macro social work: a practice in search of some theory', *Social Service Review* 51(2) : 207–27.

Schwartz, W. (1969) 'Private troubles and public issues: one social work job or two?', *Social Welfare Forum*, New York: Columbia University Press: 22–43.

Schwartz, W. (1976) 'Between client and system: the mediating function', in Roberts, R.W. and Northern, H. (eds) *Theories of Social Work with Groups*, New York: Columbia University Press.

Scurfield, R.M. (1980) 'An integrated approach to case services and social reform', *Social Casework* 61(10) : 610–18.

REFERENCES

Seebohm Report (1968) *Report of the Committee on Local Authority and Allied Personal Social Services,* Cmnd. 3703, London: HMSO.

Seed, P. (1975) Book review of Goldstein, H. *Social Work Practice: A Unitary Approach, British Journal of Social Work* 5(2) : 228–30.

Seed, P. (1976) Book review of Jones, J.W. *Giving Shape to Social Work – Use of Unitary Concepts, British Journal of Social Work* 6(3) : 426.

Sheffield, A.E. (1937) *Social Insight in Case Situations,* New York: D. Appleton-Century Co.

Sheldon, B. (1978) 'Social influence: social work's missing link', in Olsen, M.R. (ed.) *The Unitary Model: Its Implications for Social Work Theory and Practice,* Birmingham: British Association of Social Workers, pp. 39–64.

Sheldon, B. (1978a) 'Theory and practice in social work: a re-examination of a tenuous relationship', *British Journal of Social Work* 8(1) : 1–22.

Sheldon, B. (1986) 'Social work effectiveness experiments: review and implications', *British Journal of Social Work* 16(2) : 223–42.

Simey, T.S. (1968) *Social Science and Social Purpose,* London: Constable.

Simon, B.K. (1977) 'Diversity and unity in the social work profession', *Social Work* 22(5) : 394–400.

Simons, R.L. and Aigner, S.M. (1979) 'Facilitating an eclectic use of practice theory', *Social Casework* 60(4) : 201–8.

Simpkin, M. (1979) *Trapped Within Welfare: Surviving Social Work,* London: Macmillan.

Siporin, M. (1972) 'Situational assessment or intervention', *Social Casework* 53(2) : 91–105.

Siporin, M. (1975) *Introduction to Social Work Practice,* New York: Macmillan.

Siporin, M. (1978) 'Practice theory and vested interests', *Social Service Review* 52(3) : 418–36.

Siporin, M. (1978a) 'On the road to professional unity', *Social Work* 23(2) : 164–5.

Siporin, M. (1978b) Book review of Specht, H. and Vickery, A. (eds), *Integrating Social Work Methods, Social Service Review* 52(2) : 317, 319.

Siporin, M. (1979) 'Practice theory for clinical social work', *Clinical Social Work Journal* 7(1) : 75–89.

Siporin, M. (1982) 'Moral philosophy in social work today', *Social Service Review* 56(4) : 516–38.

Skidmore, R.A. (1976) *Introduction to Social Work,* Englewood Cliffs, N.J.: Prentice Hall.

Skynner, A.C.R. (1974) 'Boundaries', *Social Work Today* 5(1) : 290–4.

Smale, G.G. (1983) 'Can we afford not to develop social work practice?', *British Journal of Social Work* 13(3) : 251–64.

Smid, G. and Van Krieken, R. (1984) 'Notes on theory and practice in social work: a comparative view', *British Journal of Social Work* 14(1) : 11–22.

Smith, G. and Harris, R. (1972) 'Ideologies of need and the organization of social work departments', *British Journal of Social Work* 2(1) : 27–45.

Smith, N.J., Boas, P., and Carew, R. (1981) *Genericism in Social Work: A Contribution Towards Its Conceptualization,* Clayton, Victoria: Department of Social Work, Monash University.

268

REFERENCES

Snizek, W.E., Fuhrman, E.R., and Miller, M.K. (eds) (1979) *Contemporary Issues in Theory and Research,* London: Aldwych Press.

Souflee, F. Jr. (1977) 'Social work: the acquiescing profession', *Social Work* 22(5) : 419–21.

Sowers-Hoag, K. and Thyer, B.A. (1985) 'Teaching social work practice: a review and analysis of empirical research', *Journal of Education for Social Work* 21(3) : 5–15.

Specht, H. (1972) 'The deprofessionalization of social work', *Social Work* 17(2) : 3–16.

Specht, H. (1974) Book review of Goldstein, H. *Social Work Practice: A Unitary Approach, Social Service Review* 48(2) : 296–8.

Specht, H. (1977) In Specht, H. and Vickery, A. (eds) *Integrating Social Work Methods,* London: Allen & Unwin.

Specht, H. and Vickery, A. (eds) (1977) *Integrating Social Work Methods,* London: Allen & Unwin.

Statham, D. (1978) *Radicals in Social Work,* London: Routledge & Kegan Paul.

Stein, H.D. (ed.) (1968) *Social Theory and Social Intervention,* Cleveland: Case Western Reserve University Press.

Stein, I. (1974) *Systems Theory, Science and Social Work,* Metuchen, N.J.: Scarecrow Press.

Stevenson, O. (1971) 'Knowledge for social work', *British Journal of Social Work* 1(2) : 225–37.

Stevenson, O. and Parsloe, P. (1978) *Social Service Teams: The Practitioner's View,* London: HMSO.

Strean, H.F. (1971) *Social Casework: Theories in Action,* Metuchen, N.J.: Scarecrow Press.

Stumpf, J. (1970) 'Teaching an integrated approach in social work practice', in Ripple, L. (ed.) *Innovations in Teaching Social Work Practice,* New York: Council on Social Work Education.

Suchman, E.A. (1971) 'Action for what? A critique of evaluative research', in O'Toole, R. (ed.) *The Organization, Management and Tactics of Social Research,* Cambridge, Mass.: Schenkman.

Teigiser, K. (1983) 'Generalist social work practice in the 1980s', paper presented at the National Association of Social Workers Symposium, Washington, D.C., November.

Thomas, D. and Shaftoe, H. (1974) 'The patch system: does casework need a neighbourhood orientation?', *Social Work Today* 5(16) : 483–6.

Thomas, E. (ed.) (1967) *Behavioural Science for Social Workers,* New York: Free Press.

Tilbury, D.E.F. (1977) *Casework in Context: A Basis for Practice,* New York: Permagen Press.

Timms, N. (1968) *Language of Social Casework,* London: Routledge & Kegan Paul.

Timms, N. and Timms, R. (1977) *Perspectives in Social Work,* London: Routledge & Kegan Paul.

Tomlinson, J.R. (1977) *Is Band-Aid Social Work Enough?* Darwin: Wabbly Press.

REFERENCES

Triseliotis, J. (1978) 'Beyond the unitary approach', *Social Work Today* 9(35) : 20–2.

Turner, F.J. (ed.) (1974) *Social Work Treatment: Interlocking Theoretical Approaches*, New York: Free Press.

United Nations (1950) *Training for Social Work: An International Survey*, New York: United Nations, February, pp. 18–20.

Van Krieken, R. (1980) 'Casework recycled – on Ron Baker's *The Interpersonal Process in Generic Social Work*', *Australian Social Work* 33(4) : 30–4.

Varley, J.E. (1980) 'The applicability of genericism to school social work', *Australian Social Work* 33(1) : 25–38.

Vickery, A. (1973) 'Specialist: generic: what next?', *Social Work Today* 4(9) : 262–6.

Vickery, A. (1974) 'A system approach to social work intervention: its uses for work with individuals and families', *British Journal of Social Work* 4(4) : 389–404.

Vickery, A. (1976) 'A unitary approach to social work with the mentally disordered', in Olsen, M.R. (ed.) *Differential Approaches to Social Work with the Mentally Disordered*, Birmingham: British Association of Social Workers, pp. 113–24.

Vickery, A. (1977) 'Use of unitary models in education for social work', in Specht, H. and Vickery, A. (eds) *Integrating Social Work Methods*, London: Allen & Unwin.

Vickery, A. (1977a) 'Social work practice: divisions and unifications', in Specht, H. and Vickery, A. (eds) *Integrating Social Work Methods*, London: Allen & Unwin.

Vickery, A. (1979) 'A unitary model for social work practice', unpublished paper available from the author.

Vinter, R.D. (1967) 'Problems and processes in developing social work practice principles', in Thomas, E.J. (ed.) *Behavioural Science for Social Workers*, New York: Free Press.

Vinter, R.D. (1967a) 'Essential components of group work practice', *Readings in Group Work Practice*, Ann Arbor: University of Michigan.

von Bertalanffy, L. (1968) *General Systems Theory*, New York: Braziller.

Vreugdenhil, E. (1981) *A Discussion of the Relevance of the Generic Approach to Field Practice in Social Work*, MSW Qualifying Project, School of Social Work, University of New South Wales.

Vreugdenhil, E. (n.d.) 'Gatekeepers and territories: a participant observation study of social work practice', Ph.D. thesis in preparation, School of Social Work, University of New South Wales.

Wallace, D.W. (1980) *A Description and Appraisal of the Evaluation Practices of N.S.W. Government Community Workers*, MSW thesis, School of Social Work, University of New South Wales.

Watts, R. (1977) 'Invitation to conviviality: a first report on a learning situation', *Contemporary Social Work Education* 1(2).

Watts, R. (1978) 'The Emperor's new clothes: a review of systems theory in social work theory', paper presented at SAANZ Conference.

Webb, D. and Evans, R. (1972) 'Developing a client-centred sociology', *Community Care* 201: 20–2.

REFERENCES

Webber, R. (1977) 'Using a unitary approach in student placements', *British Journal of Social Work* 7(4) : 455–68.

Weber, M. (1949) *The Methodology of the Social Sciences*, Glencoe, Ill.: Free Press.

Weiss, S. (1966) 'Alternative approaches in the study of complex situations', *Human Organization* 25(3) : 198–206.

Whittaker, J.K. (1974) *Social Treatment: An Approach to Interpersonal Helping*, Chicago: Aldine.

Wilkes, R. (1978) 'Some philosophical implications of the unitary approach', in Olsen, M.R. (ed.) *The Unitary Model: Its Implications for Social Work Theory and Practice*, Birmingham: British Association of Social Workers.

Willer, D. (1967) *Scientific Sociology: Theory and Method*, Englewood Cliffs, N.J.: Prentice Hall.

Woodroofe, K. (1962) *From Charity to Social Work*, London: Routledge & Kegan Paul.

Wooldridge, P.J. (1971) 'Theory, meta-theory and scientific research', in O'Toole, R. (ed.) *The Organization, Management and Tactics of Social Research*, Cambridge, Mass., Schenkman.

Working Definition of Social Work (1958), *see under*: National Association of Social Workers Committee on the Working Definition of Social Work Practice for the Commission on Social Work Practice.

Wrong, D.H. (1961) 'The oversocialized concept of man in modern sociology', *American Sociological Review*, 26 : 183–93.

Yanoov-Chetkow, B. (1980) 'Some notes on a "systems" analysis of social work practice', *Contemporary Social Work Education* 3(2) : 179–190.

Yessian, M.R. and Broskowski, A. (1977) 'Generalists and human-service systems – their problems and prospects', *Social Service Review* 51(2) : 265–88.

INDEX

acceptance of the individual 140, 151
Addams, Jane 178
agencies 86, 87, 98, 149, 172
agreement *see* consensus
Alexander, C.A. 184, 187
analogistic method 213–14, 218–19
Anderson, J.D. 165, 166, 168
Armstrong, J. 147, 170, 194–5, 229
assessment 78, 103, 121, 125, 198, 218, 230–1, 234
assumptions 19, 21, 27–35 *passim*, 44, 45, 49–55, 142, 147, 153, 154, 155, 157, 229–33 *passim*, 244–5; background 28–9, 30, 31–2, 33, 49, 157

background assumptions *see* assumptions
Baer, B. 198
Bakan, D. 29, 30
Baker, R. 4, 43, 46, 69, 144, 148, 151, 171, 174, 175, 177, 189, 193, 197, 198; common base of 127, 129; and society 145–7; 'unitary' in 168, 169, 170; universality of 130–1
bargaining 7, 100, 104, 149
Bartlett, H.M. 2, 4, 43, 69, 92, 104, 111, 126, 130, 132, 133, 138, 147, 151, 155, 179, 181, 196, 197, 226; common base of 127, 128, 129; framework reviewed 70–82; nomenclature in 160–2, 163–4, 165, 168, 171
behaviour change 39, 59, 112, 113
behaviour, relation to values 152; theories of 229
behaviourism 29–30
Berger, P.L. 19
Bisno, H. 109, 126

Blyth, M.J. 19, 20
Boehm, W.W. 181–2
Brennan, W.C. 38, 40
Breshers, J.M. 25
Briar, S. 40–1, 182–4, 186, 187
Brieland, D. 179, 180
British Association of Social Workers 1, 188
Bromberger, S. 31
Buck, R.C. 207, 213
Buckley, W. 205, 209
Burrell, G. 50–2, 153, 154
Butrym, Z. 115
Bywaters, P. 170, 172, 175, 189–90

Carew, R. 39, 40
case based nature of social work 191
cases 102–3, 218
casework 7, 87, 146, 170, 179, 182, 183, 188, 190, 194, 198; 'generic' related to 163, 165, 179–80
Chamberlain, E. 27
Chambers, Clark 178
change 245
change agent system 98–9, 100, 103, 109–10, 149
change, behaviour *see* behaviour change
change, social *see* social change
change, structural *see* structural change
change system 86–7
Chicago Meeting (1981) 1, 186
class 195
client and non-client 5, 7, 38, 58–9, 141, 146, 147, 148, 149–50, 151, 152, 172, 175–6, 177, 190, 211; in Bartlett 77; in Goldstein 85–7, 140; in Middleman and Goldberg 111–12, 113, 116,

For Product Safety Concerns and Information please contact our EU
representative GPSR@taylorandfrancis.com
Taylor & Francis Verlag GmbH, Kaufingerstraße 24, 80331 München, Germany